Coptic Legal Documents
Law as Vernacular Text and Experience
in Late Antique Egypt

Medieval and Renaissance
Texts and Studies
Volume 377

Arizona Studies in the
Middle Ages and the Renaissance

Volume 32

COPTIC LEGAL DOCUMENTS
LAW AS VERNACULAR TEXT AND EXPERIENCE
IN LATE ANTIQUE EGYPT

Translated by
LESLIE S. B. MACCOULL

ACMRS
(Arizona Center for Medieval and Renaissance Studies)
Tempe, Arizona
in collaboration with
BREPOLS
2009

© Copyright 2009
Arizona Board of Regents for Arizona State University
and Brepols Publishers, n.v., Turnhout, Belgium

ASMAR Volume 32: ISBN 978-2-503-53380-3   D/2009/0095/172

Library of Congress Cataloging-in-Publication Data
Coptic legal documents : law as vernacular text and experience in late antique Egypt / translated by Leslie S.B. MacCoull.
   p. cm. -- (Medieval and renaissance texts and studies ; v. 377) (Arizona studies in the middle ages and the renaissance ; v. 38)
  Includes bibliographical references and index.
  ISBN 978-0-86698-425-6 (alk. paper)
  1. Law--Egypt--History--To 1500--Sources. 2. Egyptian law--Sources. 3. Roman law--Sources. 4. Copts--Legal status, laws, etc.--History--To 1500--Sources. I. MacCoull, Leslie S. B.
  KRM134.C67 2009
  932'.023--dc22
                                                                    2009052797

∞

This book is made to last.
It is set in Adobe Caslon Pro,
smyth-sewn and printed on acid-free paper
to library specifications.
Printed in the United States of America

*In loving centenary commemoration
of
Mirrit Boutros Ghali
(b. 1908—✝ 1992)
who did not live to see
the teaching of Coptic culture at a university in Cairo*

*"Something died out by this river: but it seems
less than a nightingale ago."*
(Lawrence Durrell, 1940)

Table of Contents

Acknowledgments — xiii
Abbreviations — xv
Note on Translation — xvii
Map: Egypt in Late Antiquity — xviii
Introduction — xix

Documents

P.Cair.Masp. II 67176r + P.Alex. inv. 689, cession of land, 4 November 569 — 1

P.Lond. V 1709, arbitration of inheritance, ca.570 — 4

P.KRU 105, donation of village land for a monastic foundation, 576-578 — 8

P.Mich. inv. 6898, mutual cession of land, 632 (?) — 11

P.KRU 77, preamble to a will, 4 December 634 — 18

P.Vat.Copti Doresse 2, sale of house property, 639 (?) — 19

P.Vat.Copti Doresse 5, sale/transfer of landed property, 640 (?) — 21

P.Vat.Copti Doresse 3, division of house and land, 624 or 654 — 24

P.Vat.Copti Doresse 1, sale/cession of part of a wheeled vehicle, 625/26 or 640/41 (?) — 26

P.KRU 75, testament, 7th c. — 29

P.KRU 65, testament, late 7th c. — 36

P.CLT 1, document of release, 13 November 698 — 42

P.CLT 4, document of release, 18 November 702 — 48

P.CLT 2, agreement concerning a monastic donation, 25 November 703 (?) — 51

P.CLT 5, legal relief concerning money dispute, 24 November 711 — 54

P.KRU 34, sale of silver object, 15 January 713	60
P.KRU 9, sale of part of a courtyard, 4 March 715	62
P.KRU 35, settlement of inherited-property division, 6 October 719	65
P.KRU 55, business agreement, 7 October 720 (or 735?)	69
P.KRU 66/76, testament, before 722	71
P.KRU 10, sale of landed property, 8 December 722	78
P.KRU 25, sale of half of a house, 722/23	82
P.KRU 47, division of sold house property, 722/23 (or 737/38)	85
P.KRU 68, testament, May-June 723	88
P.CLT 6, service agreement, 9-10 February 724 (or 739?)	93
P.KRU 51, settlement among neighbors over wall-building, 27 March 724	97
P.KRU 36, settlement of inheritance dispute, 4 June 724 (or 723?)	99
P.KRU 37, settlement of division of inheritance, 724	103
P.KRU 50, document of release in land dispute, 22 August 724	107
P.KRU 17, donation of house property to a woman for her dowry, early 725 (?)	111
P.KRU 45/46, division of a house, 24 April 725 (or 740?)	113
P.KRU 21, sale of half of a house with its land, 12 June 725	116
P.KRU 67, testament, 2 November 725	120
P.KRU 42, settlement of division of house property, 725/26	127
P.KRU 49, surrender of collateral against money loan, 17 January 728	130
P.KRU 44, settlement of inherited house property and dowry, 10 September 728	131
P.KRU 3, sale of inherited landed property, 728/29	136
P.KRU 69, testament, 18 August 729	138
P.KRU 27, sale of textile works, ca. 730 (?)	141
P.KRU 5, sale of inherited land, 24 March 733	144
P.KRU 13, sale of house property, 30 November 733	147
P.KRU 12, sale of house property, 8 December 733	151

P.KRU 74, testament, 28 December 733 — 153

P.KRU 88, donation of a child oblate, 8 March 734 — 157

P.KRU 78, donation of a child oblate, 28 September–27 October [early 8th c.] — 160

P.KRU 104, document of self-oblation by an adult, 771/72 — 163

P.KRU 106, donation of property to a monastery, 31 May 734 — 166

P.KRU 18, sale, 1st 1/3 of 8th c. — 174

P.KRU 38, settlement of inheritance, 26 February 738 — 177

P.KRU 19, transfer of house property, 5 November 747 — 180

P.KRU 54, acknowledgement of receipt of donation, 24/25 September 748 — 183

Glossary — 185

Bibliography — 189

Index — 201

Acknowledgments

My first thanks go to Terry Wilfong of the University of Michigan (Ann Arbor), author of *Women of Jeme*, who not only did not mind my continuing to work on this material but also warmly encouraged the idea of making documents like these available to as wide an audience as possible. It is because of him and other brilliant younger researchers that someone who began in Coptic studies over forty years ago, when such work not only was outré but was actively discouraged, can be assured that matters are in better hands than ever. (As Gaston Zananiri wrote, 'Laissez-moi vieillir avec amour.')

Next I am grateful to Arizona State University and its Center for Medieval and Renaissance Studies, for providing proof that late antiquity is a profession that *can* be practiced in a warm climate. Its publication series keeps those involved with the east blessedly aware of the western dimension of all they do. And Hayden Library's Interlibrary Loan staff never gave up.

I thank Lucia Papini and Rosario Pintaudi of Florence for passing on to me images of the Vatican Coptic documents at the New York papyrology congress of 1980. The complete edition is eagerly awaited (and see the update by H. Förster at the Ann Arbor papyrology congress of 2007).

Of all old friends I most thank Kent Rigsby, formerly of Duke University. For forty-four years his wry and incisive wit has never failed pithily to sum up the root of the matter and point me toward interesting paths. Also, his aid with the Thesaurus Linguae Graecae has been indispensable. Other old friends are no longer alive: Maxwell Vos, Juli Bellet, Michael Kenny, John Oates. They are daily remembered.

Most gratitude goes to those younger scholars who have both taken the field into their able hands and taken the trouble to send me their illuminating works: Heike Behlmer and Malcolm Choat of Sydney, Jennifer Cromwell of Liverpool and Oxford, Jean-Luc Fournet of Strasbourg and Paris, Eitan Grossman of Jerusalem, Monika Hasitzka of Vienna, Caroline Humfress of London, Arietta Papaconstantinou of Paris and Oxford, T.S. Richter of Leipzig. And one we miss: the late Sarah Clackson of Cambridge, who revolutionized the field in a short span of thirty-seven years on the planet. "The Road goes ever on and on; / Let others follow it who can."

Roy Rukkila and Karen Lemiski helped with computer know-how, encouragement, and insights from other fields (always the way for classicists to know what they think they know). And the staff of the ASU Computing Commons saved a low-tech person from her worst nightmares. Eugene Cruz-Uribe (formerly) of Flagstaff and Lucy-Anne Hunt of Manchester aided me in rereading texts published nearly a century ago. Frank Campbell of the American Numismatic Society, a friend for forty-two years, helped me find needed material on coinage after 641. And John Cotsonis of Holy Cross Hellenic College and Michael Lang of the Brompton Oratory (presently at the Vatican) provided helpful remarks. Finally, an illuminating visit to an exhibit of Tibetan Buddhist art at the Phoenix Art Museum made me acquainted with a deity all papyrologists should invoke, "The Protector of Discovered Texts."

This volume was produced to honor the one-hundredth birthday of Mirrit Boutros Ghali, who founded the first learned society devoted to Coptic studies (giving them, as has been said with brilliant appositeness, their "lettres de noblesse") and fought without success all his long life to see Coptic studies taught at a university in Egypt — an activity still not without controversy and peril. He thought a surname was a qualification. He thought the person who paid the bill could control the content. In these misprisions he was of his time and place. But he was beautiful:[1] and that was everything. May his memory be eternal.

and

"In memory of . . . the works of art, of the books, thoughts, and feelings that perished under the reign of evil . . .".[2]

---

[1] ". . . the one to whom all hard-won gifts should be conveyed in tribute, the inheritor who would redeem through his beauty the sacrifice of a life . . ." (R. Scruton, *England: An Elegy* [London, 2000], 34).

[2] P.O. Kristeller, in *Kristeller Reconsidered*, ed. J. Monfasani (New York, 2006), 19-20.

ABBREVIATIONS

Crum, *CD*	W.E. Crum, *A Coptic Dictionary* (Oxford, 1939; repr. 1962, 2005)
CSBE 2	R.S. Bagnall and K.A. Worp, *Chronological Systems of Byzantine Egypt*, 2nd ed. (Leiden, 2004)
Förster, *WB*	H. Förster, *Wörterbuch der griechischen Wörter in den koptischen dokumentarischen Texten* (Berlin-New York, 2002)
Godlewski, *Phoibammon*	W. Godlewski, *Le monastère de Phoibammon* (Warsaw, 1986)
ODB	*Oxford Dictionary of Byzantium*, ed. A. Kazhdan et al., 3 vols. (New York, 1991)
Richter, *Sprache*	T.S. Richter, *Rechtssemantik und forensische Rhetorik: Untersuchungen zu Wortschatz, Stil und Grammatik der Sprache koptischer Rechtsurkunden* (Leipzig, 2002; 2nd ed. 2008)
Seidl, "Eid"	E. Seidl, *Der Eid im römisch-ägyptischen Provinzialrecht*, 2 vols. (Munich, 1933-1935), 2:137-60, "Der Eid im koptischen Recht"
Till, *D&P*	W.C. Till, *Datierung und Prosopographie der koptischen Rechtsurkunden aus Theben* (Vienna, 1962)
Till, *Erb*	W.C. Till, *Erbrechtliche Untersuchungen auf Grund der koptischen Urkunden* (Vienna, 1954)
Till, *KRUTheb*	W.C. Till, *Die koptische Rechtsurkunden aus Theben* (Vienna, 1964)
Timm, *Ägypten*	S. Timm, *Das christlich-koptische Ägypten*, 6 vols. (Wiesbaden, 1984-1992)
Wilfong, *Women*	T. Wilfong, *Women of Jeme: Lives in a Coptic Town in Late Antique Egypt* (Ann Arbor, 2002)

Papyri and ostraca are cited according to J.F. Oates et al., *Checklist of Editions of Greek, Latin, Demotic, and Coptic Papyri, Ostraca, and Tablets*, continually updated online at http://scriptorium.lib.duke.edu/papyrus/texts/clist.html

Note on Translations and Conventions

In presenting these documents I have tried to follow the format used in B. Porten, ed., *The Elephantine Papyri in English* (Leiden, 1996). Indicated in each document heading are its date (as accurately as is known), its place of origin, the parties to the transaction, the object of the transaction (where stated), the number of witnesses, and the name of the scribe (where preserved). Signs of the cross (+) in the texts indicate crosses made by notaries and/or signatories. These documents being papyri, they are lacunose and have bits no longer readable; omissions in the translations, occasionally with indications of their size, are signalled by ellipses (. . .). Translations are as literal as possible, retaining features of the Coptic language (such as resumptive forms) and even on occasion its word order, in order to give a flavor of these texts as they were generated by scribes who were products of a long process of evolution of their practice and of personal training. Though there may already exist English translations of some passages that read more smoothly as English, I want to try to convey to the reader the differentness of this world, its unaccustomed feel. On the other hand, I have chosen to keep forms of names familiar in English—'Mary', not 'Maria'; 'John', not 'Iôannês'—where substituting literal transliteration would sound paradoxically awkward. Throughout the legal texts I have tried to render the same (especially Greek) term by the same English word; see the Glossary. I indicate in brackets where specific phrases—such as especially the invocation formulae—are in the Greek language, not in Coptic per se (recalling once again the striking presence of Greek loanwords throughout the Coptic language in all its contexts and registers). I hope all this will aid readers to discern both the consistency through time of long-lasting notarial traditions and the reflections of change in the parties' historical situations.

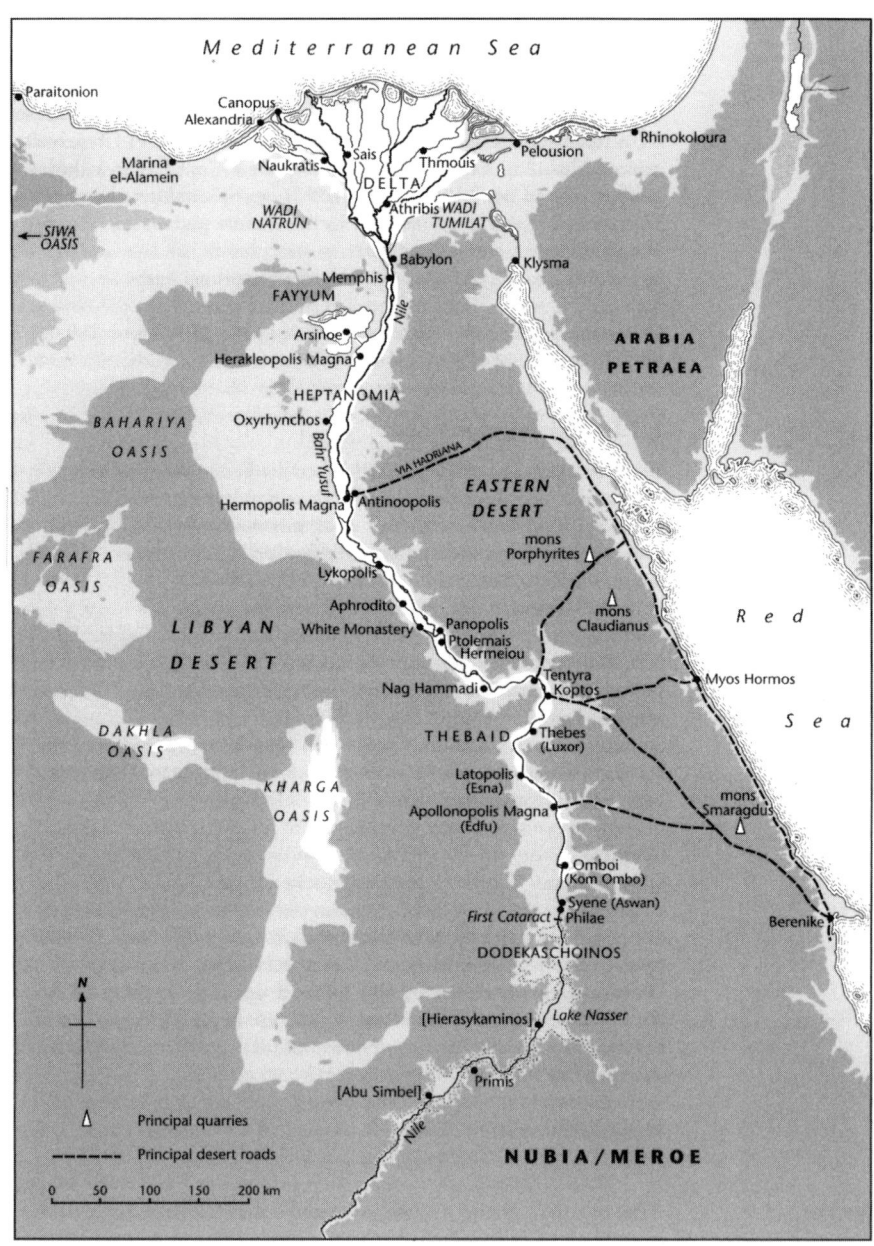

Egypt in Late Antiquity.

From R. S. Bagnall and D. W. Rathbone, *Egypt from Alexander to the Copts: An Archaeological and Historical Guide* (London, 2001). Used by permission.

Introduction

> Voici l'heure néfaste au savant qui travaille, . . .
> S'il interroge encore un poudreux papyrus,
> Il n'en déchiffre plus les occultes rébus,
> Car le soir vient, le soir trouble, où son coeur défaille . . .

In the first third of the nineteenth century, long after papyrus documents in Greek had accidentally been discovered in Egypt,[1] some other documents were found by chance in the upper Nile valley, at a site built amidst the ruins of the Pharaonic temple at Deir el-Bahri (western Thebes) that had been transformed into a Christian monastery in late antiquity.[2] The papyri were passed on to English and German travellers and officials.[3] These texts were in Coptic, chronologically the most recent form of the Egyptian language.[4] A related piece that happened to be in Greek, which educated Englishmen could read, was translated into English as a "curiosity of law," as it was described.[5] But these texts, dating mostly from the seventh and eighth centuries, remained for the most part obscure for a further hundred years and more. Being legal documents—wills, contracts, sales, and so on—they were studied by jurists, mostly German and Italian, who were concerned with the absorbing question of the reception of Roman law, especially Justinianic codified law, in the provinces of the empire.[6] However, they have not been read by those of less narrow specialization, and their being in Coptic walled them off from those possessing only the knowledge of more mainstream classical languages. The texts from the Thebaid site, the town of Jeme (west of the

---

[1] The first being P.Schow (N. Schow, *Charta papyracea Graece scripta Musei Borgiani* [Rome, 1788]).

[2] R.S. Bagnall and D.W. Rathbone, *Egypt from Alexander to the Copts: An Archaeological and Historical Guide* (London, 2004), 194–95.

[3] See Godlewski, *Phoibammon*, 54–56.

[4] Champollion's famous decipherment of Egyptian hieroglyphics (1822) had been aided by his knowledge of Coptic.

[5] C. Goodwin, "Curiosities of Law: Conveyancing among the Copts of the Eighth Century," *Law Magazine and Law Review* 6.12 (1859): 237–48. (His dating turned out to be off: it is actually from the early seventh century.)

[6] L.S.B. MacCoull, "Law," in *The Coptic Encyclopaedia*, 8 vols. (New York, 1991), 5:1428–32.

Nile across from Luxor),⁷ were translated into German by W.C. Till in 1954 and 1964;⁸ just ten were translated into English when they were published as *P.CLT* in 1932. More Coptic-language legal texts were published in scattered fashion over the twentieth century, including some earlier ones from the Middle Egyptian site of Aphrodito (on the west bank of the Nile between Assiut and Sohag)⁹ where Greek-language documents (known to papyrologists as *P.Cair.Masp.* and *P.Lond.* V) had been found before the First World War, plus a few strays from Jeme. The language barrier has continued to prevent their being more widely known by historians of late antiquity and the early Middle Ages.¹⁰

In this volume I present in annotated English translation a selection of fifty of these documents, in chronological order, taking the reader on a tour of the culture and the persons that produced them. I have tried to select the most representative and most interesting of their kinds. The number of fifty was not pre-selected or arbitrary; it reflects how this work unfolded after decades of immersion in this genre of Coptic cultural production. (In the specific case of the documents of child donation, now beginning to attract the scholarly attention they deserve after long languishing in the attics of juristic specialization,¹¹ I have not translated the entire corpus of them here: such a work, with cultural commentary, will be the task of a younger scholar well versed in the currently fashionable matters of gender and property.)¹² The texts are not grouped thematically: that was the approach taken by earlier, juristically-oriented work—witness Till's separating off the wills in a separate study (Till, *Erb*). What I find absorbing is the process of continuity-plus-change through time. It will be easy to see in these texts how the majestic and codified law of the Christian Roman empire was engaged with by living people in their everyday transactions, and how there was continuity even when a transformed Egypt became subject no longer to that empire but to the rule of the Islamic caliphate. These legal documents provide mini-narratives of human lives as people sought to safeguard their property, carried on family disputes, and invoked the powers of heaven to adjudicate their cause.

---

⁷ Bagnall and Rathbone, *Guide*, 193.
⁸ Till, *Erb* and idem, *KRUTheb* (see Abbreviations).
⁹ Bagnall and Rathbone, *Guide*, 156 (map).
¹⁰ Cf. C. Wickham, *Framing the Early Middle Ages: Europe and the Mediterranean 400–800* (Oxford, 2005), 420 on the language barrier.
¹¹ L.S.B. MacCoull, "Child Donations and Child Saints in Coptic Egypt," *East European Quarterly* 13 (1979): 409–15 first took up the subject after Schiller and Till.
¹² Bearing in mind the salutary balance expressed in W. Treadgold, *The Early Byzantine Historians* (New York, 2007), xiv.

Society and law

We are fortunate for Egypt as for no other region of the late antique and early medieval world to have preserved enormous quantities of the paperwork of government and of daily life. Personal and official letters, petitions, bills, wills, tax registers and receipts, pawn tickets and shopping lists, and the reports of family members all taking one another to court and hiring notaries and advocates to achieve their goals[13]—all enable a closeup view of the actualities of life impossible anywhere else. These documents, mostly on papyrus, have given rise to the discipline of papyrology and to a way of doing history that has led to great advances in the past thirty to forty years.[14] From these texts historians have traditionally tried to discern the workings of the Ptolemaic-, Roman-, and Byzantine-ruled society (and even later) of polyethnic, multilingual Egypt. However, that traditional approach has previously tended to be 'top-down', focused on governing agency,[15] rather than 'bottom-up', looking at what is emergent from what we see individual agents actually doing. If you were interested in 'the law' as it was dictated to be, you wanted to see how, and whether, people affluent and literate enough to commission documents to record and safeguard their transactions were obeying the law, manipulating it, or evading it for their own reasons. Earlier readers of these texts, few as they were, did not take the document framers'-eye view.[16] What is taking place now is the making of a yet newer picture of late antiquity,[17] thinking "... in terms of law as a set of social practices rather than as primarily the law of the emperor."[18]

After earlier scepticism, it has now also been satisfyingly and definitively shown that Egypt was like any other late Roman region in being a place where the emperor's writ indeed ran.[19] The question is how. Entrants into monastic communities were supposed to make arrangements for their immovable property,

---

[13] C. Humfress, "Cracking the Codex: Late Roman Legal Practice in Context," *Bulletin of the Institute of Classical Studies* 49 (2006): 251–64; and cf. T. Gagos and P. van Minnen, *Settling a Dispute: Towards a Legal Anthropology of Late Antique Egypt* (Ann Arbor, 1994).

[14] See R.S. Bagnall, *Reading Papyri, Writing Ancient History* (London, 1995).

[15] C. Humfress, "Law in Practice," in *A Companion to Late Antiquity*, ed. P. Rousseau (Oxford, 2009), 377–91.

[16] C. Humfress, *Orthodoxy and the Courts in Late Antiquity* (Oxford, 2007), 116: "... it would be a mistake to focus solely on whether laws and legal principles were 'applied', 'vulgarised' or even 'developed' in late antiquity. We should ask first how they were handled in practice."

[17] C. Humfress, "Law and Justice in *The Later Roman Empire*," in *A.H.M. Jones and the Later Roman Empire*, ed. D.M. Gwynn (Leiden, 2007), 121–42.

[18] Humfress, "Law in Practice."

[19] J. Beaucamp, "Byzantine Egypt and Imperial Law," in *Egypt in the Byzantine World 400–700*, ed. R.S. Bagnall (Cambridge, 2007), 271–87; cf. J. Urbanik, "Dioskoros and the

yet we see monks retaining their own residences and transferring them.[20] Ties with blood relatives still in the world caused further complications.[21] Ordinary laypeople could transfer land to the possession of a monastery and then swap to get it back. Testaments endow monastic charities and provide for intercessions for the souls of the deceased. And above all, questions of inheritance, most especially with regard to the children of composite families made up of the offspring of multiple marriages, never cease to vex. Was there a valid will or not? Who benefits? In the documents generated by routine transactions[22] we see all this happening, complete with emotional baggage, as though with a time machine.

Islamic rulers replaced Christian ones as Egypt's overlords; yet an enacted legal tradition went right on. We can follow families through their archives that span the conquest in A.D. 641: family members continue to travel up and down the Nile valley, quarrelling with and suing one another,[23] and even appealing for help to representatives of the Islamic government while continuing to produce, as evidence in court, deeds invoking the Christian Trinity and specifying fines in Byzantine-style currency. As has been said about a later epoch, ". . . the assumption that 'the empire of the Romans' was part of God's design for mankind . . . was widespread among eastern Christians from Egypt to northern Rus. And it was something which Muslim powers had to accommodate within their own spectrum of political thought."[24] The framers of these post-conquest documents swore oaths "by the holy and consubstantial Trinity and by the well-being of our lords the rulers who rule over us at present," all the while continuing to endow monastic foundations, dower and marry off their children, and even donate some of those children as oblates to the monasteries that had come to carry such a heavy charge of power and identity for Egyptian Christians.

Law (on Succession)," in *Les archives de Dioscore d'Aphrodité cent ans après leur découverte*, ed. J.-L. Fournet (Paris, 2008), 117–42.

[20] See E.R. O'Connell, "Transforming Monumental Landscapes in Late Antique Egypt: Monastic Dwellings in Legal Documents from Western Thebes," *Journal of Early Christian Studies* 15 (2007): 239–73, here 263–65.

[21] For excellent western comparanda (from a slightly earlier epoch) see J.J. O'Donnell, *Augustine: A New Biography* (New York, 2005), 166–69.

[22] For a western parallel compare S. Keynes, "The Fonthill Letter," in *Words, Texts and Manuscripts*, ed. M. Korhammer (Munich, 1992), 53–97, esp. 54–55, 96–97.

[23] A splendid example—too lengthy to include in this volume—is found in the 'Budge papyrus' and its relatives (a bilingual, Greek and Coptic, archive): A.A. Schiller, "The Budge Papyrus of Columbia University," *Journal of the American Research Center in Egypt* 7 (1968): 79–117.

[24] J. Shepard, "The Byzantine Commonwealth 1000–1500," in *The Cambridge History of Christianity*, 5: *Eastern Christianity*, ed. M. Angold (Cambridge, 2006), 3–52, here 34–35.

We begin in a world that is a Miaphysite[25]-majority province of the Dyophysite Christian Byzantine empire, in which Egyptians document their family and business transactions complete with invocations of the "Christ-loving kings" in Constantinople (*P.KRU* 105). We end our survey in a world in which the pagarch of the district is named Mamet (Muhammad) and termed an *amir* (*P.KRU* 106). Something has happened over time. It used to be fashionable to take the "eternal unchanging Egypt" approach and view the population as not caring very much who was in power, pharaohs or Persian kings or Roman emperors or Byzantine emperors or Umayyad, Fatimid, Mamluk, or Ottoman Muslim governors or British officials or heads of a republic. Nowadays it is fashionable to think that the Muslim conquest of Egypt in the mid-seventh century, with the new rulers keeping the old local officials in place, did not make for much antagonism on the part of the non-Muslim majority. Does a chronological read through these documents support this position? Religious invocations heading documents had been de rigueur since the reign of the Byzantine emperor Maurice (*CSBE 2*, 99). By A.D. 698 or so the framers of *P.CLT* 1 could, if they read Greek, see at the head of their document a bilingual invocation in both Greek and Arabic stating that "There is no God but God alone; Muhammad is the messenger of God." Probably the framers of *P.KRU* 38 of A.D. 738, a document that begins with an invocation of the Trinity and simultaneously honors the "rulers who have power over the whole earth through the counsel of God Almighty," did not read Arabic and so were unaware that the writing support on which the document they kept was engrossed was stamped likewise with the proclamation (also found on coins) that "Muhammad is the messenger of God." Did obliviousness make them simply not care? The reader may form his or her own impressions.

Vernacular legal documents

I have borrowed a version of my subtitle from that of Patrick Wormald's magisterial work of 1999, *Legal Culture in the Early Medieval West: Law as Text, Image and Experience*. Law in late antique Egypt was equally simultaneously text and experience, as already spoken of above. Indeed, the law was experienced as a written textual object that was, or could be, *emphanizei*, brought out into the light of plain sight in court as evidence to prove title against all comers. Yet the production of legal documents in Coptic, the Egyptian vernacular, in a province that had used Greek for government, learning, transactions, and even religion for at

---

[25] I use "Miaphysite" throughout to designate the Egyptian church after the split in patriarchal succession following 536, as the older term "Monophysite" is no longer employed in scholarship.

least six hundred years, is a very new phenomenon.²⁶ One could as a default option have one's instrument engrossed in Greek, as had been the normal practice of Egypt's propertied classes since Alexander. Yet to make the choice of Coptic implies that such a choice was seen as advantageous to the party making it. The agent's choice of what language to use was socially significant.²⁷

The Egyptian language, formerly written in hieroglyphic, hieratic, and demotic writing systems, came to be written in the Greek alphabet (plus extra signs) early in the common era. This, what we designate 'Coptic', was used for horoscopes, translations (occasionally), and religious texts: the Bible was translated piecemeal starting in about the third century.²⁸ Above all, it was the choice for private letters, especially by women,²⁹ who may not have been up to choosing a Greek-writing letter scribe or expressing themselves in a personal missive in Greek.³⁰ As far as legal transactions, and recording them, was concerned, to opt for Coptic for your land sale, your bequest, or your inheritance division showed something about your priorities and about what sort of outcome you desired. However, notwithstanding the female letter-writing phenomenon, statistics that would link the use of Coptic in legal documents with the parties' gender do not

---

²⁶ See L.S.B. MacCoull, "Why Do We Have Coptic Documentary Papyri Before A.D. 641?," in *Actes du huitième Congrès international des études coptes*, ed. N. Bosson and A. Boud'hors, 2 vols. (Leuven, 2007), 2: 751–58; also J. Gascou, "L'Égypte byzantine (284–641)," in *Le monde byzantin*, ed. C. Morrisson et al. (Paris, 2004), 403–36, here 413–14; and now Richter, *Sprache*, 2ⁿᵈ ed., x, xv–xvii; M. Choat, "Language and Culture in Late Antique Egypt," in *A Companion to Late Antiquity*, ed. Rousseau, 342–56, and J. -L. Fournet, "The Multilingual Environment of Late Antique Egypt," in *Oxford Handbook of Papyrology*, ed. R. S. Bagnall (Oxford, 2009), 418–51, here 430–45; A. Papaconstantinou,"Dioscore et la question du bilinguisme dans l'Egypte du VIe siècle," in *Les archives de Dioscore d'Aphrodité*, ed. Fournet, 77–88.

²⁷ I am grateful to Eitan Grossman for illuminating e-mail discussion on this subject, and to T.S. Richter for an advance copy of his "Greek, Coptic, and the 'Language of the Hijra': Rise and Decline of the Coptic Language in Late Antique and Medieval Egypt," in *From Hellenism to Islam: Cultural and Linguistic Change in the Roman Near East*, ed. H. Cotton (Cambridge, forthcoming); also idem, *Sprache*, 2ⁿᵈ ed., xxi, xxiii–xxv.—Interesting western comparanda on vernacular legal documents can be found in M. Herbert, "Before Charters? Property Records in Pre-Anglo-Norman England," in *Charters and Charter Scholarship in Britain and Ireland*, ed. M.T. Flanagan and J.A. Green (New York, 2005), 107–19.

²⁸ Cf. R.S. Bagnall, *Egypt in Late Antiquity* (Princeton, 1993), 253–57; Richter, "Greek, Coptic."

²⁹ R.S. Bagnall and R. Cribiore, *Women's Letters from Ancient Egypt, 300 BC–AD 800* (Ann Arbor, 2006); cf. T. Wilfong, "Gender and Society in Byzantine Egypt," in *Egypt*, ed. Bagnall, 309–27; T.S. Richter, "Coptic Letters," *Asiatische Studien / Etudes Asiatiques* 62 (2008): 739–90.

³⁰ See R. Cribiore, *Gymnastics of the Mind: Greek Education in Hellenistic and Roman Egypt* (Princeton, 2001), 74–101.

seem to work out overall.³¹ In bilingual archives,³² in which some documents about one and the same matter are in Greek and others in Coptic,³³ it does not appear that in this period women by preference had the Coptic ones drawn up as against men opting for Greek.

The choice within a bilingual society to use, for recording transactions in a medium worthy of preservation, a language variety that itself was a kind of hybrid is an interesting phenomenon. The way English is a Germanic language with a vocabulary that is heavily Latin, Coptic is a 'Hamitic' or Afroasiatic language with a vocabulary that is almost one-third Greek loanwords. Coptic developed a legal register that was indeed heavily Greek, as a glance at this volume's glossary will instantly make plain. Code-switching went on within the text of any given individual document; registers too are switched, often between a solemn scriptural register for the 'arenga' (rhetorical-narrative introduction) or *prooimion* and a more colloquial one for the details of the family narrative;³⁴ bilingual notaries switched languages often without changing scripts, writing both languages in the same hand. Egypt was of course a society that had been writing-intensive for a very long time. Egyptians, used to transacting personal affairs in Greek for over half a millennium, as far as their vernacular was concerned developed two types of pragmatic literacy, a religious one and a legal one. (If these 'descended' in any way from the earlier use of demotic in temples and in contracts, I cannot judge.) In both of these media they took account of changes in their world, physical, administrative, and mental.³⁵

The documents we peruse here are nearly all in the classic form of the Roman-Byzantine *diploma*.³⁶ They embody a perpetual witness to a transaction that has taken place, by way of enacting that transaction as it happens in time. They

---

³¹ L.S.B. MacCoull, "The Bilingual Written Environment of Late Antique Egypt: Did Gender Have Anything to Do With It?," *DIOTIMA*, http://www.stoa.org/diotima/essays/fc04/MacCoull.html.

³² Cf. I. Gardner, "Report on the Editing of both the Coptic and the Manichaean Texts from Ismant el-Kharab," in *The Oasis Papers 3*, ed. G.E. Bowen and C.A. Hope (Oxford, 2003), 201–5, here 203.

³³ Cf. L.S.B. MacCoull, "Further Notes on Interrelated Greek and Coptic Documents of the Sixth and Seventh Centuries," *Chronique d'Egypte* 70 (1995): 341–53.

³⁴ It was what has been termed "a persuasive display of acquired skills": V. Burrus and R. Lyman, "Shifting the Focus of History," in *Late Ancient Christianity*, ed. V. Burrus (Minneapolis, 2005), 1–23, here 8.

³⁵ "It would only have been natural for . . . individuals to deploy, with regard to their private economic transactions, techniques and terminological forms derived from their experience of imperial administration. . . . men whose native tongue is likely to have been Coptic . . . had a natural tendency . . . to fall back upon well-known phrases and formulations": P. Sarris, "On Jairus Banaji's *Agrarian Change in Late Antiquity*," *Historical Materialism* 13 (2005): 207–19, here 215–16.

³⁶ Oddly enough, δίπλωμα/ⲇⲓⲡⲗⲱⲙⲁ is not in Förster, *WB*.

are framed by the parties themselves (not by a ruling authority), parties of the first part addressing ("writing to") parties of the second part. They begin with a formal religious invocation after that became legally required.[37] Thus they included elements of what western scholars label both the 'diploma' and the 'writ' (except that they are not first-person proclamations/instructions by rulers)—close to what are loosely called 'charters'.[38] They were, above all, evidential.[39] Some provide dating by the regnal year of the Byzantine emperor, also after that was required;[40] after the seventh-century conquest, no practice of dating by reigns of Muslim rulers is ever found. Nearly all documents give an indiction, specifying one year within the fifteen-year tax cycle begun by Constantine.[41] This date specification both helped the people who preserved them to keep their records organized and made it easier for their descendants (and their advocates) to locate them and use them as proof-materials. (Not all explicit dating information is preserved in the documents in this selection, however.)

Legal documents were, of course, time-spanning devices for data storage and retrieval. Families, government offices, and monasteries kept archives of documents they might need to prove title or otherwise provide evidence in case of future disputes.[42] Most documents, written *transversa charta* or rotulus-style parallel to the short edge of a long strip of papyrus, were rolled (or sometimes folded) up and kept in boxes, baskets, or ceramic jars. (The use of the codex form, even for non-literary writings, did not often lead to large-scale copying of documents into codices; storing separate pieces together seems to have been the preferred method, at least in our period.) Monasteries had what has been termed a "bureaucratic room" for records storage;[43] such facilities continued to

---

[37] *CSBE 2*, 99–109, 290–99.

[38] Cf. R. Sharpe, "The Use of Writs in the Eleventh Century," *Anglo-Saxon England* 32 (2003): 247–91, here 247–50; and D. Bates, "Charters and Historians of Britain and Ireland: Problems and Possibilities," in *Charters and Charter Scholarship in Britain and Ireland*, ed. Flanagan and Green, 107–19.

[39] The favorite debate among earlier juristic scholars was over whether they were performative of the action or recording the action: the answer seems to be both. They certainly possessed what has been called "semiotic impact" (Herbert, "Before Charters?" 110). Cf. Richter, *Sprache*, 2nd ed., xvi.

[40] *CSBE 2*, 43–47, 252–71.

[41] *CSBE 2*, 7–21.

[42] Bagnall, *Egypt in Late Antiquity*, 161–70; cf. Godlewski, *Phoibammon*, 57.

[43] B. Layton, "Rules, Patterns, and the Exercise of Power in Shenoute's Monastery: The Problem of World Replacement and Identity Maintenance," *Journal of Early Christian Studies* 15 (2007): 45–73, here 49. On document format see also J.-L. Fournet, "Disposition et réalisation graphique des lettres et des pétitions protobyzantines: Pour une paléographie 'signifiante' des papyrus documentaires," in *Proceedings of the 24th International Congress of Papyrology*, ed. J. Frösen et al., 2 vols. (Helsinki, 2007), 1: 353–67, esp. 359–62.

serve Christian communities for centuries after the power governing them was no longer a Christian one. The papyri preserved until today were largely kept in such archives, secular or ecclesiastical.[44] Did the use of the Coptic language for certain documents aid in data retrieval for people who needed to find the deed to their house in order to have it brought to court—in the frequently-used verb quoted above, *emphanizei*, brought out into plain sight? It is hard to draw such a conclusion, unless it might have been the case that people given the task of document finding were more familiar with the vernacular than with Greek as time went on.

Different types of oralities, different kinds and degrees of literacies, and their interactions played large roles in the generation of these documents. The document was viewed as the fixing in written words of an act performed orally by the parties. Often we read the framer's words stating that he or she "had it [the document] read aloud to me"—even "read aloud in the Egyptian language"—"and I approved it." (We even have examples in which the document was dictated in Coptic but written down in Greek [such as *P.Lond.* I 77].) While the legal language embodying such acts strove to be univocal—that is its function, to be precise—the orthography of legal terms and expressions in Coptic, varying as it is analyzed through the different optics of late Greek phonology and Coptic dialect, appears multiplex to the reader, and probably was almost polysemous to the hearer as the text was read out. As time goes on, through the chronological reach of Coptic documents we can watch the development of a flexible and practical medium of extra-Byzantine forensic rhetoric[45] even more closely than is possible through Greek-language documents. After Greek was prohibited for public acts around the turn of the seventh to eighth century, Coptic continued to be used as it had been under the later Byzantine rulers, and continued to develop.

Do these documents indeed reflect real life? If so, how and to what extent? Do they interact with reality, helping to effect change? Do they reflect actual changes in legal procedure, in the ways people formally interacted, or do they just embody different ways of recording what went in during the business of

---

[44] For the workings of such a monastery and its integration into the life of its surrounding community see S.J. Clackson, *Coptic and Greek Texts Relating to the Hermopolite Monastery of Apollo* (Oxford, 2000). For monasteries as producers of texts see C. Kotsifou, "Books and Book Production in the Monastic Communities of Byzantine Egypt," in *The Early Christian Book*, ed. W.E. Klingshirn and L. Safran (Washington, DC, 2007), 48–67. I have not yet seen A. Maravela-Solbakk, "Monastic Book Production in Christian Egypt," in *Spätantike Bibliotheken, Leben und Lesen in den frühen Klöstern Ägyptens* (Vienna, 2008).

[45] Hence the first half of the full title of Richter's monograph (see Abbreviations), *Rechtssemantik und forensische Rhetorik*. See Humfress, *Orthodoxy and the Courts*, 77–78, 93–96, 106–32. I shall return to this subject below.

negotiating affairs and writing down compromise solutions?⁴⁶ Reading chronologically may suggest answers to questions of this kind. The tradition of Coptic-language documentary prose— a functional style for instruments that accomplished something— was worked out over time by its practitioners.⁴⁷ Scholars of an earlier era used to be suspicious of what they considered 'fossilized' formulas, phrases that were repeated by rote by the notaries who had learned them from memory. When disputes and their settlements were recorded in this vernacular medium, were the formulas really 'fossils' or did they attest to something that 'really happened'? Even the act of choosing formulas from models—what come to be termed formularies⁴⁸—can still reflect real life; and in the Jeme material in particular one can see a locally-based and community-based reality at work in the pleonastic documentary style. Interpreting the significance of formulas in this document repertory is full of interest: for example, what did a sanction clause mean to its writer and to its audience? A potential contract breaker was threatened with a heavy fine, oaths were sworn in and upon holy places,⁴⁹ and yet in another year's time the parties were back at loggerheads again. Once again, it is fascinating to follow out the continuities—with law being a sacred presence comparable to that of the actual scriptures themselves in the courtroom⁵⁰— while tracing the ways people mentally adjusted to their changing world. It used to be stated that Coptic-language documentation comes into its own only after 641, but this was far from the case. The choice of Coptic for legal documents can probably be traced to the earlier sixth century; securely dated instruments begin, as far as we have now, with the first text in this volume, an item from the archive of the well-known jurist and poet Dioscorus of Aphrodito,⁵¹ explicitly dated to

---

⁴⁶ "Documentary criticism is a work of modesty, and the document, closely scrutinised, reminds us every day that it does not exactly say what it says or what we wish it would say, but instead what people wanted the reader to think": J. Bingen, "Normality and Distinctiveness in the Epigraphy of Greek and Roman Egypt," in idem, *Hellenistic Egypt*, ed., trans., and intro. R.S. Bagnall (Berkeley, 2007), 256–78, here 278.

⁴⁷ Richter, *Sprache*, esp. 1–8; and cf. C. Sirat, *Writing as Handwork* (Turnhout, 2006), 267–71, 319–25, 437–42 on scribal/notarial practice in the sense of practicing.

⁴⁸ Cf. N. Oikonomides, "Formularies," *ODB* 2: 797–98.

⁴⁹ See Humfress, "Law in Practice" and "Law and Justice in *The Later Roman Empire*"; also eadem, "Law and Legal Practice in the Age of Justinian," in *The Cambridge Companion to the Age of Justinian*, ed. M. Maas (Cambridge, 2005), 161–84, esp. 180; *Orthodoxy and the Courts*, 127 with n. 127.

⁵⁰ C. Humfress, "Judging by the Book: Christian Codices and Late Antique Legal Culture," in *The Early Christian Book*, ed. Klingshirn and Safran, 141–59, here 145, 148–59.

⁵¹ See L.S.B. MacCoull, *Dioscorus of Aphrodito: His Work and his World* (Berkeley, 1988), and J.-L. Fournet, *Hellénisme dans l'Égypte du VIe siècle: La bibliothèque et l'oeuvre de Dioscore d'Aphrodité*, 2 vols. (Cairo, 1999). An earlier Coptic document from the Dioscorus archive, P.Berol. 11349 (MacCoull, *Dioscorus*, 22–23), though without an explicit date, has now been dated on prosopographical grounds to 549/550: J.-L. Fournet, "Sur

569. Coptic-language documents, alongside other Coptic-language non-literary and literary materials, are now integrated into the mainstream discourse of the history of late antique Egypt, a state of affairs scholars have striven for over the last few decades.[52] Coptic-language documentary materials indeed continue until the tenth century, when Arabic begins to be used for everyday transactions[53] as well as for governance. The present selection goes down to just before the Abbasid regime replaced that of the Umayyads in 750—a choice that tries not to get involved in the 'how late did late antiquity go?' debate.[54]

The worlds we come to see

In this collection we start in the landscape of Byzantine Egypt at the end of Justinian's reign, a landscape we know well from documentary papyri. Once dismissed in 'Chesterbellocian' terms as a 'servile state',[55] this society is now known for the wealth of its economy and the richness and complexity of its social,

---

les premiers documents juridiques coptes," in *Actes des 13e Journées coptes de Marseille (juin 2007)* (forthcoming): see Richter, *Sprache*, 2nd ed., xxv.

[52] S.J. Clackson, "Papyrology and the Utilization of Coptic Sources," in *Papyrology and the History of Early Islamic Egypt*, ed. P. M. Sijpesteijn and L. Sundelin (Leiden, 2004), 21–44.—Wickham, *Framing the Early Middle Ages*, is a revelation; and the contributors to *Egypt*, ed. Bagnall, use both Greek and Coptic evidence, as well they should.

[53] Just one small-seeming but telling change: in Greek and Coptic sale documents the contract is framed in the first person by the seller ("I, N., am writing to you, M., to state that I am selling you my (x). . ."), and in leases it is first-person by the lessee ("I, N., am leasing from you. . ."), whereas in Arabic-language sale documents the contract is a first-person formulation by the buyer, and in leases by the lessor: G. Frantz-Murphy, "A Comparison of the Arabic and Earlier Egyptian Contract Formularies (5)," *Journal of Near Eastern Studies* 48 (1989): 97–107, here 105; eadem, "Land-Tenure in Egypt in the First Five Centuries of Islamic Rule," in *Agriculture in Egypt*, ed. A.K. Bowman and E. Rogan, Proceedings of the British Academy 96 (Oxford, 1999), 237–66, here 242. This is indeed a mental shift.

[54] Cf. M. Mavroudi, review of G. Fowden, *Qusayr 'Amra: Art and the Umayyad Elite in Late Antique Syria* (Berkeley, 2004), *Journal of Roman Archaeology* 19 (2006): 731–38, here 737–38; also R.S. Bagnall, "Periodizing When You Don't Have To: The Concept of Late Antiquity in Egypt," in *Gab es eine Spätantike?* (Frankfurt, 2003), 39–49. The debate goes on: cf. P. Athanassiadi, "Antiquité tardive: construction et déconstruction d'un modèle historiographique," *Antiquité tardive* 14 (2006): 311–24; A. Marcone, "A Long Late Antiquity?" and E. James, "The Rise and Function of the Concept 'Late Antiquity'," *Journal of Late Antiquity* 1 (2008): 4–19, 20–30 respectively.

[55] H.I. Bell, "The Byzantine Servile State in Egypt," *Journal of Egyptian Archaeology* 4 (1917): 86–106.

intellectual, and religious culture.[56] And, once the domain of specialists in papyrology, it has now been integrated into the normal historical discourse about late antiquity.[57] Egypt under the last century of Byzantine rule had developed an autonomous Miaphysite church that had become a powerful property-owner and a center of loyalty. Miaphysite monasteries were almost like towns with their own dependents,[58] and their abbey churches functioned something like 'minsters' in England a bit later.[59] Estate economies were an especial point of meeting between lay and church powers,[60] being rationally managed to the benefit of both.[61] Late antique structures like these, which we can track thanks to papyri and especially to fiscal and legal instruments, laid the foundations for what continued in the smaller Byzantine empire[62] after the losses of the mid-seventh century.

We come especially to know families of magnates like the Apions of Oxyrhynchus, holders of high imperial office,[63] and families of provincial landowners who were lawyers and literati, transmitters of the classical and Christian *paideia*, like Dioscorus of Aphrodito from whose locality come the first seven of our documents. Persons like these engaged with the legal processes and legal structures present to them in a fashion that was also deeply involved in the religious

---

[56] Gascou, "L'Égypte byzantine"; *The Cambridge Companion to the Age of Justinian*, ed. Maas; P. Sarris, *Economy and Society in the Age of Justinian* (Cambridge, 2006); and now *Egypt*, ed. Bagnall, and G. Ruffini, *Social Networks in Byzantine Egypt* (Cambridge, 2008).

[57] Wickham, *Framing the Early Middle Ages*, esp. 22–25, 242–53, 411–19.—This monograph actually has sections entitled 'Aphrodito in the Sixth Century' and 'Jeme in the Eighth Century', a state of affairs that could only have been dreamed about forty years ago.

[58] Clackson, *Apollo*. For a western parallel cf. C. Stancliffe, "Religion and Society in Ireland," in *The New Cambridge Medieval History*, vol. 1: *c.500–c.700*, ed. P. Fouracre (Cambridge, 2005), 397–425, here 408–9, 414–15.

[59] Cf. J. Blair, *The Church in Anglo-Saxon England* (Oxford, 2005), esp. 80–91.

[60] Cf. K. Bowes, "Personal Devotions and Private Chapels," in *Late Ancient Christianity*, ed. Burrus, 188–210, esp. 200–9 on landowners' churches on their estates.

[61] Cf. E. Papagianni, "Legal Institutions and Practice in Matters of Ecclesiastical Property," and J. Lefort, "The Rural Economy, Seventh-Twelfth Centuries," in *Economic History of Byzantium*, ed. A. Laiou, 3 vols. (Washington, DC, 2002), 3:1037–47 and 1:225–304 respectively; K. Smyrlis, "The Management of Monastic Estates: The Evidence of the Typika," *Dumbarton Oaks Papers* 56 (2002): 245–61, esp. 260–61 and tables 2 and 3; A. Harvey, "Economy," in *Palgrave Advances in Byzantine History*, ed. J. Harris (London, 2005), 83–99; and the papers in *Monastic Estates in Late Antique and Early Islamic Egypt: Ostraca, Papyri, and Studies in Honour of Sarah Clackson*, ed. A. Boud'hors et al. (Cincinnati, 2008).

[62] Cf. L. Neville, *Authority in Byzantine Provincial Society, 950–1100* (Cambridge, 2004).

[63] See now T. Hickey, *Economic Decision Making and Fiscal Participation in Late Antique Egypt* (forthcoming) for the Apions' estates and offices.

and ecclesiastical changes happening all around them[64]—in a province where the emperor was trying to enforce a brand of 'right thinking' that was not shared by the majority. The legal world of these people was that of the on-the-ground practice of notaries, often bilingual, who stocked their family archives with the papers they would need in their multigenerational disputes. In the present collection we begin with lay-monastic transactions, dowry problems, and property transfers and divisions of normal types—and also the donation of village land to endow a monastery, plus a monastic will. Clearly these monasteries were vital to the society. In sixth-century Aphrodito, the father of Dioscorus the lawyer-poet, the former village headman Apollos, founded a monastery dedicated to the Apostles, into which he retired; after his death in 546 his son Dioscorus took over as lay curator.[65] He mediated between the monastic community and the village community, corresponding with neighbors about matters of finance and helping to settle disputes. Bridging the centuries, there were further south at Jeme two monasteries dedicated to the martyr Phoibammon: a smaller one founded in the 570s (*P.KRU* 105) and the larger one that grew from the Christian reconfiguration of the pharaonic temple; they were joined by the St Paul monastery, and our documents owe their survival largely to them.

Egypt was conquered[66] by Muslim Arab invaders in 641 and made a part of a new empire—its granary, and a source for material supplies, human resources, and ideas about governance.[67] We know from documents what post-conquest life was like in two towns in particular: Aphrodito, with its mostly Greek tax records,[68] and Jeme (also referred to by its older Greek name of Kastron Memnonion), from which most of our Coptic-language documentary texts come.[69] The reader encounters people making a living in a world where the town's chief official, the *prôtokômêtês* (headman) or *dioikêtês*, is now also designated by the Coptic-language title *lashane*; where taxation always weighs heavy; and where there is now an *amir* representing both the provincial governor in Fustat and the

---

[64] Cf. Humfress, "Law and Justice."

[65] L.S.B. MacCoull, "The Apa Apollos Monastery of Pharoou and its Papyrus Archive," *Le Muséon* 106 (1993): 21–63.

[66] And it is still unclear how this could have happened: for a downbeat view see Sarris, *Economy and Society*, 229–34.

[67] H. Kennedy, "Egypt as a Province in the Islamic Caliphate, 641–868," and T. Wilfong, "The Non-Muslim Communities: Christian Communities," in *The Cambridge History of Egypt*, 1: *Islamic Egypt, 640–1517*, ed. C.F. Petry (Cambridge, 1998), 62–85, 175–97 respectively; P.M. Sijpesteijn, "The Arab Conquest of Egypt and the Beginning of Muslim Rule," in *Egypt*, ed. Bagnall, 437–59; G. Frantz-Murphy, "The Economics of State Formation in Early Islamic Egypt," in *From al-Andalus to Khurasan: Documents from the Medieval Muslim World*, ed. P.M. Sijpesteijn et al. (Leiden, 2007), 101–14.

[68] Wickham, *Framing the Early Middle Ages*, 134–40 is a good introduction.

[69] Wilfong, *Women*, and Wickham, *Framing the Early Middle Ages*, 419–28, are good guides.

caliph in remote Damascus. Yet still the monasteries, small and large, are closely related to the lives of ordinary families, helping to arbitrate their quarrels and look after their children. The pieces translated here comprise wills, agreements, donations (of property and of persons), sales, pledges, inheritances and their partitions, neighbors' and relatives' disputes, and similar windows into the texture of life.

Our documents come, thanks to the accidents of preservation and discovery, from regionally concentrated areas, here Aphrodito in Middle Egypt (earlier) and Jeme in Upper Egypt (later). We must always be aware of the difficulties consequent upon trying to generalize from data from one region and then applying those conclusions to another region and/or to Egypt as a whole.[70] However, this sort of extrapolation is what papyrologists do, and with our increasing data (in a world in which gathering those data is ever more dangerous) the further finds have tended to bear out the extrapolations. Thematic as well as personal/archival connections can be traced by the reader through the indices of personal and place names.

Workpoints[71]

In these pages the reader meets human beings engaging with the law on the ground, commissioning the writing of—and sometimes themselves writing—texts that simultaneously embody and enact their experiences: experiences, that is, embodied and enacted in the vernacular.[72] Their whole society can be glimpsed between the lines. Underneath it all is a whole body of education, of *paideia*, that long endured, fused as it became with Christian learning.[73] In

---

[70] Bagnall, *Reading Papyri, Writing Ancient History*, chap. 3, "Particular and General," 32–54.

[71] I purposely borrow Lawrence Durrell's word from *The Alexandria Quartet*. Durrell may be somewhat out of fashion at the moment (he is due for a critical renaissance), but he was—on the basis of personal experience— the first imaginative writer in English to draw attention to the Copts, their history, and their culture, and his deliciously acute renderings have been helpful to more than one Coptic specialist (cf. L.S.B. MacCoull, "Christians *Like Yourself*: Copts in the *Quartet*," forthcoming in *Genius Loci*). The dedicatee of this book ("Nessim")—though he had his disagreements with Durrell—would have understood. I am grateful to Michael Haag, who is preparing a new Durrell biography, for e-correspondence.

[72] Cf. Gardner, "Report," 203: "Coptic usages themselves may reveal the social and cultural worlds of their authors to an extent that has not previously been envisaged."

[73] E.J. Watts, *City and School in Late Antique Athens and Alexandria* (Berkeley, 2006), esp. 213–22, 229–30, 237–56; Fournet, *Dioscore*, 1: 262–64, 317–25, 2: 684–90; Humfress, *Orthodoxy and the Courts*, 108: "A formal training in rhetoric . . . shaped and reproduced an *ethos* for the literate elite."

Egypt the educated elite were lastingly familiar with the notion that, in the law, a person could serve God, like Robert Bolt's Thomas More, "wittily, in the tangles of his mind." Both notarial and monastic training combined and helped to promote ". . . a form of learning with new textual and intellectual priorities" that ". . . was not an alternative to traditional forms, because it functioned in a [new] way."[74] From Egypt we have preserved on papyrus, written by such elites, a succession of actual petitions from individuals that vividly sum up just what concrete cases rulers and subjects were grappling with[75]—petitions that could actually change matters.[76] Just such bottom-up maneuvers were at work in the documents translated here.

Parallels to structures and procedures in the early medieval west are not far to seek. It is scholars and students outside the narrow specialisms of papyrology and ancient law, heavily concentrated in the realm of the eastern empire as they are, that this compilation hopes to serve. Those familiar with charter material from Anglo-Saxon England, Merovingian Francia, or early medieval Ireland will find these texts at once a bit strange and oddly familiar in tone. Their framers are telling stories—angled stories, stories with spin,[77] carefully designed to leave out no detail however small. Their notaries are working at the everyday meeting-point of institutional justice and trained compositional efficacy.[78] It is hoped that these texts will begin to receive the wide reading they deserve.

---

[74] A.H. Becker, *Fear of God and the Beginning of Wisdom: The School of Nisibis and Christian Scholastic Culture in Late Antique Mesopotamia* (Philadelphia, 2006), 6: an important comparandum.

[75] J.-L. Fournet and J. Gascou, "Liste des pétitions sur papyrus des Ve-VIIe siècles," along with J. Gascou, "Les pétitions privées," and J.-L. Fournet, "Entre document et littérature: la pétition dans l'antiquité tardive," all in *Les pétitions à Byzance*, ed. D. Feissel and J. Gascou (Paris, 2004), 141–96, 93–103, 61–74 respectively. (Unfortunately the "Liste" is not arranged in chronological order.) These petitions are all in Greek, though, and we may indeed here be up against a register phenomenon. I know of no Coptic-language petitions to the authorities, Byzantine or Muslim, before or after 641; and after the second decade of the eighth century, petitioning would probably have had to be done in Arabic—through the agency of a bilingual drafter—to be acceptable.

[76] Humfress, "Cracking the Codex," going back to Valentinian's Novel 21.2.

[77] For a recent treatment of this aspect of the documents of donation of children to monasteries mentioned above, see T.S. Richter, "What's in a Story? Cultural Narratology and Coptic Child Donation Documents," *Journal of Juristic Papyrology* 35 (2005): 237–64.

[78] For western comparanda see e.g. R. Firth Green, "Literature and Law," in *A Companion to Medieval English Literature and Culture c.1350–c.1500*, ed. P. Brown (Oxford, 2007), 292–306, esp. 292, 294, 296–97. I have learned much from R.C. Stacey, *Dark Speech: The Performance of Law in Early Ireland* (Philadelphia, 2007), esp. 1–14, 48–49, 54–55, 78–80, 92–94, 96–98, 102–5, 120–21, 146–48, 157–59, 165–67, 176–80,

The tradition of Christian legal *paideia* described and manifested here could have continued to serve Egypt even after Christians were no longer the majority of its population. It could have played a role of resistance like that of the classics in mid-twentieth-century eastern Europe.[79] Yet it did not. Khedive Ismail in the nineteenth century said "Mon pays s'appartient à l'Europe," and the dedicatee of this volume said "La conciliation passe par la Méditérranée"; but others have gone another way.[80] However, the most recent research reminds us that by as late as "in 800 a high proportion of the city-level aristocratic families of the late empire were still around, speaking . . . Coptic. . .,"[81] and their legal homeland was the legal text. In the documents collected here we can track the astringent, idiosyncratic sensibility of a living world.[82] Whatever else may have happened, as late ancient provincial people passed from a world in which law distinguished *honestiores* and *humiliores* to one in which 'personal status law' came to obtain, their texts have endured, perhaps to point to future possibilities. These texts witness to and embody the cognitive resources of Coptic culture.[83] J.R.R. Tolkien once quoted another scholar as saying "'Languages are the chief distinguishing marks of peoples. No people in fact comes into being until it speaks a language of its own: let the languages perish and the peoples perish too, or become different peoples. But that never happens except as the result of oppression and distress'."[84] Conclusions may be drawn.[85]

208–13, 218–20, 224–34, 238–43, 249; 224: ". . . the power of the vernacular was a key aspect of the vernacular of power."

[79] J. Axer and K. Tomaszuk, "Central-Eastern Europe," in *A Companion to the Classical Tradition*, ed. C.W. Kallendorf (Oxford, 2007), 132–55.

[80] R.S. Bagnall, "Egypt and the Concept of the Mediterranean," in *Rethinking the Mediterranean*, ed. W.V. Harris (Oxford, 2005), 339–47.

[81] Wickham, *Framing the Early Middle Ages*, 168 (and cf. 254).

[82] ". . . not simply as the assent to a series of intellectual propositions but rather as richly embodied cultural systems": D. Krueger, "The Practice of Christianity in Byzantium," in *Byzantine Christianity*, ed. idem (Minneapolis, 2006), 1–15, here 3.

[83] Compare the salutary warnings in V. Karalis, "Greek Christianity After 1453," in *The Blackwell Companion to Eastern Christianity*, ed. K. Parry (Oxford, 2007), 156–85.

[84] Quoted in J. Lobdell, "Welsh Language," in *J.R.R. Tolkien Encyclopedia: Scholarship and Critical Assessment*, ed. M.D.C. Drout (New York, 2007), 705–6, here 705.

[85] Cf. J. Timbie, "Coptic Christianity," in *Blackwell Companion to Eastern Christianity*, ed. Parry, 94–116, here 95; A. Papaconstantinou, "Historiography, Hagiography, and the Making of the Coptic 'Church of the Martyrs' in Early Islamic Egypt," *Dumbarton Oaks Papers* 60 (2006): 65–86, esp. 67–69, 72, 78–79; and 82–84 on language; eadem, "'They Shall Speak the Arabic Language and Take Pride in It': Reconsidering the Fate of Coptic After the Arab Conquest," *Le Muséon* 120 (2007): 273–99; and Richter, "Greek, Coptic, and the 'Language of the Hijra'"; also idem, "Greek and Coptic in Late Antiquity," in *Law and Society in Ptolemaic, Roman, and Byzantine Egypt*, ed. J.G. Keenan et al. (Cambridge, forthcoming).

P.Cair.Masp. II 67176r + P.Alex.inv. 689
Cession of Land

DATE: 4 November 569

PLACE: Aphrodito

PARTIES: Anoup son of Apollo and Julius son of Sarapammon, brothers, both sons of Mesianê; Papnoute, monk of the monastery of the Apostles of Pharoou founded by Apollos father of Dioscorus[1]

OBJECT: Inherited monastic cell

WITNESSES:[2] [none]

SCRIBE: Dioscorus of Aphrodito

PUBLICATION: L.S.B. MacCoull, "A Coptic Cession of Land by Dioscorus of Aphrodito," in *Acts of the Second International Congress of Coptic Studies* (Rome, 1985), 159–66, repr. in eadem, *Coptic Perspectives on Late Antiquity* (Aldershot, 1993), no. VII; eadem, *Dioscorus*, 36–39; cf. Richter, *Sprache*, 2nd ed., xxiv.

This is the earliest extant Coptic-language legal document to bear a specific absolute date.[3] That date is written at the end, not in an opening dating formula as specified by Justinian's Novel 47 of A.D. 537;[4] by the reign of Justin II, that emperor had altered the phraseology somewhat. The situation of this document

---

[1] Further data on the parties to this document and the second, fourth, and sixth through ninth documents in this collection will be found in the forthcoming Aphrodito prosopography being made by G. Ruffini (I thank him for sending a draft version).

[2] These deserve attention: see K.A. Worp, "Witness Subscriptions in Documents from the Dioscorus Archive," in *Les archives de Dioscore d'Aphrodité*, ed. Fournet, 143–53.

[3] An earlier document without explicit date has been prosopographically dated to 549/50: J.-L. Fournet, "Sur les premiers documents juridiques coptes" (forthcoming), and Richter, *Sprache*, 2nd ed., xxv.

[4] *CSBE 2*, 45.

is one in which two sons of the same mother (by two different fathers)[5] are about to enter monastic life in the monastery founded by Apollos, the late father of the lawyer-poet Dioscorus, dedicated to the Apostles[6] at the site known as Pharoou.[7] Dioscorus himself, acting as the monastery's caretaker, is helping to resolve a dispute with one of the monastery's officials, Apa Papnoute, over ownership of a monastic residence. Although entrants were supposed to renounce both their property and their blood family upon joining a monastery,[8] all our documentation shows that this norm was a long way from being observed.[9] A factor in the dispute is who is indeed the owner of the property, the mother or her two sons jointly? Only the legal owner would have the capacity to enter into an agreement with the monastic official. Apparently the decision reached is that the mother, who has urged her sons to become monks, has settled the property upon them and they thus can go shares with the superior.

[fr. 1] [. . . having established] a cession (with?) Apa Papnoute . . . so as to be its [owner?] lawfully for ever, she agreeing . . . if my sons also, having become monks, are to inherit the cell,[10] not returning the matter to her. Accordingly she said in the cession that if they become monks they are to share in this way, but if not, no heir is to have a case,[11] neither person of mine[12] nor stranger. But if they enter the mon[astic life] . . . writing to them . . . producing . . . It happened that an additional week of the fifteenth (indiction) year past (566) intervened. But when they heard these things, namely Anoup son of Apollo and Julius son of Sarapammon, they brought a countersuit[13] against them, (to the effect) that their mother was not the owner, but rather the sons were (the owners). They made an agreement (of) cession which was drawn up with Apa Papnoute. I found . . . showing[14] that Apa Papnoute was to agree . . . with the heirs. But the sons with . . . were to . . .

---

[5] See P. van Minnen, "Dioscorus and the Law," in *Learned Antiquity*, ed. A.A. MacDonald et al. (Leuven, 2003), 115–33.

[6] Papaconstantinou, *Saints*, 56–58, esp. here 57.

[7] MacCoull, "The Apa Apollos Monastery of Pharoou (Aphrodito) and its Papyrus Archive."

[8] Layton, "Rules, Patterns, and the Exercise of Power in Shenoute's Monastery," 60; *Nov.Just.* 5.5 (from A.D. 535).

[9] Cf. O'Connell, "Monastic Dwellings," 263–65.

[10] Here *ri* (ⲣⲓ). See D. Brooks-Hedstrom, "Divine Architects: Designing the Monastic Dwelling Place," in *Egypt*, ed. Bagnall, 368–89.

[11] Literally "matter," *hôb* (ϩⲱⲃ), calquing the Roman-law *res*.

[12] Quoting Mesianê's direct words here.

[13] *antidikologein* (ἀντιδικολογεῖν): cf. Förster, *WB*, 62, though not this form.

[14] *sêmainein* (σημαίνειν): Förster, *WB*, 723.

I Papnoute, at all times when you have ... yourselves over the cell, and ... nothing in improvement. ... other men ... [fr. 2] ... they did not sell it without consideration,[15] but even if it had been without consideration, the boundaries[16] were warranted for them concerning ... the consideration. As the Lord put it into my heart that they should inherit, ... Apa Papnoute and Anoup son of Apollo and Julius son of Sarapammon are to inherit the above simultaneously, half and half, according to the right[17] of those of our house. (As for) the half of Apa Papnoute, should anyone proceed against (him) over their sale ... (they would risk?) their property with one another ... Concerning the payment sent to me, I have given it ... Only if no improvement has been made to the cell is Apa Papnoute not to seek for a ... from them. Let the cell be ready at all times, serviceable for them in good order[18] ... with one another without quarrelling. For they are in harmony together[19] according to our scrutiny[20] ... our counsel that we (have taken). For because Anoup and Julius, the sons, have entered the monastic life according to the counsels of Mesianê their mother, they are to share[21] with Apa Papnoute, rightly and justly [Greek], going half-and-half simultaneously, accordingly for the rest, according to this plan[22] that is decided and without dissembling.[23]

+ Give it to the God-loving "Great Men"[24] of the mountain of Pharoou and its whole village, from Dioscorus, most humble son of Apa Apollo of Pharoou. + [Greek] The Holy Trinity.[25] And guard me through your prayers from above ...

+ Hathyr, new moon, third indiction, fourth year of the reign and consulate[26] of our most divine master Flavius Justin, semper Augustus, imperator. [Greek]

---

[15] *askopôs* (ἀσκόπως): Förster, *WB*, 115.

[16] Probably from *fossatus*, a boundary: not listed in S. Daris, *Il lessico latino nel greco d'Egitto*, 2nd ed. (Barcelona, 1991).

[17] *dikaion* (δίκαιον): Förster, *WB*, 192–95, esp. here 193–94.

[18] *ep'ordinon* (ЄΠΟΡΔΙΝΟΝ): Förster, *WB*, 587.

[19] *symphônein* (συμφωνεῖν): Förster, *WB*, 770–71.

[20] *dokimasia* (δοκιμασία): Förster, *WB*, 207.

[21] *metechein* (μετέχειν): Förster, *WB*, 518.

[22] *typos* (ΤΥΠΟC), here, it seems, in its earlier signification (cf. Förster, *WB*, 827–28); cf. below, note on *P.CLT* 1.

[23] *hypokrisis* (ὑπόκρισις): not in Förster, *WB*.

[24] We will encounter this expression later in 8th-century Jeme (cf. Wilfong, *Women*, 7, 89, 127). These respected individuals can be either lay (or clerical) officials or monastic leaders.

[25] See L.S.B. MacCoull, "'The Holy Trinity' at Aphrodito," *Tyche* 6 (1991): 109–11.

[26] For both of these, *CSBE* 2, 94–95, 210 (**2A**); and cf. 47–48.

P.Lond. V 1709

Arbitration of Inheritance

DATE: *c.*570

PLACE: Antinoopolis

PARTIES: Victorine and Phoibammon, children of the late John, a deacon and official; Philadelphia, their younger half-sister, and Amanias, their widowed stepmother

OBJECT: Household goods, house property, grain, money

WITNESSES: 5 [named]

SCRIBE: Dioscorus of Aphrodito

PUBLICATION: MacCoull, *Dioscorus*, 45–47; cf. Richter, *Sprache*, 2nd ed., xxiii.

Dioscorus has been called in to sort out the quarrels of half-siblings over inheritances from their deceased father, a deacon of Antinoopolis. The deacon John's first wife, the mother of his two eldest children Victorine and Phoibammon, died; he got married again, to a woman named Amanias by whom he had a younger daughter, Philadelphia, Victorine and Phoibammon's half-sister. Although Victorine is already married (to a husband named Aphous known from *P.Cair.Masp.* I 67006 v), there seems to be a difficulty over her dowry. She and her brother Phoibammon are about to take their stepmother Amanias and their half-sister Philadelphia to court for their having wrongly appropriated all of John's property, including what should have gone to them, Phoibammon and Victorine, as the first-born. The trouble is that John died without leaving a testament in writing, having made only an oral declaration.[1] Philadelphia is apparently now trying to produce a donation document from her father making the property over to her, but the elder children are scornful of this obvious ploy. Amanias too is determined that her daughter, not yet of age, shall win out. It seems that she and her daughter have gone to live in the south, and have had to return to Antinoopolis to thrash out the dispute.

This is a first-person law report, not a document in epistolary style. Unfortunately, it is fragmentary, and Dioscorus' decision is not known.

---

[1] See D. Simon, "Intestate Succession," *ODB*, 2:1004.

+ According to the style² of an arbitration³ I have heard the case⁴ of the (legal) matter⁵ of Phoibammon the weak⁶ and Victorine his sister, children of the late John the deacon, former supervisor⁷ of the honored house of the most magnificent⁸ patrician Athanasius,⁹ (who are) seeking a judgement with regard to their sister Philadelphia whom their father engendered with his second wife Amanias. They are asking me for an oath¹⁰ at the same time, so that I may hear their (legal) matter that they have with one another, and they have requested me for a single agreement.¹¹

They informed me that they had drawn up a *compromissum*,¹² and then came to me in person because they were burdened,¹³ so that I might investigate¹⁴ their (legal) matter that they were disputing about¹⁵ and suing¹⁶ one another concerning it, according to the way that the Lord will inform me (as to) its solution. I listened to them, according to their lawsuit with one another. This is the nature¹⁷ of their matter: Phoibammon on the one hand, and Victorine his sister, children of John the deacon by his first wife, are disputing with Philadelphia the daughter of his second wife, who is their paternal (half-)sister, saying that she took all the household goods¹⁸ of their father. She had power over them (the goods), together with her mother, up to and including even his house. They had power over them,

---

² *tropos* (τρόπος): Förster, *WB*, 824–25.

³ *mesiteia* (μεσιτεία): Förster, *WB*, 516.—The Columbia University Library houses unpublished notes by the late A.A. Schiller for a work to be titled "Arbitration in Coptic Law," and I have used them at first hand.

⁴ *hypothesis* (ὑπόθεσις): Förster, *WB*, 838: also "the circumstances."

⁵ *hôb* (ϩⲱⲃ) again calquing *res* in Roman law; cf. Richter, *Sprache*, 329–30.

⁶ Perhaps he, the only son, was disabled in some way?

⁷ *pronoêtês* (προνοητής): Förster, *WB*, 683; and see Sarris, *Economy*, 29.

⁸ *paneuphêmos* (πανεύφημος), title for a high Byzantine official: Förster, *WB*, 604–5.

⁹ Duke of the Thebaid 565–568: Fournet, *Dioscore*, 1:330–32; cf. Sarris, *Economy*, 165. For a deacon holding such a position cf. G. Schmelz, *Kirchliche Amtsträger im spätantiken Ägypten* (Leipzig, 2002), 256–61, 274–79.

¹⁰ *anash* (ⲁⲛⲁϣ): cf. Seidl, "Eid," 146–47; and below, *P.CLT* 5, note 36.

¹¹ *synainesis* (συναίνεσις): Förster, *WB*, 773.

¹² Daris, *Lessico latino*, 59.

¹³ *enochlein* (ἐνοχλεῖν): Förster, *WB*, 262.

¹⁴ *exetazein* (ἐξετάζειν): Förster, *WB*, 270.

¹⁵ *amphiballein* (ἀμφιβάλλειν): Förster, *WB*, 40–41; cf. Richter, *Sprache*, 367 (no. 306).

¹⁶ *dikazesthai* (δικάζεσθαι): Förster, *WB*, 192.

¹⁷ *mine* (ⲙⲓⲛⲉ), also a word fraught with meaning in the Christological disputes; these terms had come much to the fore in the discourse surrounding the separation of Egypt's Miaphysite church in the mid-sixth century. It is interesting to see such a term in its ordinary 'lay dress' used in legal discourse. A contemporary would have heard both fields of resonance in this word.

¹⁸ *skeuê* (σκευή): Förster, *WB*, 735–37.

saying, "We will throw you (pl.) out of the inheritance of your father," in such a way as if we were children of a whore. But we are the legitimate[19] children of his first wife, and our father went to his death without a written[20] will [Greek]. But he said, in the presence of witnesses, "My children are to divide among them all that is mine: and I order that they divide it up among themselves, one-third to each, in accordance with my poverty." But she, Philadelphia, along with her mother, has taken those household goods up until now, and they have not let us (have our shares) without trouble. So when we heard . . . we threw out (their suggestion about? or production of?) a donation document of our father . . . to Philadelphia making over to her all those household goods named[21] in writing above,[22] in every shape and form,[23] all of which he had (allegedly) given to her, and also his share of a house that he had bought as well, he having no other house but that one, and saying . . . [. . .] . . . . Phoibammon and Victorine . . . their portion . . . For his documents are in her hand, and she has power over them . . . I hope to obtain the gift . . . that our mother gave me for my dowry. . . . The first wife divided (it) . . . [. . .] . . . the property . . . in his great sickness . . . he desired . . . but he said . . . [. . .][24] . . . respectable;[25] but only . . . Victorine . . . against the (gift?) . . . to divide them . . . Our father . . . the voice . . . many men . . .[26] after his death. All the household goods belonged to his poverty. We nullified (that) and requited them, we all at once, the three heirs; but the mother of Philadelphia has taken a stand against us (two), (saying) "My daughter, though young,[27] is going to come of age and handle her affairs well with regard to you (pl.). I am not going to divide anything, nor will I let you (pl.) take anything. I have been looking for the upshot[28] of the order of the unwritten will of their father." Phoibammon produced (something) in evidence, with them witnessing it (before?) the defense attorney[29] of their city, Assiut,[30] with some witnesses saying to her [Philadelphia],

---

[19] Here *authentês* (αὐθέντης): Förster, *WB*, 122–23, here 122.

[20] For *agraphos* (ἄγραφος) see Förster, *WB*, 12.

[21] *-onomaze* (-ⲟⲛⲟⲙⲁⲍⲉ): cf. Förster, *WB*, 584 (ὀνομάζειν).

[22] Read *shrpshai* (ϣⲣⲡⲥϩⲁⲓ) for the original editor's (H.I. Bell in *P.Lond.* V) ⲉⲃⲣⲡⲕⲁⲓ. No list is preserved at the head of this document (perhaps one was attached at some point).

[23] *eidos* (εἶδος): Förster, *WB*, 227–28.

[24] The proper name originally read here is probably a ghost-name; it is not found in M. Hasitzka, "Namen in koptischen dokumentarischen Texten," www.onb.ac.at/sammlungen/papyrus/publ/kopt_namen.pdf

[25] Also misunderstood as a proper name.

[26] This fragmentary bit may refer to John's *viva voce* declaration before witnesses, already referred to.

[27] Once again misread by Bell as a proper name.

[28] *systasis* (σύστασις): Förster, *WB*, 782.

[29] *antekdikos* (ἀντέκδικος): Förster, *WB*, 61; from *ekdikos* (ἔκδικος), *defensor*: Förster, *WB*, 236; cf. Sarris, *Economy*, 210.

[30] Timm, *Ägypten*, 1:235–51.

"His [Phoibammon's] father said before his death that they were to divide it up, each one (getting) one-third, (but) with no fifth[31] for Philadelphia." He revealed from the . . . , that of those witnesses the *defensor* said, "What, or what portion of what, are they giving her?" But these are the witnesses: Paul son of Azarias, deacon of the prisons,[32] and Mena son of Flavius [N.], and Mena son of Sie, former supervisor of . . ., and N. son of N., and Constantine son of Cyrus the honey-seller; these are all of them.

And Colluthus . . . namely Philadelphia . . . especially . . . the need of all men. But Victorine is crying out saying "Pay me my dowry; if the inheritance belongs to you (Philadelphia) . . . These are they: twelve artabas of wheat and everything that he gave me, and what was my mother's, a portion[33] of the support money[34] that he promised[35] for the dowry that was to be given to me: give it to me." She (Philadelphia) said bad things about him (John), (to the effect that) he expelled her, even though . . . the household goods . . .

Philadelphia . . . exchanging with . . . your sister . . . four places . . . dowry . . . of the first marriage . . . [movable and] immovable and [self-moving] . . . to their reckoning[36] . . . But Victorine is contesting . . . what was given to her . . . with the gift to the bridegroom[37] . . .

---

[31] Reading the number five here instead of the verb "to give". Does this envision five possible heirs, the three children, the widow, and a charity?

[32] *signon* (σίγνον): Förster, *WB*, 726–27; Daris, *Lessico*, 103. See S. Torallas Tovar, "The Police in Byzantine Egypt," in *Current Research in Egyptology 2000*, ed. A. McDonald and C. Riggs (Oxford, 2000), 115–23; cf. Sarris, *Economy*, 131–32; Schmelz, *Kirchliche Amtsträger*, 295–96.

[33] Here *shaat* (ϣⲁⲁⲧ).

[34] *chorêgia* (χορηγία): Förster, *WB*, 876.

[35] *syntaze* (from *syntassein* / συντάσσειν): Förster, *WB*, 780.

[36] *gnôsis* (γνῶσις): Förster, *WB*, 151–52.

[37] On the meaning of *sheleet* (ϣⲉⲗⲉⲉⲧ) see Wilfong, *Women*, 138, 141.

P. KRU 105

Donation of Village Land for a Monastic Foundation

DATE:[1] between 576 and 578

PLACE: Thebes

PARTIES: Village, clergy, and *lashane* (village headman)

OBJECT: Landed property

SUM [fine]: 6 oz. gold

WITNESSES: 6

SCRIBE: Damian,[2] *grammatikos*

PUBLICATION: *P.RevilloutCopt.* 4 ['Boulaq 5']; A. Steinwenter, "Zur Edition der koptischen Rechtsurkunden aus Djême," *Orientalia* 4 (1935): 377–85; Till, *KRUTheb*, 188–90

This document is rightly seen as the foundation instrument for the first of the two Phoibammon monasteries in the Thebes region.[3] It was originally linked to the larger and later one, that in the pharaonic temple, but more likely it was the act of founding its smaller, earlier predecessor (MacCoull, "A Date"). The deed is executed by an entire village acting as a body represented by its officials.[4] Crum, at first followed by Steinwenter,[5] originally dated this document to the later sixth century; Steinwenter later changed his mind and influenced Till to place it in the second half of the seventh, but that seems impossible owing to the mention of the "Christ-loving kings", who have to be Byzantine emperors, not Muslim overlords.[6] In this text we see the village acting to transfer land to the

---

[1] L.S.B. MacCoull, "A Date for *P.KRU* 105?," paper at the 25th International Congress of Papyrology (Ann Arbor, 2007).

[2] Corrected from 'Dakianos' initially on the basis of Revillout's facsimile, and subsequently on that of a photograph for which I thank Eugene Cruz-Uribe.

[3] M. Krause, "Zwei Phoibammon-Klöster in Theben-West," *Mitteilungen des deutschen archäologischen Instituts Kairo* 37 (1981): 261–66.

[4] See A. Papaconstantinou in *Journal of Juristic Papyrology* 32 (2002): 92.

[5] A. Steinwenter, "Die Rechtsstellung der Kirchen und Klöster nach den Papyri," *Zeitschrift der Savigny-Stiftung für Rechtsgeschichte, kanonistische Abteilung* 50 (1930): 1–50, here 14.

[6] See Godlewski, *Phoibammon*, 63–64, 81.

collective ownership of what appears to be an already existing monastic community, a group who "have taken care for" the site "since it was a desert." (This expression would be more likely to designate an original settlement, not a huge structure already in place that was simply being re-used.) The community has the authority to appoint a superior of its own choosing, who upon succeeding is also to become owner of the property; from this incomplete text we do not know the identity of the superior at the moment the document was drawn up.

. . . that will come after you, God and yourselves willing, according to what may be necessary, because of the fact that you are owners[7] of the whole *topos* of Apa Phoibammon, so as to dwell in it, build on it or tear down,[8] or receive men to yourselves there, anyone who will walk in the fear of God for the whole time of your life and of the one you shall assign to the *topos* after you to serve it in the work of charity to the poor. And no man shall be able (to transgress this), and anyone who dares to will (incur) the judgement of God and will pay to account of fine, according to the damages that our Christ-loving lords the kings[9] have defined, six ounces of gold;[10] after the fine he is to appear and acknowledge every matter written in this document, because we find that you are the ones who took trouble for the *topos* from the first; you established it since it was a desert. Because of this, the one whom you shall assign to the *topos* after you depart from the body, he shall rule over the place, according as we have written above.

No man shall be able to go to law against this in court or before a place of judgement, because it has seemed good to us in this way. And we all together have established this document which will be secure and warranted and effective and have validity in all places where it may be produced in evidence, before any rule or authority. And they asked us, we agreed.

+ We, the whole village, through the most pious priests and Papnoute the most honorable *lashane* [village headman], we assent to this document. +++

Jeremiah, archpriest,[11] I assent to these words.

---

[7] Lit. "lords", as throughout.

[8] We will encounter versions of this owners'-rights clause many times.

[9] I conclude that this refers to Justin II and Aelia Sophia (cf. *CSBE 2*, 288, XXXVIII (f) and (g)). For 'Christ-loving' as an epithet of plural Byzantine co-rulers cf., e.g., *Inscriptions grecques et latines de la Syrie*, vol. 6, ed. J.P. Rey-Coquais (Paris, 1967), no. 2984, lines 10–11. (I thank Kent Rigsby for directing me to the Packard epigraphy website.)

[10] Fines (and other sums) were still being reckoned in ounces of gold in documents of the Byzantine period: e.g., *P.Lond.* V 1730.22; I 77.54 (the testament of Abraham of Hermonthis, dated to c.600[-610], of which more below: see L.S.B. MacCoull, "Apa Abraham," in *Byzantine Monastic Foundation Documents*, ed. J.P. Thomas and A.C. Hero, 5 vols. [Washington, DC, 2000], 1: 51–58).

[11] See Schmelz, *Kirchliche Amtsträger*, 37.

Joseph son of Mythia, priest of the Apostles'[12] (Church), I assent to these words.

+Kyrikos son of Joseph, priest, I assent to these words.+

+++ I Joseph son of Abraham, priest of St Victor's,[13] I assent to these words.—I Daniel, priest, I wrote for him as he did not know how;[14] he made three crosses with his hand.[15]

+ I Daniel son of Andrew, priest of St Mary's,[16] I assent to these words as I heard them.+

+ I Abraham son of Lelou, priest, I assent to these words.

+++ Apa Victor son of Pouôhe, priest, I assent to these words.

+ Elisha son of Hatre, deacon, I assent to these words.+

+ Peter son of Moses, deacon, I assent to these words.+

+ Papnoute son of Isaac, deacon, I assent to these words.+

++ David son of Ezekiel, deacon, I assent to these words.

+ Ezekiel son of Pahom, I bear witness.

Abraham son of Enoch, I bear witness.

Peter son of Jeremiah, I bear witness. +++

Kame son of Pabos, I bear witness.

[Greek] Written by me, Damian, on my own behalf.

+ Geton son of John, I bear witness.

+ John son of Joseph, I bear witness.+

[Greek] By me, Damian, *grammatikos*, who also executed this document; being asked, I wrote for Papnouthi the village headman[17] as he did not know letters (*grammata*); he wrote three crosses with his hand.

---

[12] Papaconstantinou, *Saints*, 56–57, esp. here 57.

[13] Papaconstantinou, *Saints*, 62–68, esp. here 64.

[14] An illiterate priest? See the introduction to this document. Possibly this means that Joseph was literate in Greek but not in Coptic.

[15] Other than the early, medieval-England-oriented study by C. Sisson, "Marks as Signatures," *The Library*, 4th ser. 9 (1928): 1–37 (I thank Caroline Humfress for this reference), I have not found a prescription in Roman law for this practice.

[16] See A. Papaconstantinou, "Les sanctuaires de la Vierge dans l'Égypte byzantine et omeyyade," *Journal of Juristic Papyrology* 30 (2000): 81–94, here 88–89 (no. 17).

[17] Here *prôtôkomêtês* (πρωτωκομήτης) in Greek, not *lashane* (ⲗⲁϣⲁⲛⲉ) in Coptic.

P.Mich.inv. 6898
Mutual Cession of Land

DATE: 632 (?)

PLACE: Aphrodite

PARTIES: Thaumastê (also acting for her late son Paul) and her daughter Anastasia, on one part; Colluthus and Mark, sons of Christopher, on the other part

OBJECT: Agricultural property with buildings thereon

SUM [fine]: 36 solidi

SCRIBE: Apa Rasios (Rashe)[1]

WITNESSES: 5

PUBLICATION: A. Alcock and P.J. Sijpesteijn, "Early 7th Cent. Coptic Contract from Aphrodito," *Enchoria* 26 (2000): 1–19; *SB* 26. 16647; *KSB 3*, 1369; a re-edition by H. Förster is forthcoming

This document and its relatives have occasioned no small controversy (see Richter, *Sprache*, 2nd ed., xxiii-xxv). After the initial publication, the authors of which opted for a seventh-century date, the present writer, noticing text misreadings and details such as the oath clause, the types of fiscality mentioned (the taxes in grain and money and on river transport), and the prosopography, attempted to date it rather to the sixth.[2] These suggestions were later modified with a further dating schema according to which the 'second Aphrodito dossier' is seventh-century and spans the conquest.[3] I have tried to take these conclusions into consideration and re-revisit the document group with a yet further dating plan.[4]

---

[1] Known as the scribe (in Greek) of *P.Mich.* XIII 662, most recently dated (Bagnall and Worp, "Dating") to as late as 645 (for him see J.M. Diethart and K.A. Worp, *Notarsunterschriften im byzantinischen Ägypten (ByzNot)*, 2 vols. [Vienna, 1986], 1: 31 [Aphrodite 17.1.1], 2: Tafel 4). Comparing the hand this scribe used to write Greek and the hand he used to write Coptic is instructive.

[2] L.S.B. MacCoull, "P.Mich.Inv. 6898 Revisited: A Sixth-Century Coptic Contract from Aphrodito," *Zeitschrift für Papyrologie und Epigraphik* 141 (2002): 199–203; also M. Hasitzka, "Einige Korrekturen zu P.Mich.Inv. 6898," *Enchoria* 27 (2001): 200–1.

[3] R.S. Bagnall and K.A. Worp, "Dating the Coptic Legal Documents from Aphrodite," *Zeitschrift für Papyrologie und Epigraphik* 148 (2004): 247–52.

[4] L.S.B. MacCoull, "More on Documentary Coptic at Aphrodito," *Chronique d'Égypte* 82 (2007): 365–74.

Settling the question definitively must await the full edition of the Vatican Coptic papyri (see below) that belong to this group. In general for Aphrodito transactions see Ruffini, *Social Networks*, chaps. 3 and 4.

In these instruments we look in on the property transactions of a woman named Thaumastê, daughter of the late Paul. She has been married twice: first to the late Constantine, with whom she had a son named Paul after his grandfather; apparently this son did not live long. Subsequently she was remarried, to a man named Jacob, who engaged in further property transactions (see below) and fathered a daughter with Thaumastê named Anastasia before himself dying. Thaumastê here is transferring a complex set of landed and built properties between herself and two brothers, Colluthus and Mark, sons of Christopher, an Aphrodito 'contributor' or substantial proprietor. We also observe the interesting interrelations of the population with a famous monastic house. Thaumastê's late father Paul had donated some property to the Monastery of Shenoute in the Panopolite;[5] the monastery had subsequently sold land back to the Aphrodito family, thus getting a cash profit for itself and enabling the entrepreneurial families to carry on further land transactions. Everyone benefited, and the monastic institution became even more closely inwoven into society—here a society already traumatized by ten years of Persian occupation, if the provisional dating suggested here can stand.

. . . and interchanging with one another . . . (we) the aforenamed, Thaumastê daughter of the late Paul and Anastasia her daughter, contributors,[6] we are willing to give to you . . . the aforenamed Colluthus and Mark, sons of Christopher . . . ; we cede to you in every cession and exchange and concession[7] and interchange, from now for ever, and this is our wish arising from just equity and authority . . . not held back. This is what happened . . . from our parents . . . by sale . . . in the east field of the village of Aphrodite in the allotment of Talôl, . . . with the well being dug, together with the watchman's hut and the tower[8] and the house and the enclosure and the livestock pen and the granary and the orchard and the place for vegetables and the palm trees and all the trees whether yielding

---

[5] See R.-G. Coquin et al., "Dayr Anbā Shinūdah," *Coptic Encyclopaedia*, 3: 761–69; cf. below, notes 12 and 16 to this document.

[6] *syntelestês* (συντελεστής): Förster, *WB*, 780–81; A. Laniado, "Συντελεστής: notes sur un terme fiscale surinterpreté," *Journal of Juristic Papyrology* 26 (1996): 23–51; M. Mirković, "Ktetores, syntelestai et l'impôt," in *Les archives de Dioscore d'Aphrodité cent ans après*, ed. Fournet, 191–202. See Sarris, *Economy*, 99, 157.

[7] *synchôrêsis* (συγχώρησις): Förster, *WB*, 763–64.

[8] G. Descoeudres, "Wohntürme in Klöstern und Ermitagen Ägyptens," in *ΘΕΜΕΛΙΑ: Studien Peter Grossmann zum 65. Geburtstag*, ed. M. Krause and S. Schaten (Wiesbaden, 1998), 69–80, discusses monastic towers but not those like here on lay-owned property.

fruit or not, and the fields outside and . . . and all the rights[9] of the fourth portion within and without, in accordance with the ancient boundaries round about, and according to the way our parents dwelt in it, and according to the force of the sales that took place, established in every place according to their force . . . again in all cession and interchange, from now for ever, unto all time.

This is the half of the portion given to me, me, Thaumastê, and Paul my son, from Constantine, viz., the one-twelfth of the common place called Byllê Field, which is in the field west of the village of Aphrodite, in the allotment of Anoup, with the half of the portion that Constantine gave me, me, Thaumastê, and the late Paul my son, (consisting in) the old well and the watchman's hut and the tower and the house and the livestock pen and the adjoining part and the granary and the place for vegetables and the orchard and the jujubes and the palm trees and all the trees whether yielding fruit or not, with the fields outside, with all the rights of that twelfth part of the place we spoke of above, within and without, in accordance with the ancient boundaries round about, and according to the way it has been dwelt in since Constantine, with the twelfth part of the place for catching fish. We have not left behind anything unceded to you in what we agreed before, viz., the fourth portion of the place called "The Oil-Seller's," with the fourth portion and all the rights within and without, in accordance with the ancient boundaries round about, and according to the way it has been dwelt in since our parents, with the sales that took place, established in every place according to their force, along with the twelfth part of the common place that we spoke of above, that is called Byllê Field, with the twelfth part of all the rights, within and without, in accordance with the ancient boundaries round about, in a word,[10] as it was dwelt in since Constantine, and as we afore ordained, according to place.

And these are the neighbors of the whole place entire, called "The Oil-Seller's," with its four corners round about:[11] south, the public facade; east, what they call on the east the "Circle" of the field of Antaa; north, the corner to the east is the boundary of the field of Antaa while the corner to the west is the boundary of the one of . . .; west, the corner to the south is the boundary of the field of Komes while the corner to the north is the boundary of the one of Tasinou. Again, these are the neighbors of the other place, entire, called Byllê Field: south, the corner to the east is the boundary of the New Field while the corner to the west is the boundary of "The Oil-Seller's"; east, the corner to the north is the Birds of the Place of the Elder's Roof while the corner to the south is the boundary of Little Bês; north, the boundary of the field of Panchirme; west, the corner to the north is boundary of Kalopou while the corner to the south is the boundary of Panlane. These are the neighbors round about.

---

[9] *dikaiôma* (δικαίωμα): Förster, *WB*, 196.
[10] *hapax haplôs* (ἅπαξ ἁπλῶς): "to make a long story short": Förster, *WB*, 71–72, 76.
[11] Here the boundaries are given in the order south, east, north, west.

And we agree that we have ceded to you the twelfth part of Byllê Field, that was given to us from Constantine, and the other twelfth part that came to us by a written document of sale from the holy monastery of Apa Shenoute the archimandrite,[12] viz., the sale of the sixth part of the whole place, entire, called Byllê Field, in accordance with the boundaries round about.

+ We too, the aforenamed Colluthus and Mark, approaching with each other, sons of Christopher, the afore[said], . . . ; I (Colluthus) wish to represent myself, and I represent Mark; I am ready[13] to risk[14] all my property,[15] movable and immovable, until he comes from abroad, if he appears according to the force of this interchange. We willingly cede to you, you the aforenamed Thaumastê and Anastasia her daughter, contributors, the (right?) in what you have ceded, and we cede to you in all cession and in all concession and in all exchange, from now for ever unto all time, viz. what belongs to us and what came to us by a written document of sale from the holy monastery of Apa Shenoute the priest and archimandrite and prophet[16] that is in the mountain of Atripe, that came to it, the holy monastery, by a written donation document by the hand of the late Paul, so that this sale might be drawn up and warranted in every place where it may be produced in evidence, according to its force: viz., the fourth portion of the place called Byllê Field which is in the field west of the village of Aphrodite in the allotment of Anoup, and the fourth portion together with the old well and the watchman's hut and the tower and the house and the enclosure and the livestock pen and the adjoining part and the fields and the place for catching fish, and the half-portion of the new well and the orchard and the place for vegetables and the gardens and the palm trees, together with the half-portion of the late Jacob, within and without, according to place in accordance with the ancient boundaries round about, and in accordance with the force of the written document of sale drawn up for us by the holy monastery of Apa Shenoute, it having been drawn up in every place according to its force. And we have not left anything behind whatsoever unceded to you in what we agreed to above, viz. the half of the portion of Jacob, viz the fourth portion of the common place named Byllê Field, with all its rights within and without, according to the ancient boundaries round about, and according to the way we afore ordained it.

---

[12] The famous "White Monastery" in the Panopolite (cf. above).

[13] *hetoimos* (ἕτοιμος): Förster, *WB*, 299–301.

[14] *kinduneuein* (κινδυνεύειν): Förster, *WB*, 413–14.

[15] *hypostasis* (ὑπόστασις): Förster, *WB*, 842.

[16] Shenoute's typical title: see S. Emmel, *Shenoute's Literary Corpus*, 2 vols. (Leuven, 2004), 1: 12–13, and R. Krawiec, *Shenoute and the Women of the White Monastery* (Oxford, 2002), 56–66, and J. Timbie, "Shenoute," *ODB*, 3: 1888; also cf. C. Schroeder, "Prophecy and *Porneia* in Shenoute's Letters: The Rhetoric of Sexuality in a Late Antique Egyptian Monastery," *Journal of Near Eastern Studies* 65 (2006): 91–97, here 84–90; and eadem, *Monastic Bodies: Discipline and Salvation in Shenoute of Atripe* (Philadelphia, 2007).

And these are the neighbors of the whole place entire, called the Byllê Field, with its four corners round about:[17] south, the corner to the east is the boundary of the place called the New Field while the corner to the west is the boundary of the place called "The Oil-Seller's"; north, the boundary is the place called the field of Panchirme; west, the corner to the north is the boundary of the place called Kalopou while the corner to the south is the boundary of the place called Panlane. These are the boundaries round about.

This is so that each of us severally (enjoys) all ownership over the apportionment[18] to each one of us, to dwell therein as we have afore ordained, so that each one inhabits his/her apportionment as they wish, to administer it, manage it, build on it, bringing to it the power and making it have the power to give it with rent[19] or without rent, to give it to their children and their children's children, to make use of it, survey it, dwell in it, as they wish, making it so that no man be able to hinder us or proceed against us for ever unto all time. And so as to warrant this with one another about the apportionment that we have made with one another, for ever unto all time, and so that each one of us be contributory[20] with regard to his/her apportionment, being assigned therefor according to place, whether tax in grain[21] or tax in gold[22] or tax on river transport[23] or any other *titulus*[24] at all to come upon it according to the force of the public tax codex[25] and as matters are arranged apportionment by apportionment. And we are to begin from this reckoning[26] of the fifth indiction, for the harvest of the D.V. sixth indiction and the one coming after it, and for ever to all time.

Anyone who wishes, contrary to us, over the two portions, to transgress this written document which is an interchange, subsequently at any opportunity or time, anyone who might dare to do this is to pay to account of fine, for the transgression that he has committed, thirty-six gold solidi, = AV sol. 36, and subsequent to the fine he is to acknowledge this written document as being drawn up and warranted in every place where it may be produced in evidence, according to its force.

---

[17] Here the boundaries are given in the order south, north, west, [east omitted].
[18] *meris* (μερίς): Förster, *WB*, 533.
[19] *misthôsis* (μίσθωσις): Förster, *WB*, 524–25.
[20] *syntelein* (συντελεῖν): Förster, *WB*, 780–81.
[21] *embolê* (ἐμβολή): Förster, *WB*, 250.
[22] *chrysikon* (χρυσικόν): Förster, *WB*, 887–88.
[23] *naulon* (ναῦλον): Förster, *WB*, 539.
[24] Daris, *Lessico latino*, 111.
[25] *Codex* ΔΗΜΟCΙΟΝ: see Daris, *Lessico latino*, 64 for 'codex'. On the *dêmosion* or land tax and its function in the taxation system and process see Sarris, *Economy*, 184; Hickey, "Economy"; and C. Zuckerman, *Du village à l'empire: autour du registre fiscale d'Aphroditô (525/526)* (Paris, 2004), 34–40. By this time in the war-ridden reign of Heraclius, tax income was especially vital to the empire.
[26] *kanôn* (κανῶν): Förster, *WB*, 376–77.

And we are ready, we, Thaumastê and Anastasia her daughter, to act as contributors with regard to the contributorship of the sown-land that we gave to N. ... the ... (late? N.?)[27] in the place called "The Oil-Seller's", whether for tax in grain or tax in gold or tax on river transport or any other *titulus* at all to come upon it, with respect to you, brought to bear over the matter as has seemed good.

And subsequent to these things we swear by the name of God Almighty and the victory[28] and well-being of our lords who have power[29] to observe and keep to the force of this written document which is an interchange, it being drawn up in every place according to its force. And we have also drawn up a single copy,[30] willingly and being persuaded, by our very own free choice, without any duress[31] or deception or necessity or misleading,[32] with no seizure, with the land tax commenced that I have completed lawfully. And we who know how to write ourselves are subscribing with our own hands, while for any who does not know how, a subscriber will write. And we are requesting some other respectable[33] people to bear witness to it ...

... and risking for one another all our own property, movable and immovable and self-moving,[34] it being pledged[35] ... approaching one another ... concerning this ... written document ... (which is) complete in its sequence of clauses.[36]

+ I Colluthus son of Christopher, contributor, I assent to this written document of interchange as it is written.

We Thaumastê daughter of Paul, and Anastasia daughter of Jacob, her daughter, with God's help,[37] we assent to the written document of interchange

---

[27] Makare could also be a proper name, not "the late".

[28] *nikê* (νίκη): cf. Förster, *WB*, 541 (though not citing such a formula).

[29] A problematic formula: cf. *CSBE 2*, 284 (XXXI [a]), 285 (XXXII [a], XXXIV [c]), 286 (XXXIV [d], [e], [g], 287 (XXXVI {a], [b], XXXVII [b]); but also 289 (XXXIX [g]. [h]).

[30] *ison* (ἴσον): Förster, *WB*, 354.

[31] *bia* (βία): Förster, *WB*, 134–35; elsewhere calqued by "compulsion", *ji nchons* (ϫⲓ ⲛϭⲟⲛⲥ).

[32] *planê* (πλανή): Förster, *WB*, 649.

[33] *eleutheros* (ἐλεύθερος): Förster, *WB*, 247–48; and W.C. Till, "ⲉⲗⲉⲩⲑⲉⲣⲟⲥ = 'unbescholten',*" Le Muséon* 64 (1951): 251–59.

[34] On this stereotyped clause see Richter, *Sprache*, 209–10, and L. Papini, "Notes on the Formulary of Some Coptic Documentary Papyri from Middle Egypt," *Bulletin de la Société d'Archéologie Copte* 25 (1983): 83–89.

[35] *enechyron* (ἐνέχυρον): Förster, *WB*, 260–61.

[36] *akolouthia* (ἀκολουθία): Förster, *WB*, 26.

[37] P. Luisier, "ⲥⲩⲛ ⲑⲉⲱ: Signification et destin d'une formule d'invocation en Egypte," in Κορυφαίῳ Ἀνδρί: *Mélanges offerts à André Hurst*, ed. A. Kolde et al. (Geneva, 2005), 339–46, does not take documentary data sufficiently into account in his interpretation of this expression.

according to its force.—+ Pahôm son of Apollo, most humble priest and D.V. hegoumenos, they requested me, I wrote for them.

+ Peter son of the late Permô, most humble priest, I bear witness to this written document of interchange according to its force.

+ I Apatêr son of Sarapion, and . . . , I bear witness to this written document of interchange according to its force.

+ I Anastasius son of Victor, I bear witness to this written document of mutual interchange according to its force.

+ I George son of the late Isaac (?), I bear witness to this written document of mutual interchange according to its force.

+ I Peter son of Constantine, I bear witness to this written document of mutual interchange according to its force.

+ [Greek] Written by me, Apa Rasios, with God's help notary (*symbolaiographos*).[38]

---

[38] Förster, *WB*, 766.

P.KRU 77

Preamble to a Will

DATE: 4 December 634

PLACE: Jeme

PARTY: Victor, priest and superior of the St Phoibammon monastery, testator

PUBLICATION: *SB* I 4319; Till, *Erb*, 204 and idem, *KRUTheb*, 144ff., incorrectly; corrected by M. Krause, "Die Testamente der Äbte des Phoibammon-Klosters in Theben," *Mitteilungen des deutschen archäologischen Instituts Kairo* 25 (1969): 57–67, esp. 61, 66

This text consists mostly of the Greek-language opening to a Coptic-language testament, the body of which is now mostly lost. Fortunately preserved is the absolute-date clause with its phraseology from the reign of Heraclius and his son. See *CSBE 2*, 96–97, 271 (correcting Heraclius junior's regnal year to 22); Godlewski, *Phoibammon*, 67, 68, 69; and Schmelz, *Kirchliche Amtsträger*, 298–99, 303. After the naming of the official, the language switches from Greek to Coptic, and the day, month, and indiction year are repeated. We do not know what this monastic superior was bequeathing, or to whom; nor the scribe's name, nor the witnesses.

[Greek] [In the reign of our greatest] benefactor, [Flavius Heraclius semper Augustus, imperator,] year twenty[-five, and of the consulate of] our most pious master, {and} year twenty-four, and of Flavius Heraclius New Constantine the God-crowned, year twenty-three, Choiak 8, indiction 8; in the *topos* of the prize-bearing martyr Abba Phoibammon in the mountain of [Kastron Memnonion] in the nome of Hermonthis; under John son of David,[1] most honored headman.[2]
. . . [Coptic] Today being the eighth day of the month of Choiak, in the year 8.

Victor son of Cyriac and his mother Sanêth, most humble priest and superior[3] of the holy *topos* of Abba Phoibammon the holy martyr, this one that lies in the mountain of Jeme in the nome of the city of Hermonthis, + he is the one who is writing in this way, laying down a testament that is to be untransgressable by law and . . . [

---

[1] Till, *D&P*, 234.
[2] *prôtokômêtês* (πρωτοκωμήτης): Förster, *WB*, 703.
[3] Till, *D&P*, 236.

P.Vat.Copti Doresse 2
Sale of House Property

DATE: 639 (?)

PLACE: Aphrodito

PARTIES: Jacob, second husband of Thaumastê, seller; [buyer(s) not preserved]

OBJECT: Agricultural property with buildings and irrigation works

SUM: 11 gold [units]

WITNESSES: [not preserved]

SCRIBE: George (?) [restored from P.Vat. Copti Doresse 3 below]

In this document we follow more of the affairs of Thaumastê's family (see P.Mich. inv. 6898 above). Her second husband, Jacob, is here selling property he has acquired by inheritance, property that originally had belonged to Constantine, Thaumastê's deceased first husband (presumably she, as the widow, inherited it and then her subsequent husband became its actual owner).[1] The agricultural property is complex here too, with drying- and threshing-floors, outbuildings, irrigation works, and provision for viticulture (reeds for uprights for the vines, a winepress).

The right margin is not well preserved, hence there are disconcerting lacunae, especially in the oath clause.

[beginning not preserved]
... and the tower and the granary ... round about ... with one another ... according to its boundaries ... and the livestock pen on the south side, and the fields ... the place for vegetables[2] ... they set up on the east ... that we set up. + I on the one hand, the one who ... on the south and west. I set up the dam ... the boundaries again of what I set up ... (called by?) his name, Jacob. I set up in the fields of Kalopou,[3] and I set up the granary on the west ... of the field ... not to transgress ... on the north. ... these boundaries: the tower and the enclosure and the stream (water-channel) toward the south and the pond and some places of building[4] and some columned porticoes[5] and the different kinds

---

[1] On this kind of transfer see van Minnen, "Dioscorus and the Law."
[2] *lachanon* (λάχανον): Förster, *WB*, 465–66.
[3] Cf. above in P.Mich. inv. 6898.
[4] Presumably builders' workshops.
[5] From *paradromê* (παραδρομή): not in Förster, *WB*.

of pastures and the watchman's hut . . . I, Jacob, (am specifying) the boundaries of the small (property), and subsequently of the parts of the level fields as we marked them out, up until now, dividing them up for ourselves as we wished. . . . one by one . . . to him and his sons, . . . up to the harvest[6] of this thirteenth indiction; [swearing] in the name of God Almighty and the well-being of [not preserved] (to abide by this) division[7] for ever unto (all) time, so as to . . . without fear. And if anyone should wish to transgress [this, he is to pay a] fine of 11 gold [keratia or solidi?], = [11 *n.*] (It is) established . . . I have received it, not quarrelling or withholding[8] . . . and have completed them according to the law . . . so that we warrant it for ever.

And from the parcel on the south up to the columned porticoes, likewise I have set up some garden- or vineyard-land parcels . . . north and further north to the head of the property . . . property with its other eighteen . . ., and its north being . . . north to the present boundaries . . . from now . . . with one another. And again similarly I have set up . . . leading into the watchman's hut at the north side . . . on the north, to draw water; according to its boundaries . . . Antinoopolis (?). I have set up according to what came to me . . . from (our?) sister. I set up the apportionment[9] . . . up to the tower to the north up to the present boundary. And I have set up other properties . . . with the trimesion which I got . . . and again I have set up fields on the south for planting (?) . . . from the north side . . . up to the boundary of the place for kindling (?), north to the canal and up to the middle of the . . . of the enclosure (pen) (interlinear: `and again its door is towards the drying-floor (or solarium)[10] all together´) . . . up to the canal from the covered well. . . . Likewise again . . . I, Jacob, inherited it, (if you should) enquire about them. And likewise again I set up reed-[patches] . . . (from) the aforementioned Constantine. I set up some fields . . . the field of Kalopou . . . towards the boundary . . . to draw water . . . in the fields to the south of the water-source . . . a winepress. And I set up . . . facing it. + I Jacob the aforewritten, . . . in the middle of . . . set up to the east of the fields . . . facing south toward the water-source, in accordance with their boundaries . . . of the water-source. And again I set up amid the . . . and likewise again I set up a threshing-floor . . . and the pond with what belongs to it, and the drying-floor . . . I set them up so that they drain between the tower and the cistern . . . the level (field) to the south up to the canal . . . [

---

[6] *karpos* (καρπός): Förster, *WB*, 380–81.

[7] *merismos* (μερισμός): Förster, *WB*, 513–14.

[8] *apaitein* (ἀπαιτεῖν): Förster, *WB*, 69–70.

[9] *meris* (μερίς): Förster, *WB*, 513.

[10] *hêliastêrion* (ἡλιαστήριον): Förster, *WB*, 323. ἱλαστήριον can also mean a part of an irrigation machine (*P.Oxy.* LXX 1985.11, 33).

P.Vat.Copti Doresse 5
Sale/Transfer of Landed Property

DATE: 640 (proposed; also 625, during the Persian occupation? or 665?)

PLACE: Aphrodito

PARTIES: Taham daughter of Prômauô, widow, seller; Colluthus and Mark, sons of Christopher the contributor, buyers

OBJECT: Landed property with buildings

SUM: 3 solidi

WITNESSES: 3 (+)

SCRIBE: Theodore (?)

PUBLICATION: Cf. Papini, "Formulary"

In this document a woman, Taham, states that she is acting in accordance with a sale instrument (acquired from the heirs who inherited the land) originally executed by her late husband, to transfer land with its buildings to the brothers Colluthus and Mark, sons of Christopher, of the family we have already encountered. While she has already paid the land tax (*dêmosion*), they, the acquirers, are to be responsible for the money tax and transport tax (*chrysikon* and *naulon*).

[beginning lost] . . . with my hand in the presence of subscribers . . . receiving . . . as it is written . . . from Colluthus and Mark, brothers . . . (and?) contributors, so that you (pl.) have power over and be owners of . . . the fields and the place of . . . and the small field and that house there and the watchman's hut with its legal obligation (?), so as to make it healthful[1] within and without, according to its ancient boundaries round about, in short,[2] according to the force of the written document of sale which my late husband . . .; and Mark took it so it might become established, like a son (?), to fence it off so you (pl.) might dwell there, so you could build on it, live in it, plant it and harvest from it, improve it,[3] give it as a gift, sell it, rent it out or let it rent-free, give it to your sons or daughters and their children and/or those who come after you;[4] you could make cash profit on

---

[1] *hygiazesthai* (ὑγιάζεσθαι): not in Förster, *WB*.
[2] *hapax haplôs* (ἅπαξ ἁπλῶς): Förster, *WB*, 71–72, 75–76.
[3] Here *beltioun* (βελτιοῦν): not in Förster, *WB*.
[4] Or "your successors."

it,[5] farm it,[6] or deal with it in any fashion you wish, with no man hindering you nor being able to obstruct[7] you . . . at any time . . . .. But I shall warrant it for you with every warrant unto all time.

Anyone who will wish to proceed against you (pl.) over this matter at any time or occasion, whether myself or my heirs or my heirs' heirs or any man at all whosoever, whether someone belonging to me or an outsider to me, he is to pay the price of this sale, that you, the buyers, have paid today, . . . and subsequently is to pay [a fine . . .]; . . . it (the document of sale) is to be warranted and valid in every place where it may be produced in evidence.

I have drawn it up of my own free will, well persuaded, of my own free choice, . . . with no deception or (compulsion) or seizure or circumscription . . ., without trickery . . .; as far as the old tax[8] is concerned, I have paid it in full legally. I requested subscribers to subscribe for me, and likewise some other respectable[9] witnesses to witness to the concluding[10] (of the sale) and the warranting of the written document of sale of the property at hand[11] that is mine, movable and immovable and self-moving, being pledged[12] . . . They asked me, I agreed to this same (sale). . . .

From today I hand over[13] to you by this written document of sale which my late husband Mark received from them, the heirs of the late Psousire,[14] according to its force, so that it might be established in every place according to its force. They asked us, we agreed.

Again I present these other words in this way to you, Colluthus and Mark together, sons of Christopher the contributor, so that you (pl.) complete the contribution of the half-portion of the place that my son spoke of in this year, . . . (complete with) tax in money and transport tax . . . according to the force of the codex[15] . . . And if a measuring[16] takes place, you (pl.) will again be willing, just like the whole village, and you will begin from the assessment[17] of this

---

[5] *chrysousthai* (χρυσοῦσθαι): not in Förster, *WB*.

[6] *nemesthai* (νέμεσθαι): Förster, *WB*, 540.

[7] *empodizein* (ἐμποδίζειν): Förster, *WB*, 251.

[8] *dêmosion* (δημόσιον): the land tax (Förster, *WB*, 171–73). Again see Hickey, "Economy."

[9] *eleutheros* (ἐλεύθερος) again.

[10] *eleusis* (ἔλευσις): not in Förster, *WB*.

[11] From *hypokeisthai* (ὑποκεῖσθαι): Förster, *WB*, 838–39.

[12] *enechyron* (ἐνέχυρον): Förster, *WB*, 260–61.

[13] From *paradidômi* (παραδίδωμι): Förster, *WB*, 614.

[14] A name not in Hasitzka, "Namen in koptischen dokumentarischen Texten."

[15] Cf. above, P.Mich. inv. 6898. This seems to refer to the Aphrodito census of c. 523/24: see Zuckerman, *Du village à l'empire*, 35–40.

[16] *metrêsis* (μέτρησις), a cadastral survey: not in Förster, *WB*.

[17] *kanon* (ⲕⲁⲛⲟⲛ; κανών: Förster, *WB*, 376–77.

fourteenth indiction to the harvest of the D.V. fifteenth indiction that will come after it and unto all time; I agree. +

+ I Taham daughter of Prômauô assent to this written document of sale according to its force, and I bear witness to the complete paying-in,[18] viz. of three gold solidi, and I shall warrant it for you with every warrant for ever. +—+ I Apa Victor son of the late Phoibammon, Taam asked me, I wrote for her. +

+Victor (son of) Apatêr, priest, I bear witness to this written document of sale, and I bear witness that they have received the paying-in of three gold solidi.

+I Theodosius son of Menas, I bear witness to the sale, and I bear witness to the price which is complete, viz., three gold solidi.

I Mark son of [N.] . . .

Written by me, Theodore (?).

---

[18] *katabolê* (καταβολή): Förster, *WB*, 386–87.

P.Vat.Copti Doresse 3
Division of House and Land

DATE: 624 (during the Persian occupation?) or 654?

PLACE: Aphrodito

PARTIES: Constantine and [N.]

OBJECT: House with landed property

SUM: [fine amount not preserved]

WITNESSES: 6+

SCRIBE: [same as that of P.Vat.Copti Doresse 5, Theodore?]

In this lacunose document a man named Constantine is dividing up a house and some land he has inherited, with parties whose names have not been preserved. Hardly anything remains of the specifics of property boundaries and the like. The left margin of the papyrus is lost and the right damaged, so there are gaps in the text. No trace of the fact that Egypt has been conquered by an alien invading force of different religion can be inferred from what we have here. It will be seen that family archives do indeed span the mid-seventh-century conquest without a qualm.

[beginning lost] . . . [its boundaries] round about . . . which I inherited . . . which I also inherited . . . they are to be in common for us, half and half . . . (with) its roof-beams . . . but the part that we are to agree about[1] is on the east of the (dwelling?), . . . explaining it as being useful[2] [to] those who come after you or after me, for ever. So as to begin[3] . . . those who will come after us, for ever; we swearing by the well-being of the kings[4] that we will observe the mutual agreement[5] that we have taken care to have drawn up in one single conviction[6] (to be) un(alterable?),

---

[1] Here not *homologein* (ὁμολογεῖν) but *tôt* (ⲧⲱⲧ), "come to consent about."

[2] *chrêsimon* (χρήσιμον): Förster, *WB*, 884.

[3] *archesthai* (ἄρχεσθαι): Förster, *WB*, 110.

[4] This is crucial for dating. Under the Persian occupation documents either have no ruler given or else can mention "the King of Kings" (cf. *CSBE 2*, 106). Plural Byzantine emperors could be meant, in the date spans 565–618/19 and 629/641; but that seems not to work out. It has been insisted (Bagnall and Worp, "Dating") that this formula has to refer to (plural) Muslim rulers. See Seidl, "Eid," 141 (with caution!) and below on *P.KRU* 65, n. 6.

[5] *symphônon* (σύμφωνον): Förster, *WB*, 771–72.

[6] *gnômê* (γνώμη): Förster, *WB*, 151.

an agreement of property division[7] with account of . . . so the division takes place . . . in two (parts?) yet unanimously. We desire it with no necessity incumbent upon us, but rather we wish to establish (it) taking the risk[8] together about the apportionment[9] at any time. . . . [And if anyone contravenes this arrangement he is to pay] . . . a fine . . . as made clear (above?). I have divided (it), and so that each one is to be owner of what is his. I have given them names so that they may dwell there . . . the one they call "John's palm tree." . . . We agree. . . . and I guarantee to you that . . . likewise to the north of the field established as "Phane's field" (?) . . . agreeing together with one another. They asked us, we agreed.

+ I Constantine son of [N.], [I agree to this according to its] force.—I George son of [N.], I wrote for him as he did not know how. +

Megethos (?) son of Paul, I assent.

I Jacob son of [N.], I assent.

I Abraham [

[traces of names of possibly as many as four more witnesses] . . . according to its force.

I N., landowner,[10] . . .

---

[7] *merismos* (μερισμός).
[8] *kindyneuein* (κινδυνεύειν): Förster, *WB*, 413–14.
[9] *meris* (μερίς).
[10] *ktêtôr* (κτήτωρ): not in Förster, *WB*; see Sarris, *Economy*, 99 ("man of property").

P.Vat.Copti Doresse 1
Sale/Cession of Part of a Wheeled Vehicle

DATE: 625/6 (during the Persian occupation?), or 640/41?, or 665/6?

PLACE: Aphrodito

PARTIES: Tsyra daughter of Sabine and N., and her son David, sellers/donors; Colluthus, son of the late Christopher the *syntelestês*, buyer/recipient

OBJECT: Wheeled vehicle or portion thereof

SUM: [price] 1 1/6 gold solidi

[fine] 3 ½ gold solidi

WITNESSES: 3

SCRIBE: Jacob son of George

PUBLICATION: cf. Papini, "Formulary"; now republished in H. Förster, "Ein koptischer Kaufvertrag über Anteile an einem Wagen: Edition von P.Vat.Copti Doresse 1," *Aegyptus* 84 (2004): 217–42.

Here we return to the family of Christopher of Aphrodito and its affairs. In this document Christopher the *syntelestês* (contributor) is deceased,[1] so it postdates those other items in the bilingual dossier mentioning him—some in Greek,[2] others in Coptic (above)—in which he appears as still alive. The framer of the document, also the co-seller, is Tsyra, daughter of Sabine, and (confusingly) widow of a different deceased Christopher; her co-seller is her son David who had inherited the item from his late father; the buyer is Colluthus son of 'the other' deceased Christopher, the *syntelestês*. The oath clause mentions plural rulers: see above on P.Vat.Copti Doresse 3 for the problems this involves.

The item being transferred, sometimes termed a "farm cart" or "wagon,"[3] seems rather grander than that since it has a bench to lie down on (a *krabaktion*), and perhaps should rather be called a "carriage". (For a detailed examination of the vehicle and its parts, with comparanda, see Förster, "Kaufvertrag," 226–28.)

---

[1] As he is in the Greek-language document *P.Mich.* XIII 662 (written by the same [bilingual] scribe, Apa Rasios, as P.Mich. inv. 6898 above), now dated to 645 by Bagnall and Worp, "Dating."

[2] Such as *P.Mich.* XIII 664, datable to 600 (in the reign of Maurice), in which Christopher buys a share in a grain-measure from a widow named Judith.

[3] See C.E.P. Adams, *Land Transport in Roman Egypt* (Oxford, 2007), 67, 81.

The repeated mentions of a "fourth portion" (*tetarton meros*; readings are clear), together with a "fifth" in line 12, remain puzzling. We see female agency in the way Tsyra acts on her son's behalf (though the vehicle's owner by inheritance, perhaps he was under-age): in lines 25–26 and 36–37 she expressly represents David.

No signature of either Tsyra or Colluthus remains; David signs (through the agency of a subscriber), by way of confirming the waiver of his claims to (part-)ownership of the vehicle he had inherited.

[beginning lost] . . . [I Tsyra] daughter of Sabine and [N.,] [. . .] according to the force of this written document of the men of the village of Aphrodito[4] all together, I am writing to Colluthus, son of the other, the late Christopher, contributor, himself also a man of the same village: Greetings. As follows: I agree and am willing and put my trust[5] in this written document which is a sale, with unchanged and unrepented opinion,[6] without trickery, out of my own free choice, sw[earing by God] Almighty and the well-being of our lords who have power[7] that I am selling to you, you the aforewritten by name, Colluthus son of the late Christopher the contributor, and I am ceding to you and conceding[8] to you in all perpetual cession, that which belongs to David my son, namely the fifth portion of the wagon/vehicle of my husband, with its iron wheel(s)/attachments and all its interior (fittings)[9] of wood, and its reclining bench,[10] and all its interior (fittings), as aforesaid, which came to him from his late father Christopher. And again I am selling you, for ever unto all time, the fourth portion, thusly, of these, so that you may be their owner for ever unto all time, with no other exceptions than (what) I first agreed to. And these are they: the vehicle of my husband, with its ten iron wheel(s)/attachments and all its fittings, according to the way it was crafted, with the fourth (portion) in this way: so you may be their owner, to sell, give to your children and children's children, bequeath, treat in any fashion you wish, rent out or let rent-free, acting in any fashion at all you may wish.

And no man is to be able to go to law with you or lay a complaint[11] upon you, neither myself nor my heirs, nor is any man belonging to me ever to be able to go to law with you over this matter at any time, because I have received the complete price, which is one solidus and half a trimesion, gold, = AV sol. 1 1/6. The price, in gold, I have received it myself (with) the (co-)seller, David son of Christopher,

---

[4] Called here by its Coptic name, Jkôw (ⲬⲔⲰⲞⲨ): Timm, *Ägypten*, 3: 1438–61.
[5] ⲠⲒⲐⲈ (restored by Förster; from πείθειν): Förster, *WB*, 632–33.
[6] *gnômê* (γνώμη).
[7] Seidl, "Eid," 139, 142 (frequent at Aphrodito: 142 n. 1).
[8] *synchôrein* (συγχωρεῖν): Förster, *WB*, 763–64; note the distinction between this term and the following where a complementary noun would be expected.
[9] Or "containers," from *ôrb* (ⲰⲢⲂ).
[10] *krabaktê* (ⲔⲢⲀⲂⲀⲔⲦⲎ), = *krabaktion* (κραβάκτιον): Förster, *WB*, 441 with n. 46.
[11] ⲈⲄⲔⲀⲖⲈⲒ: Förster, *WB*, 224.

by hand, I Tsyra daughter of Sabine and N., assuming to myself the risk[12] along with you[13]—for you are the (co-) seller to Colluthus son of the other Christopher—because I have received its price that is complete and of (full) measure in the presence of witnesses who will bear witness. And I am risking vis-a-vis you all that is mine, movable and immovable, being deposited[14] and justly pledged,[15] such that I am acting in the way I have written before, for the putting forth[16] of this written document and the warranty of the sale, so as to take upon myself the warranty for you. They asked me, I agreed, because I have set up all these words in this way. And if I should wish to proceed against you (Colluthus), either myself or my son David, we are to pay to account of fine three and a half gold solidi for the transgression that has occurred;[17] and after the fine, are to acknowledge the written document of sale that has taken place, drawn up according to its force. They asked me again, I agreed.

+ I David son of the late Christopher—represented by myself, Tsyra his mother—, I assent to this sale according to its force.—+ I Victor son of the late Phoibammon,[18] she asked me, I wrote for him.

+ I Theodosius[19] son of the late Macarius, I bear witness to the sale according to its force.

+ Victor son of Apatêr, D.V. priest,[20] I bear witness to the sale according to its force. +

+ John, priest and hegoumenos, I bear witness to the sale according to its force.[21]

+ I Jacob son of George,[22] bear witness, I who also wrote the body of the text. +

[verso:] [Greek]
+ Sale that has taken place from David son of Christopher by me,[23] Tsyra his mother, of a fifth portion of his father's vehicle,[24] at a price of 1 1/6 gold sol.

---

[12] From *kindyneuein* (κινδυνεύειν): Förster, *WB*, 413–14.
[13] Here Tsyra turns to address David.
[14] *enechyron* (ἐνέχυρον): Förster, *WB*, 260–61.
[15] From *hypothêkê* (ὑποθήκη): Förster, *WB*, 838.
[16] ⲉⲭⲑⲏⲥⲓⲥ: cf. Förster, *WB*, 313; but close to ἔκθεσις, a promulgation.
[17] Lit. 'that they have done'—a Coptic periphrastic passive-voice construction.
[18] Also signs P.Vat.Copt. 5 above.
[19] Also signs P.Vat.Copt. 5 above.
[20] Also signs P.Vat.Copt. 5 above.
[21] This witness signs in a very large, slowly written hand.
[22] Not recorded for Aphrodito by Diethart and Worp, *ByzNot*.
[23] She uses the formula δι' ἐμοῦ used by notaries.
[24] Here ἅμαξα in Greek.

P.KRU 75

Testament

DATE: 7th c.

PLACE: Monastery of Epiphanius, Thebaid

PARTIES: Jacob son of David, and Elias son of Samuel, monks, testators; Stephen, monk, heir designate

OBJECT: Inherited monastic dwellings

SUM [fine]: 6 oz. gold

WITNESSES: 6

SCRIBE: [not named]

PUBLICATION: Till, *Erb*, 198–204; cf. idem, *D&P*, 236; O'Connell, "Monastic Dwellings," 249, 265–67

After Artur Steinwenter included this text in his study "Byzantinische Mönchstestamente," *Aegyptus* 12 (1932): 55–64, and a succession table for superiors of the Epiphanius monastery was given in Till, *D&P*, 236, Martin Krause studied it in three articles: "Testamente der Äbte"; idem, "Zwei Phoibammon-Klöster in Theben-West"; and idem, "Die Beziehungen zwischen den beiden Phoibammon-Klöstern auf dem thebanischen Westufer," *Bulletin de la Société d'Archéologie Copte* 27 (1985): 31–44. Godlewski (*Phoibammon*, 80) underlined the parallels to the economic resources enjoyed by the Phoibammon house. For recent summings up see C. Thirard, "Le monastère d'Épiphane à Thèbes: nouvelle interprétation chronologique," in *Études coptes IX*, ed. A. Boud'hors et al. (Paris, 2006), 367–74,[1] and O'Connell, "Monastic Dwellings."

Parallels with our very first document (that of the monastic half-brothers, their confrere, and their cell) are manifest. Here the pair of framers are vigilant against letting blood relations get control of their cell property, and promise—doubtless with an eye on homoerotic misbehavior—not to allow youths below the age of twenty to dwell with them.

[In the name of the holy consubstantial Trinity, Father, Son and Holy Ghost.] [. . .]

---

[1] Cf. also F. Calament, "Correspondance inédite entre moines dans la montagne thébaine," in *Études coptes IX*, 81–103, esp. 86–87.

[. . . We,] the most humble Jacob and Elias, the aforewritten, having been concerned about the permanent separation of soul from body for, see you, a long time, we have wished necessarily, for the advantage and profit of our souls, to understand and reckon the matters of this life as vain, to be discarded, and as dreams,[2] because we might incur the turning away and the wrath of the fearsome Judge; but having hope to obtain leniency in that time of necessity that no man can be exempted from, we have had a desire, in good thoughts and knowledge, concerning the dwelling-places (viz.[3] caves)[4] that belong to me, me, Jacob, according to the force[5] of the two testaments that were drawn up for me by my holy father Apa Psan. He for his part was their owner through the force of the testament that was drawn up for him by his holy father Apa Epiphanius. Now I have given them to you, you, Stephen. And my holy father Apa Psan, first off before Apa Elias dwelt with us, wrote the first testament for me, making me owner of all the dwelling-places, viz. caves, and the tower,[6] from the way that goes in to St Phoibammon's to the way that goes in to the cave of those remembered among the saints, Apa Abraham and Apa Ammonius, men of Esna, and up to the way to the valley and up the hill that is above the caves and that tower.[7]

When Apa Elias dwelt with us he drew up the second testament again for me, according to the force of the first one in all matters, saying in it in this way as follows: "Concerning Apa Elias son of Samuel, since he has entered in to dwell with us, you are not to be able to throw him out of the *topos*, you, Jacob, at any time provided, while he lives. But if the Lord should come for you before Apa Elias, you are to give the (dwelling-)place to him to dwell in until the Lord comes for him as well. But if he ends his life, he is not to be able to make his relative according to the flesh[8] owner of the *topos*,[9] but rather is to look for a (God-)fearing monk and give the place to him for his lifetime, as I have written above

---

[2] Cf. Job 20:8.

[3] *ēgoun* (ἤγουν): "or rather" (Förster, *WB*, 323).

[4] Cf. O'Connell, "Monastic Dwellings," 269–70.

[5] Here *dynamis* (δύναμις; Förster, *WB*, 211), not *chom* (ϭⲟⲙ).

[6] See Descoeudres, "Wohntürme in Klöstern und Ermitagen Ägyptens," and O'Connell, "Monastic Dwellings," 249.

[7] For maps of the monastic site see now Thirard, "Monastère," and O'Connell, "Monastic Dwellings." Most of these walkways and spaces were covered with texts to edify visitors as well as the residents: see L.S.B. MacCoull, "Prophethood, Texts, and Artifacts: The Monastery of Epiphanius," *Greek, Roman, and Byzantine Studies* 39 (1998): 307–24.

[8] The Greek/Coptic *katasarx* (ⲕⲁⲧⲁⲥⲁⲣⲝ): cf. Förster, *WB*, 718, though he prefers two words.

[9] For this ongoing concern in Byzantine law see J. Thomas, "Early Monastic Rules," in *Byzantine Monastic Foundation Documents*, ed. idem and Hero, 1: 21–41, esp. 22–29, 32–37. Cf. also Krawiec, *Shenoute and the Women*, 33–36, 39–44, 162–74 on how the presence of blood relations in a monastery could be disruptive; and also Layton, "Rules, Patterns, and the Exercise of Power in Shenoute's Monastery," 60.

and according to the directives of the testaments of the 'Great Men'[10] to whose feet we entered in to dwell with and whose orders in all things we follow according to the will of God."

Accordingly we have thus drawn up this testament, I Jacob not knowing whether I will go out of the body first nor whether Apa Elias will go out of the body first, because the matter is hidden from all. Accordingly we, Jacob the most humble monk and Elias a mere beginner,[11] are of one mind with each other, as befits our humility,[12] so that we may be saved and not judged concerning this matter, for we pray for this all the time. We know that Your Piety[13] is God-fearing and walks in His commandments, and we have consented with you, because we tested[14] you many times for, see you, a long time. On account of this we have consented with you, and we have given you by this writing that lies before us the care for all the caves that we recited above, and the new tower, and all the dwelling-places, and all the material located within these caves, that came to us from our holy fathers,[15] and all other items even the most humble, movable and immovable and self-moving.

We have come to this testament that lies before us and is indissoluble, being alive, in our right minds, having concern for what is ours, with our thoughts sound, acting according to our customary fashion. We have dictated[16] all matters written in the unregretted testament in the language of the people of Egypt,[17] and have given directive that it be written down,[18] looking lest suddenly we be changed out of this life and leave our affairs, that we have made clear above, unprovided for and uncared for, looking like neglectful people. So in this way

---

[10] Here senior monks, though in non-monastic contexts the same expression (Coptic *noch ñ rôme*) can denote village notables (Wilfong, *Women*, 7).

[11] Here *pistos* (πιστός) may be closer to "postulant" rather than literally just "faithful". Cf. Förster, *WB*, 647–48.

[12] See D. Krueger, "Monastic Companionship: An Early Byzantine Institution?" *Byzantine Studies Conference Abstracts* 29 (2003): 78–79. On the practice of living in pairs see N.H. Henein and M. Wuttmann, *Kellia II: L'ermitage copte QR 195: archéologie et architecture* (Cairo, 2000), 245–46, and M. Rassart-Debergh in P. Ballet et al., *Kellia II: L'ermitage copte QR 195: céramique, inscriptions, décors* (Cairo, 2003), 410–21.

[13] I.e., Stephen. This is a Byzantine honorific term of address, *eulabeia* (εὐλάβεια; Förster, *WB*, 306).

[14] *dokimazein* (δοκιμάζειν): Förster, *WB*, 207.

[15] Cf. O'Connell, "Monastic Dwellings," 265.

[16] *hypagoreuein* (ὑπαγορεύειν): Förster, *WB*, 833.

[17] Cf. *P.Lond.* I 77.12–13, in which Bishop Abraham specifies that his testament has been dictated in the *tôn Aigyptiôn phônê* ("language of the Egyptians") and written down in *Hellênikois rhêmasin* ("Greek words"), and 69, where he states that it has been interpreted (*hermêneuthenta*) to him in the *Aigyptiakê dialaleia* ("Egyptian speech").

[18] Cf. J. Beaucamp, "Tester en grec à Byzance," in *ΕΥΨΥΧΙΑ: Mélanges offerts à Hélène Ahrweiler*, ed. M. Balard et al., 2 vols. (Paris, 1998), 1: 97–107.

therefore it has seemed good and satisfactory to us, having reflected for a long time thereon, and we have proceeded to this un-undoable testament, desiring that it be valid and have power and possess all validity and be established in every place where it may be produced in evidence, at any time, so that all matters written therein come about and have validity. Moreover, we adjure anyone who may encounter and read what is written in this document, and anyone who may hear it, by the holy, consubstantial Trinity and the fearsome judgement-seat before which all of us will appear, to observe it and to the utmost guard it in every place, every chapter and portion of this testament that is immovable and un-undoable.

But if at any time it should seem good to our Lord and God that we should suffer what is human[19] and change out of this transitory life on earth, we wish and order[20] that you, you, Stephen, the most God-loving monk, at that time are to acquire and have power over the entire possession[21] forever, all the places to live,[22] viz. caves, that we have made clear above, with the tower that was built by our holy fathers Apa Epiphanius and Apa Psan, they who are remembered among the saints—and I too helped with the work on it, I, Jacob, until we finished it—, this one that lies in this same mountain of Jeme in the way that goes in to St Phoibammon's, up to the way that goes in to the cave of those remembered among the saints, Apa Abraham and Apa Ammonius, men of Esna, and up to the way to the valley and up the hill that is above the caves and that tower, those that came to us from our holy father Apa Psan just as they had in turn come to him from Apa Epiphanius: these are they whose holy bodies[23] lie in the *topos* according to the force of the testaments that our holy father Apa Psan drew up for us while he was still in the body, as he said in this way, as follows: "As he said, namely my beloved father Apa Epiphanius, 'They came to me through some written testamentary documents made by my fathers in God who were before me'." So now we too, Jacob and Elias the most humble, the aforewritten above, are delivering[24] them henceforth to you, you, Stephen, so that after we have fallen asleep you may survey[25] them and be their owner and possess them and set them in order, and administer them, manage them, build on them, dwell in them, cede them to others after yourselves, (God-)fearing monks who first look with their

---

[19] *anthrôpinon* (ἀνθρώπινον): Förster, *WB*, 59; cf. *P.Lond.* I 77.15.

[20] *ouôsh . . . auô . . . ouehsahne* (ⲟⲩⲱϣ ⲁⲩⲱ ⲟⲩⲉϩⲥⲁϩⲛⲉ) (Richter, *Sprache*, 298), translating the Byzantine law formula *boulomai kai keleuô* (βούλομαι καὶ κελεύω), "I wish and order" (*P.Lond.* I 77.16).

[21] *nomê* (νομή): Förster, *WB*, 544–45.

[22] Here *ouôh* (ⲟⲩⲱϩ) not *shôpe* (ϣⲱⲡⲉ).

[23] *leipsanon* (λείψανον): Förster, *WB*, 467–68. There is indeed evidence that the bodies of revered deceased monks were kept in places of honor: see P. Grossmann, *Christliche Architektur in Ägypten* (Leiden, 2002), 200–2.

[24] From *anadidômi* (ἀναδίδωμι): Förster, *WB*, 48–49.

[25] From *periorân* (περιορᾶν; not in Förster, *WB*) (misunderstood by Till, *Erb*, 201).

eyes to the fear of our God and Lord. At any rate[26] you are not to put in any blood relative of yours according to the flesh or take to yourselves any man of below twenty years, as our holy fathers before us gave us commandment, that is, not to give the holy place to any blood relation of ours or take to ourselves any man of less than twenty years.[27] In a word, you are to act concerning all these things, in every matter, in all possession and ownership and perpetual retention, in unhindered ownership, in the fear of God and the obedience of the monastic state.

And no one, at any time nor to come, from my family, me Jacob, or from my family, me Elias, no heir of ours, Jacob's and/or Elias's, is to be able to proceed against you under any allegation[28] whatsoever, be it brought from[29] us or from our holy fathers before us; no stranger or magistrate or judge, or any man at all, in a word, is to be able to proceed against you, you, Stephen, the one whom we have cited many times, or to dislodge[30] Your Piety concerning all these things or those you will render[31] to those after you, namely the places to live that we gave you and the material and yet the books that my father gave me and I have in turn given to you, you, Stephen.

And anyone who speaks against or opposes this our wish that has been set down, at any occasion or time, or makes any motion against you or your chosen successor to whom you may have given the place—at any rate you will not have given it to any blood relative of yours according to the flesh, as we for our part were not able to give it to our blood relative, according to the law[32] given us by

---

[26] *mentoi ge* (μέντοι γε): Förster, *WB*, 512–13.

[27] On this kind of monastic prohibition, meant to discourage homoerotic relations, see J. Thomas in *Byzantine Monastic Foundation Documents*, ed. idem and Hero, 1: 35, 141, 263, also 3:939–43, and the index (vol. 5) s.vv. boys; disciples, adolescent; youths. Cf. Schroeder, "Prophecy and *Porneia*"; eadem, *Monastic Bodies*, 36–39; on the female side, T. Wilfong, "'Friendship and Physical Desire': The Discourse of Female Homoeroticism in Fifth-century CE Egypt," in *Among Women*, ed. N.S. Rabinowitz and L. Auanger (Austin, 2002), 304–29; Krawiec, *Shenoute and the Women*, 26, 37–38, 42, 148; and now (for both sexes) R. Greenfield, "Children in Byzantine Monasteries," in *Becoming Byzantine: Children and Childhood in Byzantium*, ed. A. Papaconstantinou and A.-M. Talbot (Washington, DC, 2009), 253–82, esp. 260–61, 267, 271–73. There are western parallels: R.D. Fulk, "Male Homoeroticism in the Old English *Canons of Theodore*," in *Sex and Sexuality in Anglo-Saxon England*, ed. C.B. Pasternack and L.M.C. Weston, MRTS 277 (Tempe, 2004), 1–34.

[28] Till, *Erb*, 202 misprints *apophasis* (ἀπόφασις) for *prophasis* (πρόφασις), "pretext" (Förster, *WB*, 700).

[29] From *diapheresthai* (διαφέρεσθαι): Förster, *WB*, 189–90.

[30] Literally "move".

[31] From *apodidōmi* (ἀποδίδωμι: Förster, *WB*, 79). There is a nice nuance between *ana-* (ἀνα-) and *apo-* (ἀπο-).

[32] *nomos* (νόμος): Förster, *WB*, 548–49. See A. Steinwenter, "ΝΟΜΟC in den koptischen Rechtsurkunden," in *Studi in onore di A. Calderini e R. Paribeni*, 2 vols. (Milan, 1957), 2: 461–69; and Beaucamp, "Imperial Law."

our holy fathers in their testaments not to give the place to our relative according to the flesh—anyone who may dare, then, to proceed against you at any time, you or the one you may have given the place to or your successor, be he from our blood relatives or from strangers or any man at all, moving against you or your successor (purportedly) according to the commandment of our holy fathers that they gave us and we have passed on to you, you, Stephen, in writing, in this written testamentary document, no point and chapter in this testament being undoable, first of all that person is to have no profit of the daring he has done, but is to be liable to the holy oath written in this testament,[33] and is to pay to account of fine to the honorable magistrate, by way of penalty, six ounces of gold, = AV oz. 6, and is to provide so far as he is able out of his own property. Subsequently he is to appear and acknowledge this testament according to its force; and thereupon he will be examined[34] before the judgement-seat of the Lord God Who is no respecter of persons and will be judged concerning this matter.

And on top of all these things we swear by the Holy Trinity that we placed at the head of this document[35] that no transgression will befall it in its entirety, but rather it shall be immovable for ever as we have drawn it up, for your security, it being secure and valid in every place where it may be brought forward,[36] read by any rule or authority having lawful lordship. As far as the subscription of the one who will subscribe for us, and credible witnesses who will witness at our request subsequently, are concerned,[37] they asked us about all these things: we established them and we set them down in such a way as to be observed. They asked us, we agreed, and we set it down.

+ I Jacob son of David, monk, and Elias, God-loving faithful postulant, son of Samuel, reckoned[38] to Kastron Jeme and dwelling on its holy mountain, we assent to this testament in all matters written therein, with the oath and the fine, as it stands above. And I have dismissed it.

+ I George son of Patermoute, most humble monk and priest—beyond my deserts—of the holy *topos* of St Menas[39] in the mountain of Jeme, as our God-loving holy fathers Apa Jacob the monk and Apa Elias the God-loving postulant supervised me, I wrote for them as they did not know how to write with their own hands, and I too also bear witness.

+ John son of Papnoute, most humble archpriest of the catholic church of Jeme,[40] I bear witness.

---

[33] Cf. Seidl, "Eid," 147–48.
[34] *exetazein* (ἐξετάζειν): Förster, *WB*, 270.
[35] The invocation (not preserved; restored here).
[36] Here not the usual *emphanizein* (ἐμφανίζειν) (see Glossary).
[37] Misunderstood by Till, *Erb*, 203: this is *ejn-* (ⲉϫⲛ-), "upon", not *ajn-* (ⲁϫⲛ-), "without".
[38] From *ôp* (ⲱⲡ), "number".
[39] Papaconstantinou, *Saints*, 146–54, esp. here 147.
[40] Same as the "Holy Church"—i.e., the principal church.

+ I Moses son of Matthew, most humble priest and oikonomos of the Holy Mother of God Mary the Virgin,[41] I bear witness.—+ I Patermoute son of John, most humble lector[42] of the catholic church of Jeme, Moses the priest asked me, I wrote for him as he did not know how to write,[43] and I bear witness.

+ I Isaac, most humble monk and priest of the holy *topos* of Apa Shenoute in the mountain of Pachme,[44] the God-loving Apa Jacob the monk and the postulant Apa Elias asked me, I [bear witness at their request.]

+ I N., man of the city of Hermonthis, at present resident in Jeme, [Apa Jacob the monk and] Apa Elias the postulant asked me, [I bear witness] at their request.

---

[41] Papaconstantinou, "Sanctuaires de la Vierge," 89 (no. 17bis).

[42] For this rank see Schmelz, *Kirchliche Amtsträger*, 38–39, and E. Wipszycka, "Les ordres mineurs dans l'Église d'Égypte du IVe au VIIIe siècle," *Journal of Juristic Papyrology* 23 (1993): 181–215, repr. in eadem, *Études sur le christianisme dans l'Égypte de l'antiquité tardive* (Rome, 1996), 225–55.

[43] Presumably in Coptic.

[44] Timm, *Ägypten*, 4: 1849–52.

P.KRU 65

Testament

DATE: 2nd ½ of 7th c.

PLACE: Jeme

PARTIES: Jacob, monastic superior, testator; Victor son of the late Theodore, monk, heir designate

SUM [fine]: 5 oz. gold

WITNESSES: 7 (1 + 6)

SCRIBE: Theodore, *grammatikos*

PUBLICATION: Till, *Erb*, 152–58; cf. O'Connell, "Monastic Dwellings," 268–69

Jacob, the superior of the St Phoibammon monastery, wishes to make sure that his faithful disciple and follower Victor will succeed him in the headship and be owner of all the monastery's property of whatever kind, also continuing the customary charitable works and performing the liturgy. Documents of this type—unfortunately not extant from the sixth century; some half a dozen survive from later times—have formed the center of discussion on monastic succession in the Coptic-speaking world from early on. As has been customary since Abraham of Hermonthis himself around 600–610, the notarial practice for a testament of this kind includes an opening 'arenga' (rhetorical-narrative introduction) or *prooimion* with pious sentiments. See Krause, "Testamente der Äbte", "Zwei Phoibammon-Klöster", and "Beziehungen"; also Godlewski, *Phoibammon*, 60, 61, 69, 70–72, 80.

. . . a breath is my life,[1] and I empty out my (span of) life . . . I wish to begin rather to set down the fulfilment of my last will . . . for an unrevealed thing is the going out of this world, as is the time when death comes; what time (will it be?). . . . through their deaths and the coming forth of our offering-loving fathers . . . this present way of going in which I abide according to the command of God and . . . at the hand of my holy fathers . . . before they came to these times . . . For the rest: I call to mind my own death, that it not come / befall me (suddenly?) and contrary

---

[1] Cf. Job 17:1 and Psalm 103:29 LXX.

to my expectation . . . and I (have in mind) the work of the holy *topos* after me, with its holy offerings and the administration of the place . . . and attention.[2]

Because of this I proceed to this testament and last will, being of sound mind, with my reasoning well and established in this contract[3] in my mind. Furthermore, I am practicing my customary affairs with no necessity incumbent upon me, no compulsion nor deception nor harm nor seizure nor circumscription,[4] but proceeding thereto of my very own[5] free choice and the wish of my heart. Rather I am swearing by the holy consubstantial undivided Trinity and the well-being of those bearing rule on the earth now according to the command of God, the true Master,[6] and adjuring every man who will read out this immovable and untransgressable testament, by a fearsome oath, that he is to guard it lest any transgression happen to it, but rather it is to be untransgressable, Amen. But if I should suffer this human thing[7] that has to happen to every human being, and leave behind this transitory staying-place, as the truly wise man and ancestor of our God according to the flesh, our father David, said, "I am a sojourner on this earth, as all my fathers were" [Psalm 38:12b LXX],—for everyone that comes from the human race and exists here clearly changes out of the body in this world—and those who are exercised in the monastic life customarily call to mind God's mercy after they depart, such people take care to deserve a departure in love for humankind. Whereas, . . . doing good works and well-doing for justice all the days of their life, they wish to save their souls from the unquenchable fire [Mark 9:43–48] and the eternal punishment [Matthew 25:46], manifesting every effort . . . [. . .] . . . and to enjoy ineffable good things. But those living heedlessly and foolishly have their thoughts darkened. What is more, such a departure from this life as theirs (is to be) they have not at all thought about with their mind. But I have a care day and night concerning the separation of soul and body. I necessarily wish, in good profit and the wish of my soul, to reckon the works of this transitory life as disposable and as dreams, so that I may succeed in turning aside the condemnation of the true Judge, which is so fearsome that no indulgence even in time of necessity for any man can avail; it cannot be begged off.

---

[2] *epimeleia* (ἐπιμέλεια): Förster, *WB*, 281.
[3] *synallaxis* (συνάλλαξις): not in Förster, *WB*.
[4] Cf. *P.Lond.* I 77.6–7.
[5] The Coptic has a reflexive; I translate thus to bring it out.
[6] Cf. Seidl, "Eid," 143. Why, in place of the usually single Byzantine emperor whose *salus* was sworn by, post-conquest Muslim rulers appear in the plural in oath formulas is still debated. When there were plural Byzantine rulers, beginning with Justin II and Sophia when the empress is included with the emperor in oaths (*CSBE 2*, 284–85) through the reign of Heraclius with empress and/or sons (287), their *sôtêria* was sworn by. Perhaps the post-conquest formulas intend the plural rulers to be the caliph in Damascus plus the governor in Fustat.
[7] *anthrôpinon* (ἀνθρώπινον), as in *P.Lond.* I 77.15, and above in *P.KRU* 75.

I wish, in good thoughts I have and works and commandments that have been carried out in all observances—and these are good thoughts and things known about the holy *topos* and all its dwelling-places,[8] viz. its caves[9] that lie before us in this same mountain, that are from our fathers in God through written documents that they established, the first-commemorated at all times, our most blessed fathers Apa Abraham the bishop[10] and Apa Victor the priest and holy superior who established his testament for the holy *topos* according to its legal force with our brother the most devout Apa Peter the priest, all these having gone to their rest according to God's will,[11] for the fulfilment of time of their presence in the body, so that I too shall render them [the properties] into the hand of my beloved brother Victor as I have further tested him and praised him, seeing with his eyes in the fear of God and the obedience and discipline of the monastic state that he glimpsed through my humility as God gave it to my soul to confer the holy habit upon him as God commanded me, and again to give him what I have in keeping with my heart's wish as God gave it to my soul, that in the hour of my departure from the body toward the limit of all that is appointed, concerning the authority of the holy *topos* according as it shall be defined precisely,[12] as is made plain one by one, either in the mountain or in Egypt or in the countryside,[13] simply speaking,[14] every place belonging to the holy *topos* of the holy Apa Phoibammon, interior and exterior, simply altogether.

When I saw our brother Victor, son of the late Theodore, being faithful[15] and God-fearing, leaving his house and all that was his behind to seek perfection, as is written in the Gospels [Matthew 19:21; Mark 10:21, Luke 18:22], since he was little, he took up his cross and followed the Lord [Matthew 16:24; Mark 8:34, 10:21; Luke 9:23, 14:27]. Again, he undertook to desire to become a monk, obeying us in all things befitting the state of faith of which he was a disciple, and also (as regards) worldly things. So I, Jacob the most humble, when

---

[8] Technical term for monastic dwellings, often the monks' property, that could be sold and/or bequeathed, as we have seen in our very first document. Cf. Steinwenter, "Mönchstestamente" and "Rechtsstellung," Brooks-Hedstrom, "Divine Architects," and O'Connell, "Monastic Dwellings."

[9] On the (re-)use of caves for monastic dwellings see Brooks-Hedstrom, "Divine Architects," and O'Connell, "Monastic Dwellings," 269–70.

[10] Abraham of Hermonthis, whose testament is *P.Lond.* I 77.

[11] For the succession of abbots of St Phoibammon's see Till, *D&P*, 236, and Krause, "Testamente der Äbte."

[12] From *diastellein* (διαστέλλειν) / *diastolē* (διαστολή): Förster, *WB*, 187–88.

[13] On this clause see Richter, *Sprache*, 210, no. 45.

[14] *haplôs* (ἁπλῶς), more often the standard *hapax haplôs* (ἅπαξ ἁπλῶς), "in a word" or "to make a long story short."

[15] Till (*Erb*, 155) renders this here and elsewhere as a technical monastic term for "novice" (cf. above in *P.KRU* 75); but here I am sticking with the basic notion of literally "faithful."

I accordingly tested our brother the faithful Victor thus, in every discipline befitting God and man, because of this, in the hour when God will order me to leave this life behind and go the unavoidable way, I wish and order[16] that Victor enter upon the holy *topos* of St Phoibammon the holy martyr, this one whose holy name was earlier made plain above, to have power over this holy *topos* of St Phoibammon that lies in the mountain of Jeme, with all things belonging thereto, whether gold or silver[17] or garments or bronze or written texts[18] or books,[19] caves or excavated spaces,[20] towers or fortifications,[21] within and without the four boundaries of the holy *topos*, according to the legal force[22] of the written testaments that our holy fathers left and according to their precedent,[23] be it camels, donkeys, sheep, or goats, or houses, that are donated to the holy *topos*,[24] whether in the city of Hermonthis or the *kastron*, or village[25] or hamlet,[26] or date-palm trees, wells, fields or meadows, with their yields, freely, simply stated.

Our brother is to become and be[27] owner of everything belonging to and lying within the holy *topos*, inside and outside, on the mountain or in Egypt, movable, immovable and self-moving,[28] from small to large, from a nail stuck in the wall to a handbreadth of land with a stake in the wall, altogether, he is its owner. Victor is to become and be owner of them all for his entire life, to receive and give

---

[16] *keleue* (ⲕⲉⲗⲉⲩⲉ / κελεύειν), second element in the standard two-part legal phrase (cf. Richter, *Sprache*, 298).

[17] For this type of clause see *P.Lond.* I 77.20 (cf. 71–72).

[18] *grammation* (ⲅⲣⲁⲙⲙⲁⲧⲓⲟⲛ / γραμματεῖον: Förster, *WB*, 153–54), doubtless meant here as a plural, to indicate "documents" such as deeds and monastic testaments in the archive. Cf. *P.Lond.* I 77.20.

[19] On the St Phoibammon's library see Godlewski, *Phoibammon*, 57–59, 71.

[20] Possibly "burial shafts": O'Connell, "Monastic Dwellings," 270.

[21] *periochê* (περιοχή: Förster, *WB*, 640): interesting evidence for this. Cf. Grossmann, *Architektur*, 307–14.

[22] *dynamis* (δύναμις).

[23] *pronomion* (προνόμιον: Förster, *WB*, 684); Till renders it "privileges" (Sonderrechten: *Erb*, 156), as is the usual practice with texts of the Corpus Juris Civilis; but I think there is a case for this technical term as a loanword into Coptic denoting legal precedent. A search of the TLG (for which I thank Kent Rigsby) reveals a slow evolution of this term from the top-down notion of "privilege, exception" to the bottom-up one of "precedent", i.e., an exception that makes grounds for later ones. (L.S.B. MacCoull, "Προνόμιον, *Privilegium*, and Precedent in the Law of Christian Egypt," forthcoming.)

[24] On donations of animals see A. Biedenkopf-Ziehner, *Koptische Schenkungsurkunden aus der Thebais* (Wiesbaden, 2001), 98.

[25] Here *kômê* (κώμη): Förster, *WB*, 457.

[26] *chôrion* (χώριον: Förster, *WB*, 891): a debated term. See Sarris, *Economy*, 181 n. 16; and Hickey, "Economy."

[27] Standard pairing in legal phraseology.

[28] On this perennial legal clause see Richter, *Sprache*, 210, and Papini, "Formulary," 88.

in the whole *topos* all together, being owner in all ownership without hindrance. Moreover, he is to perform the administration of the holy *topos* in all things as he has seen me performing them, in the holy liturgy of the *topos*,[29] and care for the lamps[30] of the holy *topos* according to the custom in force from time to time, alms [lit. "blessings"] for the mouths of the poor who come by, and the namedays of our holy fathers, each one by name; and, in a word, to bring everything to completion in all obedience and every discipline befitting God and the life of monasticism, for the honor of the holy *topos* and the repose[31] of our holy fathers and the maintenance[32] and administration of the holy *topos*.

And it shall not be possible[33] for any man to proceed against you, Victor, or against the holy *topos*, neither brother nor nephew nor relative in the first or second degree,[34] neither kin nor kin of kin, nor heir of mine, nor any man at all representing me at any occasion or time, either in court or out of court,[35] in city or village or *kastron*. No person shall be able to undo this testament, neither through a command[36] nor through a great general order.[37] No man shall be able to act against (countermand) this final testament, for it has been made according to my intent. And if any man dares to proceed against this testament, first it shall profit him nothing, but rather he shall be under the judgement of the holy fearsome oath. Next he shall pay to account of fine, as the just laws have defined it, five ounces of gold,[38] = AV oz. 5, to the archon or the *lashane* who is in office

---

[29] See Schmelz, *Kirchliche Amtsträger*, 76.

[30] See Schmelz, *Kirchliche Amtsträger*, 121–23.

[31] *anapausis* (ἀνάπαυσις): Förster, *WB*, 51–52 (frequent in funerary inscriptions).

[32] *systasis* (σύστασις) (Förster, *WB*, 782), "keeping it together."

[33] Here *ouk exestai* (οὐκ ἔξεσται) in Greek.

[34] Till, *Erb*, 156 and elsewhere in his work simply transliterates the Coptic *shnoua*, *shnsnau*, literally "son of one", "son of two": this is what the terms mean.

[35] This clause (cf. *P.Lond.* I 77.43–44) has occasioned much comment. Though earlier scholars pictured an Egypt where courts were hardly resorted to, we know now (Beaucamp, "Imperial Law") that a normal legal life went on regardless of rulership.

[36] *entoleus* (ⲉⲛⲧⲟⲗⲉⲩⲥ) from *entolē* (ἐντολή), "commandment" (Förster, *WB*, 264–65).

[37] *keleusis* (κέλευσις): Förster, *WB*, 402); and from *chôreuein* (χωρεύειν) (890–91).

[38] This document probably dates from before the currency reform of 696/697 by which aniconic coins with openly Muslim inscriptions replaced the imitations of Byzantine gold still in circulation. See M.L. Bates, "Coins and Money in the Arabic Papyri," in *Documents de l'islam médiéval: Nouvelles perspectives de recherche*, ed. Y. Ragib (Cairo, 1991), 43–64; now for coinage of the transitional period see C. Foss, *Arab-Byzantine Coins* (Washington, DC, 2008), 99–105 esp. 100, 109, 112–13; and for earlier Byzantine gold hoarded after the conquest, cf. G. Gabra, "Die Münzschätze aus dem Schenute-Kloster bei Sohag," in *Ägypten-Münster: kulturwissenschaftliche Studien*, ed. A.I. Blöbaum and J. Kahl (Wiesbaden, 2003), 125–28 and Plates 5–6; and H.-C. Noeske, "Finds of Coins and Related Objects from the Monastery of Apa Shenute at Suhag," forthcoming in *Dumbarton Oaks Papers* 63 (2009).

at that time.³⁹ Thereafter he will find himself at the fearsome judgement-seat of God to be judged and punished for the wrong he has done. Then the one who has dared this is to approach and acknowledge this testament and all matters written therein.

Securing the holy *topos* for you, Victor, and setting it up in stability (lit. "establishedness"), I have drawn up this testament of my last will, to be secure, have force, and be valid in every place where it may be produced in evidence, in every rulership and authority and lordship.

They asked me, I agreed and I set it down.+

+ I Jacob, the monk and superior of the holy *topos* of Apa Phoibammon in the mountain of Jeme in the nome of Hermonthis, the aforewritten above, I assent to this will and testament, with the holy oath and the fine, as aforesaid, and I am quit.⁴⁰ +

+ I Theodore, the most humble archpriest of Kastron Jeme, I bear witness to the testament as Apa Jacob the monk spoke it to me, at his request.

I Samuel son of Joses, in Jeme by happenstance I passed by the holy *topos* of Apa Phoibammon and my father Apa Jacob asked me, I bear witness to the testament at his request.

I Pekosh son of Psmo the *lashane*, I went into the holy *topos* of Apa Phoibammon by happenstance to visit our father Jacob; he asked me, I bear witness to the testament.

I David the elder (or: David son of Hllo), by happenstance I went into the holy *topos* of Apa Phoibammon to visit our father Jacob; he asked me to witness the testament at his request.

I Phoibammon son of Victor, I bear witness to the testament at the request of our father Apa Jacob, having come in to him by happenstance.

I Kale son of Matoi, former *lashane*, by happenstance I was coming to meet our father Apa Jacob the monk and superior of the holy *topos* of Apa Phoibammon; he asked me to witness his testament.

I Pisrael son of Psate, I bear witness to the testament.

[Greek] + By me, Theodore, D.G. *grammatikos* of Kastron Memnonion; having been asked to I wrote for him and for the witnesses who did not know letters, according to the abiding *ethos* of the *kastron*, and I executed (the document). +++

---

³⁹ See Schmelz, *Kirchliche Amtsträger*, 303.
⁴⁰ From *apoluein* (ἀπολύειν: Förster, *WB*, 85), the standard Greek expression for concluding a contract being *apelusa* (ἀπέλυσα).

P.CLT 1
Document of Release

DATE: 13 November 698 (or later?)
PLACE: Jeme
PARTIES: Moses, monk; Daniel, Jacob, Athanasius, et al., monks of St Paul's
OBJECT: Money donated to St Paul's monastery for charitable purposes
SUM: 20 (7 + 13) solidi
WITNESSES: 23
SCRIBE: Psate son of (the late) Pisrael[1]
PUBLICATION: Till, *KRUTheb*, 22–27

In this document a monk named Moses, whose son, Theodore, was also a member of the monastic congregation of St Paul of Jeme, narrates the story of how he was moved by an outbreak of plague to donate the large sum of twenty solidi—at this time probably no longer Byzantine solidi with emperors' images but aniconic gold coins of the caliphate[2] or a transitional form (as per Foss, *Arab-Byzantine Coins*, 99–105)—to the monastery. The community returned some of the cash (7 sol.) to Moses, who subsequently, disturbed because his monk-son Theodore was expelled from the community for disobedience,[3] had the balance of the money (13 sol.) returned to him as well. Now Moses is again giving the money back to the monastery for charitable uses, and agrees that he will not demand any of it back. The story of these father-and-son monks continues in *P.CLT* 2 below.

A bilingual protocol is preserved at the beginning of the sheet. Now those Christian Egyptians who understood Greek read, at the beginning of an official document, a Muslim 'Bismillah' invocation also naming the current governor.

In the name of God, the compassionate (*eleêmôn*), the merciful (*philanthrôpos* [literally 'lover of humankind']); there is no God but God alone; Maamet [Muhammad]

---

[1] A well-known and active Jeme scribe: see Till, *D&P*, 185–87.
[2] On 'Abd al-Malik's currency reform — a complex process — see Foss, *Arab-Byzantine Coins*, 59–60, 107–8, 113; C. Robinson, *Abd al-Malik* (Oxford, 2005), 72–75, 79–80, 103–4.
[3] On expulsion from monasteries see Schroeder, *Monastic Bodies*, 75–81.

is the messenger (*apostolos*) of God. 'Abd al-Aziz ibn Marwan, governor. [Greek; repeated in Arabic with *rasûl* for 'messenger']

In the name of the holy and life-giving consubstantial Trinity, Father, Son and Holy Ghost.[4] In the month of Thoth, 16, of the twelfth indiction; in the mountain of Kastron Memnonion.

I Moses, the most humble monk, son of the late Plouj and Tasia, man of Shensiôn in the nome of Coptos,[5] but now being a monk in the holy mountain of Kastron Jeme, and subsequently putting in place a subscriber who will subscribe for me and requesting some trustworthy witnesses who will witness for me to this written document of agreement and release that is written to be untransgressable and unshakable and un-undoable by law, and making it more established through some of these trustworthy witnesses who will witness it for me at my very own request and to my intention:[6] I am writing to the (spiritual) sons of the late Apa Paul the anchorite, this one who is now among the saints,[7] namely Apa Daniel and Apa Jacob and Apa Athanasius and the rest of their brothers and those who will come after them in the holy mountain of Kastron Jeme: Greetings.

WHEREAS: in those years that have gone I, being in the worldly life, when I heard the renown of our holy fathers, and when God, the Good, ordered that a great dying[8] happen in our land, God, the one who seeks {and seeks} our profit at all times, I went south to the holy mountain previously named above. I entered into the obedience of our late holy fathers, the above-commemorated Apa Isaac and Apa Papas the superiors, they being the (spiritual) sons of the late Apa Paul in the former age through their great, ineffable virtue.[9] I gave twenty solidi to them. I obliged them by the name of God to receive them from me and give them as an *agapê*[10] for my poor soul,[11] so that the Lord God would not take away/alter the very thing I wished. They took them from me, but after (some) time of

---

[4] Invocation Type **2E**: *CSBE 2*, 100, 104–5, 293.

[5] Timm, *Ägypten*, 5: 2140–54.

[6] *prothymia* (προθυμία): Förster, *WB*, 681.

[7] On this holy man / monastic founder see Papaconstantinou, *Saints*, 170–71; on his monastery's placement at a Jeme locality called "Kolol" or "Koulôl", "the Cup" (*P.KRU* 48.2; 106.18, 69, 210; *P.CLT* 3.3), see now V. Ghica, "Kellis: notes toponymiques," in *Coptica—Gnostica—Manichaica: Mélanges offerts à Wolf-Peter Funk*, ed. L. Painchaud and P.-H. Poirier (Québec–Louvain, 2006), 325–37, esp. 330 n. 36.

[8] On plague outbreaks after the great pandemic of 541/42 see P. Sarris, "The Justinianic Plague: Origins and Effects," *Continuity and Change* 17 (2002): 169–82; idem, "Bubonic Plague in Byzantium: The Evidence of Non-Literary Sources," in *Plague and the End of Antiquity: The Pandemic of 541–750*, ed. L.K. Little (Cambridge, 2007), 119–32; and P. Horden, "Mediterranean Plague in the Age of Justinian," in *The Cambridge Companion to the Age of Justinian*, ed. Maas, 134–60.

[9] *aretê* (ἀρετή): Förster, *WB*, 96.

[10] Förster, *WB*, 3–5, here 5. Cf. Papaconstantinou, *Saints*, 317–18.

[11] Schiller's text in *CLT* p. 20 consistently misprints *psychê* (ⲯⲩⲭⲏ) as *tychê* (ⲧⲩⲭⲏ).

requesting they persuaded me in this matter about which I have spoken above. They received them from me. After some days went by I entered in, with my son Theodore, he being a monk there. They gave me seven solidi to spend, with my son; and when the "Great Men,"[12] my fathers in God, Apa Isaac and Apa Papas, passed away, my son for his part despised[13] the habit and was not able to keep the commandments of our holy fathers. They threw him out. He went, and after some few days I urged my holy fathers over the other thirteen solidi for a full makeup payment[14] to make up the 20 sol. They brought them, they gave them as an act of mercy[15] for my poor soul, as I had said above. And subsequently they again gave them for intercession[16] for me in their troubles and efforts, whether in clothing or necessities of the monastic life, as living following God in their great goodness that was revealed to them as a result of my difficulty,[17] they, the late Apa Isaac and Apa Papas and our fathers.

So again, now, from this very day, I also agree as before the face of God [Greek] and the angelic habit now belonging to me as well, according to the execution of the account of the thirteen solidi that I requested them to give as an act of mercy for my soul, if a man should be in need, they should give them into his hands, whether solidus or trimesion, and God would count it as a good deed for their souls that they gave it into the hands of one in need, in alms, accumulating them as God wished. And I too, when I went day by day and saw the devil envying our habit, I went and received a blessing so as not to get a great curse from God and the world, like the curse brought down on Ananias and Sapphira his wife who told lies to the apostles, and rightly so.[18]

I went, I requested your God-loving selves to receive this written document of release, secured for you and your sons in God and those who come after you at all times and in all generations. Accordingly I Moses, the aforewritten above, willingly and being persuaded without any trickery or intimidation or compulsion or deception, without any seizure or circumscription,[19] with no necessity incumbent upon me, but rather out of my very own free choice and the wish of my heart, agree, swearing[20] by God Almighty and the well-being of our lords and the angelic habit now belonging to me, before the fearsome judgement-seat of

---

[12] "Great Men" (*noch nrôme*, ⲚⲞϬ ⲚⲢⲰⲘⲈ) at Jeme could be monastic heads or lay officials. See Wilfong, *Women*, 7, 87, 89, 127.

[13] From *kataphronein* (καταφρονεῖν): Förster, *WB*, 394–95.

[14] *symplêrôsis* (συμπλήρωσις / ⲤⲨⲘⲠⲖⲎⲢⲞⲨⲤⲒⲤ): Förster, *WB*, 769.

[15] Or "alms".

[16] *proseuchê* (προσευχή): Förster, *WB*, 688.

[17] *aporia* (ἀπορία): Förster, *WB*, 86.

[18] Acts 5:1–10. The fate of this cheating couple is a favorite subject in penalty clauses. See also below in this document; and often elsewhere.

[19] *perigraphê* (ⲠⲈⲢⲒⲄⲢⲀⲪⲎ) is here miswritten as *paragraphê* (ⲠⲀⲢⲀⲄⲢⲀⲪⲎ).

[20] Here Seidl, "Eid," 143–44.

Christ, the one before which the whole creation will be brought, each one to be judged according to what he has done, whether good or evil,[21] that I gave it (the money) to them and they gave it on my behalf, not only that, but I supported[22] through them the late fathers previously commemorated. And now up to today they have given me three times over[23] for my bodily needs: but God, the Good, will repay them for them; not only (for) my humility, but also everyone who will dwell (or visit) with them, since they act with God.

Now, neither I nor my son nor daughter nor brother nor sister nor relative in the first or second degree nor kin nor kin of kin nor stranger nor man of my house nor any man representing me or my heirs or my kin's kin is to be able, at any opportunity or time, to go to law with you, God-loving holy fathers, or those who come after you at any time ever, over the matter of those twenty solidi that they gave on my behalf as I said above—not only that, but they gave me three times over. Nor shall they be able to go to law with your God-loving selves or those who come after you at any time, neither in court nor out of court, neither in city nor in nome, nor any assembly of the city or the praetorium,[24] or by any honored, venerated religious law,[25] or commandment, or by a great divine[26] constitution[27] or a great, valid, prevailing rank,[28] either magisterial[29] or ecclesiastical, in a word.

But if anyone should dare to, either my son or my heir, monk or person in the world, stranger or man of my house, first of all that person is to have no profit of it, but rather first is to become and be a stranger to the holy, venerated oath by the Father and the Son and the Holy Ghost,[30] and you are to bring him before the fearsome judgement-seat of Christ to be judged over this case,[31] and he is to receive the apportionment of Ananias and Sapphira, and he is to receive the apportionment of Judas who betrayed the Lord of All. And he is to pay to account of fine twenty-four solidi of pure gold, which he is to render out of his very own

---

[21] John 5:29; Matthew 16:27. The phraseology is repeated below.

[22] From *dapanê* (δαπάνη: Förster, *WB*, 160–61). This probably refers to food for the poor set out on feasts commemorating deceased holy men.

[23] Schiller (*CLT*, p. 23) thought *triploun* (ⲧⲣⲓⲡⲗⲟⲩⲛ) was "one-third" uniquely here; but Förster, *WB*, 823 took the common-sense approach. Moses is probably alluding to Luke 11:5–8.

[24] See Förster, *WB*, 668. This praetorium is no longer a Roman magistrate's hall!

[25] See L.S.B. MacCoull, "ⲧⲩⲡⲟⲥ in Coptic Legal Papyri," *Zeitschrift der Savigny-Stiftung für Rechtsgeschichte, kanonistische Abteilung* 75 (1989): 408–11.

[26] *etouaab* (ⲉⲧⲟⲩⲁⲁⲃ, "holy") calques *theia* (θεῖα: Förster, *WB*, 330).

[27] *diataxis* (διάταξις: Förster, *WB*, 189): an imperial law. See the Introduction, and Beaucamp, "Imperial Law."

[28] *taxis* (τάξις): Förster, *WB*, 793–94.

[29] *archontikon* (ἀρχοντικόν): Förster, *WB*, 110–11.

[30] See Seidl, "Eid," 146–47.

[31] *hypothesis* (ὑπόθεσις): Förster, *WB*, 838.

property³² into the hand of the honored magistrate. And on top of that [Greek], subsequent to the paying-in³³ of the fine, he is to furnish it and appear and acknowledge the force of this written agreement which is a release, this one which I have drawn up, securing it for your God-loving selves and those who come after you for all time, and adjuring every magistrate and holy bishop³⁴ and God-fearing judge who will encounter this written document and read what is written therein, by the holy consubstantial Trinity and the well-being of our lords, before the fearsome judgement-seat of Christ before which all creation will be brought, each one to be judged according to what he has done, whether good or evil, that they are to observe the force of this written document of legal release, this one that I have drawn up, securing it for you, God-loving holy fathers and those who will come after you for all time, it being secure and valid and warranted in every place where it may be produced in evidence.

They read it out to me in Egyptian;³⁵ I heard it with my ears, it was satisfactory. I asked a subscriber, he subscribed it for me; and I requested some trustworthy witnesses, they witnessed it for me. I let it go, it being complete in all its order.³⁶ +

✠ I Moses, most humble monk, son of the late Plouj and of Tasia, man of the district of Shensiôn in the nome of the city of Coptos, but now in Kastron Jeme, the aforewritten above, I assent to this written document of release, with the oath and the fine, and with all things written therein, as it stands.—I John son of the late Lazarus,³⁷ man of Kastron Jeme: Moses the most humble monk asked me, I wrote for him. +

+ I Pshêre, most humble priest and hegoumenos of the holy church of Jeme, I bear witness at the request of the framer.

+ I Peter son of the late Komos,³⁸ I bear witness.

+ I Jeremias son of the late Basil, I bear witness.

+ I Severus son of the late Moses, I bear witness.—I David, my father³⁹ ordered me, I wrote for him, and I wrote for Jeremias and Peter too, as they did not know how to write.

---

³² *hypostasis* (ὑπόστασις).
³³ *katabolê* (καταβολή): Förster, *WB*, 386–87.
³⁴ See Schmelz, *Kirchliche Amtsträger*, 273.
³⁵ Cf. *P.Lond.* I 77.13, 69.
³⁶ *akolouthia* (ἀκολουθία).
³⁷ Frequently found as a witness: Till, *D&P*, 108.
³⁸ A known *lashane*: see Till, *D&P*, 171–72, 234. Is he the *lashane* Peter who built a food-preparation center as a thank-offering, at a cost of 10 1/3 keratia, according to *KSB III*, 1538?
³⁹ Severus, that is; David reappears below also signing for illiterates. Misled by the appearance below of a cleric actually named Eiôt, Coptic for "father", Schiller (*CLT*, p. 27) misread this as a proper name.

+ I Bartholomew son of the late John, I bear witness at the request of Moses the monk.—I Leontius son of the late Cyriac, I bear witness at the request of Moses, and I wrote for Bartholomew as he did not know how to write.

+ I Job son of David, with his brother Di[os]corus, we bear witness.

+ I Andrew son of the late Pser, I bear witness.—I Apa Victor son of the late Papnoute, I wrote for Andrew as he did not know how to write, and I bear witness.

+ I Shenoute, most humble priest of the holy church of Jeme, I bear witness. +++

+ We, Constantine and John, former *lashane*s, sons of the late Solomon, we bear witness.—Shenoute, most humble priest of the holy church of Jeme, I wrote for them.[40]

+ I Zacharias, most humble priest of St Cyriac's,[41] I bear witness.

+ I Athanasius son of the late Papnouthios, with Cyriac son of Joseph and Victor son of the late Ezekiel and Mathias son of the late Ezekiel, we bear witness.—I David son of Severus, they asked me, I wrote for them as they did not know how to write.

+ I Eiôt, son of Shenoute the most humble priest of St Cosmas's and St Theodore's[42] in the district[43] of Pakothis,[44] I bear witness to this written document of release at the request of Moses.

+ I Gamoul son of the late Elisha, in Pshenhiai, I bear witness to this written document of release.—I, Eiôt the priest, I wrote for him as he did not know how.

+ I Severus son of the late Souai, the *lashane* of Shensiôn, I bear witness.

+ I Athanasius son of the late Antony, of Shension, I bear witness to the document as it is written.

+ I Shenetôm, the *lashane* of Pauê,[45] son of the late Jacob, I bear witness to the document as it is written. ++

+ I Psate son of the late Pisrael,[46] Moses the most humble monk asked me, I drew up this written document in Egyptian with my hand.

[Docket] + Moses son of (P)Louj, his testament.[47]

---

[40] See Schmelz, *Kirchliche Amtsträger*, 251.

[41] See Papaconstantinou, *Saints*, 132–34.

[42] Papaconstantinou, *Saints*, 129–32, esp. here 130. The notary of *P.CLT* 4 below, Kalapêsios son of Sinouthios, was also priest of their church.

[43] *enoria* (ἐνορία): Förster, *WB*, 261.

[44] Timm, *Ägypten*, 4: 1818–19.

[45] Timm, *Ägypten*, 4: 1861.

[46] Since this well-known scribe (Till, *D&P*, 185–87) here designates his father as deceased, this may move the dating of this document to a later twelfth indiction: 703 or 718?

[47] Incorrect: not a testament but a release.

P.CLT 4

Document of Release

DATE: 18 November 702

PLACE: Jeme

PARTIES: Mercurius son of the late Zacharias; Daniel, Jacob, and Athanasius, monks and superiors of St Paul's[1]

OBJECT: Millstone

SUM [price]: 2 trimesia

[fine]: 6 solidi

WITNESSES: 4

SCRIBE: Kalapêsios son of Sinouthios, priest

PUBLICATION: Till, *KRUTheb*, 28–30

Mercurius here seems to be a layman from a nearby town who has sold his inherited millstone to the St Paul's monastery. On monastic mills see A. Lucas, "The Role of the Monasteries in the Development of Medieval Milling," in *Wind and Water in the Middle Ages*, ed. S.A. Walton, MRTS 322 (Tempe, 2006), 89–127; and also, from the sixth century, *P.Cair.Masp.* II 67139 fol. 5r, 13 (L.S.B. MacCoull, "The Aphrodito Estate of Count Ammonios," *Analecta Papyrologica* 16 [2007]: 83–90).

+ In the name of the Father and of the Son and of the Holy Ghost [Greek].[2] Written in the month of Hathyr, 22, first indiction.

I Mercurius son of the late Zacharias, from Shensiôn in the nome of the city of Coptos, he is[3] writing to the most God-loving monks Apa Daniel and Apa Jacob and Apa Athanasius, superiors of the congregation[4] of our holy father Apa Paul[5] in the mountain of Kastron Jeme in the nome of the city of Hermonthis; as follows:

---

[1] Whom we have met before in *P.CLT* 1 above.
[2] Invocation Type **2J**: *CSBE 2*, 100, 104–5, 294 (= *SB* I 5558).
[3] The scribe has (inadvertently) switched from first person to third.
[4] Here not "monastery", the Greek *monastêrion*, but the Coptic *heneete*.
[5] List of superiors in Till, *D&P*, 236.

WHEREAS: I being persuaded by your fatherhood,[6] with no necessity incumbent upon me, nor intimidation nor compulsion, but rather by my very own wish and an established free choice and an unchanged reasoning, I was selling to you (pl.) my millstone, this one that I got from the inheritance of my parents, and I brought some trusted and tested representatives,[7] namely Isaac son of the late Papnouthios, to value[8] it. He set a price, according to God's justice, that you (pl.) assented to with me: he valued it at two trimesia of gold. Look, accordingly I agree that you have paid me back the two trimesia, to the fulfilment of its price. They came from your hand; they were good, and were satisfactory to your fatherhoods. Accordingly you are owners of the mill (apparatus); you have put it in the workshop of your monastery, as an improvement, and for the bread of the brothers and to give out to the table of the poor.

You have sought from me a written document of release, and I agree that neither I nor my sons nor heirs nor anyone belonging to me nor another man outside of my family, neither kin nor kin of kin nor any man, shall be able to go to law with your monastery over the millstone in this way, neither with you nor with those who come after you, for ever, at any time, because you paid me its price, which came from you.

But if it should happen at any opportunity or time at all, in any fashion whatsoever [Greek], that someone should dare to go to law with your monastery over this allegation, wishing to transgress this written document of release that has been laid down above, first of all he is to have no profit at all from any rank or authority, but rather is to pay six solidi as fine, and after the fine this written document is to be established for ever, I adjuring every rule and every authority into whose hands this written document shall come by God Almighty and the well-being of our lords who rule over us[9] not to transgress it ever, securing it for your fatherhoods. I laid it down for you and those who come after you to have validity and dominion[10] in every place where it may be produced in evidence, through the subscription of the subscriber who wrote on it and the trustworthy witnesses, agreeing in this way: +++

I Philotheos son of Pesynthios, I bear witness.

+ I Thomas son of Souai, from the *epoikion*,[11] I bear witness.

I Samuel the priest, I bear witness. +

---

[6] Abstract noun of address; can be singular or plural.
[7] Should be singular: only one person is named.
[8] *syntimazein* (συντιμάζειν): Förster, *WB*, 781 (apparently an inner-Coptic neologism).
[9] Seidl, "Eid," 141.
[10] From *kyrieuein* (κυριεύειν): Förster, *WB*, 452–53.
[11] According to Sarris, *Economy*, 115–16, this means a hamlet or place where hired agricultural laborers resided. (But see also Hickey, "Economy.")

+ [Greek] Written by me, Kalapêsios son of Sinouthios, most humble priest of St[12] Cosmas's and St Theodore's.

[Docket] + The written document of agreement of Mercurius son of Zacharias over the millstone, in the first indiction [Greek].

+ I Isaac son of the late Papnoute,[13] I bear witness.

---

[12] The scribe miswrites *amma* (ⲁⲙⲙⲁ) for *abba* (ⲁⲃⲃⲁ).

[13] The valuer, as above.

P.CLT 2

Agreement Concerning a Monastic Donation

DATE: 25 November 703 (or 748/49?)

PLACE: Jeme

PARTIES: Moses and his son Theodore, monks; Daniel, Athanasius, and Severus, monks, of St Paul's

OBJECT: Donation of 20 solidi

SUM [fine]: 36 solidi

WITNESSES: 3

SCRIBE: Theodore son of Moses, monk (as above)

PUBLICATION: Till, *Erb*, 90–92

The story of this father-and-son pair of monks, Moses and Theodore, continues. By now, almost five years after the previous document involving them (*P.CLT* 1 above), both they and the St Paul's monastery appear to be on better terms. Theodore is back in the community, as he refers to himself in the first person as "most humble monk"—so his expulsion has been rescinded.[1] Moses, suffering from an illness, has wished Theodore to take care of him, bearing in mind the charity money he, Moses, has already given to the monastery to support just such good works; and this arrangement seems to have met with the community's approval.

In the name of the Father and of the Son and of the Holy Ghost [Coptic].[2] Today being the twenty-eighth of Hathyr, of the second (indiction) year.

We, Moses and Theodore, monks, are writing to our holy fathers of the congregation of our holy, God-bearing father Apa Paul, namely Apa Daniel and Apa Athanasius and Apa Severus, as follows:

Whereas: when God wished that I [Moses] enter upon a sickness in my old age, being in my place alone, I was troubled lest God further wish that I depart[3]

---

[1] Cf. Schmelz, *Kirchliche Amtsträger*, 154–59.
[2] Invocation Type **2J**: *CSBE* 2, 100, 104–5, 294 (= *SB* I 5556), dating it to 749.
[3] *apodêmei* (ⲁⲡⲟⲇⲏⲙⲉⲓ), from *apodêmein* (ἀποδημεῖν: Förster, *WB*, 78).

to Him; I was afraid that my offering[4] would go astray. I sent for and fetched Apa Athanasius and Apa Severus: I gave what was mine to them. For the rest, when they sent for my son Theodore so he might come and look after me in my sickness, the brothers to whom I had given my offering informed me: "In so far as your son is the one who is to make the effort in your sickness, the right thing[5] is that he also administer your offering accordingly meanwhile in this matter." Everything I had given them they gave back to me, up to (and including) a single trimesion. I gave them to my son so he might give them on my behalf. Accordingly, when they had given them to us, they wished and sought for a written document, secured for them and for their whole congregation.

Now, God willing, I Moses, together with Theodore, we are writing to our holy fathers the aforenamed[6] above, that we have no legal matter[7] with you, from today on and for ever. And if anyone should dare, at any opportunity or time [Greek], to proceed against you over any of this matter, either myself or brother or sister or child or grandchild, heir or kin or kin of kin, first of all he is to become and be a stranger to the Father and the Son and the Holy Ghost. And secondly he is to furnish to the honored magistrate and is to pay a fine of thirty-six solidi of pure gold. Subsequently he is to appear and acknowledge this written document of agreement according to its force.

I Theodore the most humble, I am writing to my holy fathers, as follows: I assent and I agree, in the presence of God and the authority ordained by him, that all of what belongs to my father came to us from you in full to the end, up to (and including) a single keration.[8] And if I should dare, after this agreement, to proceed against you, I am to be liable to the judgement of the holy oath by the Father and the Son and the Holy Ghost, and I am to pay the fine of thirty-six solidi; subsequently I am to appear and acknowledge this written document according to its force. And one who encounters this written document, whether magistrate or supervisor[9] or any man ordained to any rank[10] who is not upright in true judgement according to the force of this written document, he is to come before the judgement-seat of God and receive judgement over it, and he will become liable to the curses that the holy Scriptures have defined for those who turn away from the truth.[11]

---

[4] The twenty solidi he had initially donated.

[5] *dikaion* (δίκαιον).

[6] *-onomaze* (-ⲟⲛⲟⲙⲁⲍⲉ): cf. Förster, *WB*, 584.

[7] *hôb* (ϩⲱⲃ), Coptic for "thing", again calquing the Roman-law *res*, literally "thing." Cf. Richter, *Sprache*, 329–30.

[8] Schiller (*CLT*, p. 33) miswrites "trimesion."

[9] *pronoêtês* (προνοητής): Förster, *WB*, 683. Cf. Sarris, *Economy*, 29 et alibi.

[10] *taxis* (τάξις).

[11] Ananias and Sapphira again (Acts 5:1–10), and the Deuteronomic curses (Deut. 27, 28, 29) that we will encounter in other documents.

Accordingly, securing it for you, we have drawn up (this) written document, secure and having validity [in every place where]¹² it may be produced in evidence.

+ I Andrew (son) of Phêr, in Kastron Jeme, I bear witness to the agreement.

+ I Athanasius son of Daniel, man of the same Kastron Jeme, I bear witness to the agreement.—I Theodore, most humble monk, they sought for me, I wrote for them as they did not know how to write. +

+ I Theodore son[13] of Moses, I drew up the written document of agreement with my hand at the request of my father, and I assent to it according to its force in all matters written therein.+++

+ I Dioscorus son of David,[14] I bear witness.

[Docket] Written document of Moses and Theodore his son.

---

[12] Schiller (*P.CLT* 2.23) does not allow for a long enough lacuna.
[13] Correct to *pshêre* (ⲡϣⲏⲣⲉ) in *P.CLT* 2.26.
[14] Also signs *P.CLT* 1 above.

P.CLT 5

Legal Relief Concerning Money Dispute

DATE: 24 November 711

PLACE: Jeme

PARTIES: Thomas, *lashane* of Jeme; Victor and associates, monks of the St Paul monastery

OBJECT: Money (50 solidi?) found on monastic property

SUM [fine]: 1 lb. gold

WITNESSES: 12

SCRIBE: Psate son of the late Pisrael

PUBLICATION: Till, *KRU Theb*, 30–34

Here we encounter a complex and ongoing dispute between the St Paul monastery and the St Phoibammon monastery, Jeme's two principal monastic houses, over a sum of money reportedly found by one monk. Thomas the *lashane*, acting on behalf of St Phoibammon's, appears to be trying to bring about a settlement with the complainant, Apa Victor, priest and hegoumenos of St Paul's. Immediately we see an interesting manifestation of the evidentiary value placed upon written documents.[1] Documents are used as weapons in the conflict; they are torn up and pieced back together, hidden and sought for; the intentions and mental states of their past framers (many are deceased) are called into question. These private documents continue to be in Coptic, Greek being discouraged in public records supposedly by an edict of 705/6.[2] Both sides of the dispute are here compelled to agree to a settlement, fortified with oaths.

[The fragmentary first section, possibly with *lashane* in attendance and the framer putting in place his subscribers, mentions the Apa Paul monastic community, a dispute, and Apa Jacob.]

---

[1] On the Phoibammon monastery's archive as a depository for written documents see Godlewski, *Phoibammon*, 58; cf. 72.

[2] But see P. M. Sijpesteijn, "Landholding Patterns in Early Islamic Egypt," *Journal of Agrarian Change* 9 (2009): 120–33, here 125, 126 with n. 28.

... so you (pl.) could administer it now according as your holy fathers had done. But they threw out mercy;[3] they enacted the wish of their very own hearts; they envied your honorable assembly. They drew up a written document with the most reverent[4] Apa Victor.... [damage] Shenoute said to us: "I have found fifty [solidi?] thrown out in a small ceramic vessel." I gave them to the God-bearing Apa Jacob the anchorite, the one named by name above, saying, "Take them for your monastery." But subsequently the late Zacharias son of the late Samuel and Abraham son of the late Theodore and Severus son of the late Moses, the *lashane* of that year, drew up (a document) with me as well, me, Thomas, with Athanasius, (and) ... all the "Great Men" of the *kastron*[5] which now continues through the support[6] of your holy prayers and those of your holy fathers who have gone on to God.[7] They all knew that they were representing the ones just now named by name, when they drew it up in enmity[8] and antipathy,[9] because they were dwelling in the evil of their very own deeds, being thrown out of the midst of the marvellous and glorious *koinônia*[10] by the great expulsion[11] of Apa Jacob. Apa Petronius, the new man, and all the "great men" knew that this was drawn up in enmity and antipathy and as a devilish thing [Greek].

But when they produced the document in evidence, the one spoken of before, they did not find any proof[12] in it, nor were they able to show[13] any matter in it, because it had been drawn up in antipathy and as enmity. They recognized[14]

---

[3] Or "the Spirit", if traces of a supralinear stroke could be read above the letters *pna* (ⲡⲛⲁ).

[4] *theosebestatos* (θεοσεβέστατος): Förster, *WB*, 332.

[5] See Wilfong, *Women*, 7, 87, 89, 127.

[6] *synarsis* (σύναρσις): Förster, *WB*, 776.

[7] This shows how the town of Jeme saw itself as sustained by the power of its nearby monastic communities. Cf. A. Papaconstantinou, "Notes sur les actes de donation d'enfant au monastère thébain de Saint-Phoibammon," *Journal of Juristic Papyrology* 32 (2002): 83–105, esp. here 85–89 on the importance of the intercession and miracles of St. Phoibammon, who was regarded as the recipient of donations.

[8] *echthria* (ἐχθρία): Förster, *WB*, 313.

[9] *antipatheia* (ἀντιπαθεία): Förster, *WB*, 63–64.

[10] Does this technical term in Egyptian monasticism designate a late Pachomian survival? Pachomian communities designated themselves by the term *koinônia* whereas houses of the Shenoutean 'federation' called themselves *synagôgai*. For documentary attestations see Förster, *WB*, 426, 773 respectively.

[11] *aphorismos* (ἀφορισμός): Förster, *WB*, 126 (i.e., drawing a boundary with the excluded one outside). For expulsion from the monastery cf. Schmelz, *Kirchliche Amtsträger*, 154–59, on defrocking. We have already seen Moses' son Theodore as a temporarily expelled monk of St Paul's (above, *P.CLT* 1).

[12] *systasis* (σύστασις).

[13] *deiknuein* (from *deiknumi*, δείκνυμι): Förster, *WB*, 162.

[14] *katagignôskein* (καταγιγνώσκειν): Förster, *WB*, 387.

that they (the earlier framers) did not set it down (correctly even) when they drew it up with witnesses to witness it, because they could not give it any proof-value or any security in their drawing it up in antipathy and as enmity, because the devil thus influenced their hearts.[15]

The late Zacharias sent for that Apa Victor to blame[16] him because he by chance received the counsel of little children,[17] because we all knew with one mind that they had drawn it up in antipathy and as enmity, saying "Hand over[18] the document of your God-loving selves for the investigation."[19] That Apa Victor had a piece of the document, saying "Look, here is a piece of that document that your God-loving selves tore up." Subsequently, when the late Zacharias departed from the body, we stayed on, administering after him; and in the tenth indiction year that it is now, the God-loving Apa Victor once again has gone to law, saying "I wished you to listen to my legal matter with yourselves, God-loving holy fathers." But when he informed us, we kept blaming him because we knew that he said "I did not tear a piece from that document." Rather we got up and went to his monastery. He produced the piece of that document as evidence. We read it aloud. We sent for your most holy lordship the holy father, should you wish to come to St Phoibammon's. You did not wish to do this; rather we went up with Apa Victor the priest and hegoumenos. We came into your marvellous *koinônia* with the document, in which we could not show any (good) word[20] because they had drawn it up (in) antipathy and as enmity to your holy fatherhoods (and) the four holy gospels.[21] Accordingly your fatherhood raised it up from upon your holy feet. We all sat. You took hold of[22] it, according to the force of the oath[23] that would articulate[24] the latter part of this written document. He gave your lordship, holy father, the piece of that document because there was no security in it and the legal relief[25] would not happen without us. He came to an agreement with your God-loving self for[26] every complete legal relief [Greek]. And

---

[15] Cf. John 13:2 (and 1 John 3:8a).

[16] *memphein* (from *memphomai*, μέμφομαι): Förster, *WB*, 512.

[17] Perhaps inexperienced junior members of the community.

[18] From *anadidômi* (ἀναδίδωμι).

[19] Literally "digging up."

[20] Or "matter" (the term here is *shaje*, ϣⲁϫⲉ).

[21] Cf. Seidl, "Eid," 145. Oaths on the gospels had been required in lawcourts since A.D. 531: C. Humfress, "Law and Legal Practice in the Age of Justinian," in *Cambridge Companion to the Age of Justinian*, ed. Maas, 161–84, here 179–80.

[22] Schiller (*CLT*, p. 49) translated "judged," misled by the Coptic word *hap* (ϩⲁⲡ), "judgement": but here we have the Greek verb *haptein* (ἅπτειν: cf. Förster, *WB*, 93), "grasp."

[23] Cf. Seidl, "Eid," 155.

[24] *saphênizein* (σαφηνίζειν): Förster, *WB*, 720.

[25] *apallagê* (ἀπαλλαγή): Förster, *WB*, 70.

[26] This is the Greek preposition *eis* (εἰς), not the Coptic word *eis* (ⲉⲓⲥ), "Look" as Schiller (49) thought.

subsequently he came to an agreement according to the force of the oath in every way that your most God-loving selves had asked our humility, to draw up the force of the legal relief that was worked out with our humility, in a document, in writing, you securing it for the holy *koinônia* and those who will come after you for all time, and those joined with you, enduring and blessed.

Accordingly we have come to it willingly {willingly}[27] and being persuaded, without any trickery or intimidation or compulsion or deception, with no seizure or circumscription,[28] with no necessity incumbent upon us, but rather additionally swearing[29] by God Almighty and the well-being of our lords and the salvation[30] and hope of the very fearsome judgement-seat of Christ, before which all creation will be brought, each one to be judged according to what he has done, whether good or evil, and the great sentence[31] that God the Word defined with the father of us all, Adam, as follows: "From earth, you shall sleep in earth" [Genesis 3:19],[32] this is the force of the legal relief that has been worked out with us, and we are ready for them to agree to these words and to the force of this plain legal relief before every magistrate and authority in city or *kastron*, in every place, because this is the force of the legal relief that has seemed good to us. And again we give a surety (lit. Word of God),[33] (by) the Creator of the universe, over this sentence, the One Who will justly judge, without respect of persons,[34] because the breath of everyone is in His holy hands [Job 12:10; Daniel 5:23].

But if anyone should dare, from now on or at any time, to produce words giving opposition to this capital matter,[35] that person is to have no benefit from it, but rather chiefly he is to become and be a stranger to the holy, venerated oath by the perfect, undivided Trinity that is the life of all. Subsequently he is to pay to account of fine a pound of gold, upon request, out of his very own property, into the hand of the honored magistrate. Subsequently he is to furnish it and to acknowledge the force of this written agreement document that we have drawn

---

[27] Word inadvertently repeated by the scribe.

[28] Miswritten as *paragraphê* (ⲡⲁⲣⲁⲅⲣⲁⲫⲏ).

[29] Seidl, "Eid," 144.

[30] The same word as that translated "well-being": *oujai* (ⲟⲩϫⲁⲓ).

[31] *apophasis* (ἀπόφασις).

[32] Variant of "Dust thou art and unto dust shalt thou return": *kote* "to turn" playing on *nkotk* "to sleep".

[33] A.A. Schiller, "The Coptic ⲗⲟⲅⲟⲥ ⲙⲡⲛⲟⲩⲧⲉ Documents," in *Studi in memoria di A. Albertoni* (Padua, 1935), 1: 303–45 began the discussion that was continued by W.C. Till, "Koptische Schutzbriefe," *Mitteilungen des deutschen archäologischen Instituts Kairo* 8 (1938): 71–146. See now B. Palme, "Asyl und Schutzbrief im spätantiken Ägypten," in *Das antike Asyl*, ed. M. Dreher (Cologne, 2003), 203–36; and A. Delattre, "Les 'lettres de protection' coptes," in *Akten des 23. Internationalen Papyrologen-Kongresses*, ed. B. Palme (Vienna, 2007), 173–78.

[34] Literally "taking face."

[35] *kephalaion* (κεφάλαιον): Förster, *WB*, 410.

up as security for your God-loving selves, it being secure and valid in every place where it may be produced in evidence. They asked us, we agreed.+

+ And it is clear that we are making this capital matter manifest, and we adjure every magistrate and holy bishop and God-fearing judge and *lashane* who will encounter the force of this written document and read out what is written therein, by the holy consubstantial Trinity and the well-being of our lords and the very fearsome judgement-seat of Christ, before which all creation will be brought, each one to be judged according to what he has done, whether good or evil, and the great deciding sentence that will come about without respecting of persons, to observe every part of the capital matter set down in this written text, without corrupting it.

+ A copy of the oath on the four holy gospels, by its force,[36] that we take this oath[37] upon our souls over the matter of the word that Shenoute produced, that his men did not draw up at the time when he went to depart from the body, he agreeing saying "I found some gold on the mountain of this same *kastron*," and he drew up a written document for your God-loving selves that you should take them.

And now we agree with this same oath that no one is ever to proceed against you or (what belongs to) your monastery nor to our late holy fathers who were alive then.

Month of Hathyr, 29, tenth indiction. [Greek] + Victor, I assent.

+ I Thomas son of the late John, I assent to this written document of agreement, with the oath and the fine, as it stands above. +++

+ I Komes son of the late Samuel the *lashane*, the aforewritten, I assent to this written document of agreement, with the oath and the fine, as it stands above.—+ I Psate son of the late Pisrael, he asked me, I wrote for him as he did not know how to write.

+ Shmtsnêu, I bear witness.

+ I Komes son of Hatre, I bear witness.

+ I Jeremias son of the late Elisha, I bear witness.—I Komes, he asked me, I wrote for him as he did not know how to write.

+ Jacob son of Isaac, businessman[38] from the city of Justinianopolis Kato,[39] I bear witness, having been requested to by the framer. [Greek]

+ I Cyril son of Elias, I bear witness.

---

[36] Seidl, "Eid," 145.

[37] Here *anash* (ⲁⲛⲁϣ) (cf. Seidl, "Eid," 146–47). The nuance between the two Coptic terms for "oath", *ôrk* (ⲱⲣⲕ) and *anash*, remains to be explored. *Ôrk* comes from a root meaning "to attach" (W. Vycichl, *Dictionnaire étymologique de la langue copte* [Leuven, 1983], 250), so an oath is something that connects; its similarity to Greek *horkizein* (ὁρκίζειν) was noted before the conquest. *Anash* also comes from a root meaning "to tie" (14). Sometimes both terms appear in the same document. Cf. Richter, *Sprache*, 182–84, 303.

[38] *pragmateutês* (πραγματευτής): Förster, *WB*, 667.

[39] I.e., Coptos.

+ I Athanasius son of George, with Zacharias son of Apa Victor, we bear witness.—+ Psate son of Pisrael, they asked me, I wrote for them as they did not know how to write.

+ I Abraham son of the late Theodore, I bear witness.

+ I Aaron son of the late Cyriac, I bear witness.

+ I Paham son of Constantine, I bear witness.

+ Theodore son of Solomon, I bear witness.

+ I Pchêr son of the late Cyriac, I bear witness.

+ I Psate son of the late Pisrael, I drew up this written document of agreement with my hand, and I was sitting with the most admirable[40] Thomas and Komes the *lashane*s at the time when the legal relief was worked out between the God-loving brothers and Apa Victor the priest; and they ordered me, I drew it up at their order. +

---

[40] *thaumasiôtatos* (θαυμασιώτατος), the Byzantine title: Förster, *WB*, 330.

P.KRU 34

Sale of Silver Object

DATE: 15 January 713

PLACE: Jeme

PARTIES: Martyria daughter of Victor, seller; Jeremias son of Moses, buyer

OBJECT: Silver item

SUM [fine]: 2 solidi

WITNESSES: 2

SCRIBE: [not preserved]

PUBLICATION: Till, *KRU Theb*, 132

In this document we see a woman, acting on her own behalf, selling a piece of silver to a male buyer. Was this transaction an actual sale (Wilfong, *Women*, 142) or a version of pawn?[1] On the face of things it seems a straightforward sale, with money and the item changing hands.

I Martyria daughter of Victor, woman of Jeme,[2] am writing to Jeremias son of Moses, man of Jeme, in the nome (of the city of Hermonthis). I am selling you my silver object. You gave its price to me; (I have transferred) the object to you. You are its owner, and you can deal with it and handle it in any way you wish. And if I should (proceed against you) in the matter of that silver object, either myself or someone representing me at any time at all, I shall pay two solidi as fine ... (according to [or: as stipulated in]) this document of surety. I have drawn up this written document which has validity in every place where it may be produced in evidence. They asked me and I assent to it as aforesaid,[3] I, Martyria, the aforewritten.

    Paul son of Kabiou, man of Jeme, she asked me (and I agreed ... / wrote ...).

    Twentieth of Tybi, tenth indiction year.

    Athanasius son of Peter, I bear witness: +[Athanasius].

---

[1] A comparandum would be Porten et al., *Elephantine Papyri*, 459–60 (no. D24).

[2] Wilfong, *Women*, 142, calling the silver item "jewelry"; cf. idem, "Women's Things and Men's Things: Notes on Gender and Property at Jeme," *Bulletin of the American Society of Papyrologists* 40 (2003): 213–21.

[3] The standard *hôs prokeitai* (ὡς πρόκειται), "as it stands above."

[Docket on reverse]: The written document that Martyria wrote [/had written] for Jeremias about her silver object that he bought.

P.KRU 9

Sale of Part of a Courtyard

DATE: 4 March 715 [or 730?]

PLACE: Jeme

PARTIES: Athanasius son of Pillustris, seller; his brother Enoch, buyer

OBJECT: Part of courtyard

SUM [fine]: 2 oz. gold

 [price paid]: 3 gold trimesia

WITNESSES: 4

SCRIBE: [unnamed]

PUBLICATION: Till, *KRUTheb*, 100–2

Athanasius of Jeme is having this document drawn up to enact the fact that he is selling to his brother Enoch his own portion of the courtyard he inherited from his late mother. He has requested an archpriest as one of his witnesses, alongside some others who cannot write for themselves.

(In the name of . . .) the consubstantial and life-giving Trinity.[1] Today being the eighth day of the month of Phamenoth in this thirteenth indiction year; in the presence of (N.) son of the late Basil and Peter son of the late Kômos who are in office in Kastron Jeme,[2] our Lord Jesus Christ being king over the whole world.[3]

I Thanasius [sic] son of the late Pillustris and Thêre [sic] in Kastron Jeme in the nome of the city of Hermonthis, am writing, putting in place the subscription of one who will subscribe for me and these trustworthy witnesses who will witness for me below at my very own request: I am writing to my beloved brother Enoch, my legitimate[4] brother, in the same Kastron Jeme in the same nome of Hermonthis. I am writing to you without any trickery or intimidation or compulsion or necessity upon me, but by my very own free choice.

---

[1] Not quite identical with any of the Type 2 Trinity invocation formulas in *CSBE* 2, 100–1, 103–5, 293–95; probably the Persons were named first: here the epithets come after the noun.

[2] See Till's list of *lashane*s in *D&P*, 234–35.

[3] A bold and striking phrase in the Egypt of the earlier eighth century!

[4] *gnêsios* (γνήσιος): Förster, *WB*, 151.

I am selling you my portion of my courtyard,[5] which is this one-third that lies on this low / shaded side (?), which came to me from my late mother Tthêre, according to its boundaries[6] lying round about, from the land surface up to the air space,[7] on all four sides surrounding: south, Jeremias the (scribe?); north, Ankên; east, the street down to John's house; west, the street leading in to here, that the main gate opens onto. Look, these are its boundaries around, from the land surface up to the air space, in the quadrilateral surrounding it.

But you, Enoch, are to enter upon it and be owner and give orders and have power in all ownership over my portion of the courtyard, which is one-third of that courtyard, to build on it,[8] tear it down, make additions to it, alienate it or keep it for yourself, in a word, anything you wish: such that no man shall be able to proceed against you over it, ever, neither myself nor son nor daughter of mine, nor brother nor sister, nor relative in the first or second degree, nor kin nor kin of kin, nor heir coming after me,[9] nor anyone either from my family or from outside my family, altogether. The one who shall dare at any time at all to proceed against you, either myself or anyone representing me, first off, that man will not get any good out of it, but will be liable to the fine that the just laws have defined, namely two ounces of gold to the magistrate who is in office at that time. Subsequently he is to appear and acknowledge the validity of this sale, because you have given its price to me, hand to hand, namely five trimesia[10] of pure[11] gold of full weight according to the standard of the *kastron*.[12] . . .

Thereupon I swear by God Almighty and the well-being of these our lords who rule over us now[13] not to transgress this written sale, before every rule and every authority. They asked me, I agreed, securing this sale for you, which is secure and valid in every place where it may be brought before any rule or authority,[14] as it stands.

I Athanasius, the aforewritten above, I assent to the sale in every matter written therein, as it stands.

---

[5] On the structure of Jeme houses and their partibility, see Wilfong, *Women*, 51–54.

[6] Always given for property: sometimes the order (points of the compass) varies by region, sometimes by practice of the individual notary. Here they go south, north, east, west.

[7] A stereotyped phrase from Roman law: cf. *CJ* 8.10–11 (and *Digest* 39.10).

[8] This begins a fixed, or nearly fixed, set of owner's-rights clauses regularly applied to immovable property. We will see minor variations in these documents.

[9] Or: "heir or successor."

[10] A trimesion was one-third of a (Byzantine) solidus; here it is a question of one-third of a caliphal gold coin.

[11] *obryzon* (ὄβρυζον): Förster, *WB*, 559–60; see K. Maresch, *Nomisma und Nomismatia* (Opladen, 1994), 14–28, 34.

[12] On local standards see Maresch, *Nomisma und Nomismatia*, 33–34, 36–37, 59, 82–90.

[13] Seidl, "Eid," 143.

[14] Not the usual "be produced in evidence."

+ I Komos son of the late Hatre, I bear witness.

I Anchên son of George,[15] I bear witness.—I Komes, I wrote for them as they do not know how to write.

+ I Zebedee son of George, I bear witness.—I Komes, I wrote for him as he did not know how.

+ I Stephen, most humble archpriest of the holy church of the holy Apa Isidore,[16] I bear witness at the request of Athanasius.

---

[15] Same as the neighbor on the north?
[16] See Papaconstantinou, *Saints*, 110–12, and now C. Heurtel, *Les inscriptions coptes et grecques du temple d'Hathor à Deir al-Médîna* (Cairo, 2004), 100–1.

P.KRU 35

Settlement of Inherited-Property Division

DATE: 6 October 719

PLACE: Jeme

PARTIES: Abigaia daughter of Samuel, deacon and monk, and the late Tsenoute (with Daniel her husband); Elizabeth daughter of the late Epiphanius and the late Mary, Abigaia's aunt

OBJECT: House property

SUM [fine]: 4 oz. gold = 24 sol.

WITNESSES: 14

SCRIBE: John son of the late Lazarus

PUBLICATION: Till, *Erb*, 111–13; A.A. Schiller, "A Family Archive from Jeme," in *Studi in Onore di Vincenzo Arangio-Ruiz* (Naples, 1952), 325–75.

With this document we begin to follow the affairs of Abigaia of Jeme (one of two known women with that name) and her family. See Wilfong, *Women*, 49–58, translating many passages and analyzing the entire document (also cf. Wickham, *Framing the Early Middle Ages*, 424). Here Abigaia agrees that her aunt Elizabeth can have certain specified parts of the house that she (Abigaia) has inherited, while she herself retains ownership of other parts, and yet other parts are to be held and used in common. Again we see how complex Jeme houses were, as were the relationships of their owners. And if you built an addition that inconvenienced your relatives, you could be in serious legal trouble.

[traces of the protocol, mentioning "governor" (*symboulos*) in Greek and "year" in Arabic, remain at the beginning]

+ In the name of the Father and the Son and the Holy Ghost, consubstantial, perfect and life-giving Trinity,[1] and the power[2] and establishedness and

---

[1] A variant of invocation Type **2L**: *CSBE 2*, 295.

[2] The scribe here, John son of the late Lazarus (also scribe of *P.KRU* 21 dated 725 and of *P.KRU* 38 dated 738, below, where he does it too), has conflated the phraseology of an opening invocation formula with that of an oath formula which latter is, of course "by" rather than "in the name of" the ruler(s). Compare the oath clause later in this instrument.

continuance of our lords the kings who have power over the whole earth at the command of Almighty God. Today being the eighth day of the month of Phaophi, in the third indiction year, in the presence of the most honorable, honored Victor son of the late Thomas and Ananias son of the late Abraham, *lashane*s of Kastron Jeme in the nome of the city of Hermonthis.

Greetings. I Abigaia, daughter of Samuel the deacon and monk of the mountain of Jeme and of the late Tsenoute, with Daniel my husband agreeing with me in all things,[3] (we being) persons of Kastron Jeme in the nome of the city of Hermonthis: we are writing to Elizabeth daughter of the late Epiphanius and the late Mary, persons of Kastron Jeme in the same nome. We are setting down this settlement with one another, putting in place the one who will subscribe for us and some respectable and trustworthy[4] witnesses who will witness this settlement at our very own request. Greetings.

WHEREAS: at this time we have made good faith with one another, to our hearts' content, to divide the house of our departed ones among ourselves in this way, so that each one's several portion will be clear, and we will be assigning them to you: these are they: You, Elizabeth, sister of my late mother,[5] get the room under the staircase and the dining-room[6] the door of which opens northwards toward the staircase. And you will be in charge of[7] the entire exedra[8] the door of which opens northwards towards the staircase, and the entire storage space above the exedra, with its sole air space. Whoever wishes to can build onto it up to the boundary, extending his staircase to his portion. The outside door with the entryway and the water-holder[9] and the staircase are to be in common with one another, up to when someone may build on to the house; if someone does so build, let each one have his or her staircase up to his or her portion, as we have agreed upon with one another on both sides.

---

[3] Cf. J. Beaucamp, *Le statut de la femme à Byzance (4e-7e siècles)*, 2 vols. (Paris, 1990), 1: 278–79, 2: 127–39, 257–63, 309–17.

[4] Here not the completely Greek *axiopistos* (ⲁⲝⲓⲟⲡⲓⲥⲧⲟⲥ), 'worthy of trust' or 'worthy of being trusted', but the hybrid *shoupisteue nau* (ϣⲟⲩⲡⲓⲥⲧⲉⲩⲉ ⲛⲁⲩ), 'who customarily are trusted' (literally 'whom they usually trust').

[5] See the stemma in Wilfong, *Women*, 48.

[6] *symposion* (ⲥⲩⲙⲡⲟⲥⲓⲟⲛ): cf. Förster, *WB*, 769.

[7] Literally "give orders concerning," *keleue* (ⲕⲉⲗⲉⲩⲉ).

[8] According to Wilfong, *Women*, 51 with n. 11 (following Till), this means "grain storage area" (see also the house plan on 52). Ordinarily it denotes a hall or arcade with places to sit; in a religious building, especially a basilica, it means a semicircular space with tiered seating at the far end. Or have two clauses been conflated in this reading? Cf. also *BGU* XIX 2821.

[9] Or "watercourse", a bit like Schiller's "conduit" ("Family Archive," 338), but Wilfong (*Women*, 51 with n. 12) prefers the familiar phenomenon of large water-jars on stands with runnels.

These are the boundaries of that house, in a quadrilateral: south, the house of the late Sourous; east, the house of Philotheos; north, the house of Antony son of Paul; west, Cup Street[10] and the main gate (of the town). See, these are the boundaries of that house, in a quadrilateral. And the wall in the middle is to be in common with one another, with its air space. And the south part has yielded me a trimesion of gold with respect to the north part as well, as we have come to entrust one another therewith. And you, Elizabeth, when you go through the door to the storage area above the exedra, if you wish to build on to the storage area, you are in charge of it. Only you should take the staircase into the door of the storage area, with its air space. But you, Elizabeth daughter of the late Epiphanius, from now on you are the one in charge of all these portions of the house, you and your children and grandchildren and all who come after you, to bestow them or give them away or sell them, altogether.

We have come to an agreement with one another in every particular with regard to every (legal) relief[11] from everything, willingly and with trust, without any trickery or intimidation or compulsion or necessity or deception or harm and seizure or circumscription, there being not one single necessity incumbent upon us, but rather out of our own free choice, agreeing with one another about the inheritance of our house, (the house) of our departed ones, as we have made it clear.

It shall not be possible for us or our children or heirs or successors or any man at all representing us to go to law with one another, at all. Anyone who dares to, or undertakes to transgress this settlement, is to pay four ounces of gold as fine, = AV 24 sol. pure,[12] by the standard of Kastron Memnonion, and subsequently to appear and acknowledge the validity of the settlement in all matters written therein.

And upon all these things we swear by the holy consubstantial Trinity and by the power and establishedness and continuance of our lords these kings established by God that no transgression thereof will occur, of the settlement and all matters written therein. Accordingly, we have drawn up this settlement in two (identical) copies,[13] which is to be secure and have validity in every place where it may be produced in evidence.

---

[10] Koulol Street (perhaps named after the monastic location); or "Winding Street."

[11] *apallagê* (ἀπαλλαγή).

[12] If this equation/ratio obtained at this time it would mean 1 lb. gold = 96 'solidi' (dinars) with 1 oz. gold = 6 'solidi'. In *P.KRU* 68 below (dated 723), 4 oz. gold still = 24 solidi. This is below the full 'Byzantine-style' ratio of 1 lb. gold = 72 solidi (1 oz. = 4 ½ sol.), which underwent variation in the sixth century (Maresch, *Nomisma*, 101, 151).

[13] *isotypon* (ἰσότυπον: Förster, *WB*, 354), as in Byzantine law and pre-conquest papyrus documents: e.g., *P.Cair.Masp.* I 67032.79; *P.Lond.* I 113.

They asked us, we agreed; we set it down in the month of Phaophi, the 8th, 3rd indiction ⲁⲣⲭⲏ,[14] with God's help.[15] +

I Abigaia daughter of Samuel the monk, with Daniel my husband agreeing with me in all things, I assent to the settlement, with the oath and the fine and all matters written therein, as it stands.—I John son of Lazarus, I wrote for them as they did not know how to write.[16]

I Pesyntheus son of Stephen, I bear witness.

I John son of the late Victor, I bear witness.

I Pshêre, by the mercy of God this most humble priest and hegoumenos of the holy church of Jeme,[17] I bear witness.

I Peter son of Andrew, I bear witness.

I Athanasius son of the late Jeremias, I bear witness to the settlement.—I Andrew son of the late Lazarus,[18] I wrote for him and bear witness to the settlement.

I Komes, most humble priest of the holy Apa Patermouthis[19] of Kastron Jeme, I bear witness.

I Peshate son of the late Elias, I bear witness.

I Constantine son of the late Solomon, former *lashane*, I bear witness.—Komes the most humble priest, he asked me, I wrote for him as he did not know how.[20]

I Peter son of the late Komes, former *lashane*, I bear witness. I Andrew son of the late Lazarus, I wrote for him as he did not know how to write.

Psate son of Pisrael,[21] I bear witness.

I Ananias son of the late Abraham, I bear witness.

I Komes son of the late Hatre, I bear witness.

I Epiphanius son of the late Zacharias, I bear witness.

I John son of the late Lazarus, I executed it with my own hand.

[added] We, Abraham and David, . . . [agreeing] with each other, . . . anyone who proceeds against us over the fabric[22] of the common wall with the house of Antony that we have built is to . . . [settle?] with one another as aforesaid.

---

[14] *CSBE 2*, 35, 115.
[15] Cf. (with caution) Luisier, "ⲥⲩⲛ ⲑⲉⲱ."
[16] On women's literacy, in whichever language, see Wilfong, *Women*, 61–62, 75–76.
[17] The town's principal church: see Wilfong, *Women*, 10, 12.
[18] Brother of John the notary? He also writes for the former *lashane* Peter, below.
[19] Papaconstantinou, *Saints*, 168–70. Also appears in *P.KRU* 10 below.
[20] A *lashane* who could not write (in Coptic, that is); same for the next.
[21] The well-known notary (Till, *D&P*, 185–87).
[22] *oikodomê* (οἰκοδομή): Förster, *WB*, 562.

P.KRU 55

Business Agreement

DATE: 7 October 720 (or 735?)
PLACE: Jeme
PARTIES: George son of the late Matthew; Peter son of the late Komes
OBJECT: Business expenses
SUM [fine]: 1 lb. gold
WITNESSES: 2
SCRIBE: [unnamed]
PUBLICATION: Till, *KRUTheb*, 137–38

In this document we have an agreement between two men that one has been reimbursed by the other for his expenses. As one might expect, they protect themselves against counterclaims by oaths not to demand more than what is settled here. The exact nature of the 'business' is not spelled out.

[No invocation seems preserved]
+ I George so[n of the late Matthew, man of Kastron] Jeme in the nome of the city of [Herm]onthis, am writing to Peter son of the late Komes,[1] from this same *kastron*, as follows:
   Whereas: over the matter of the business[2] that we are handling with each other, we have come to an agreement with each other as to both parties in each and every matter. Concerning the matter of the expenditures[3] that I have paid out on your behalf: what I gave you, you have repaid to me.
   Neither I nor a brother belonging to me nor any man representing me is to be able to go to law against you, neither (against) yourself nor your children nor any

---

[1] *Lashane* in 715 (*P.KRU* 9 above).
[2] *pragmateia* (πραγματεία): Förster, *WB*, 667.
[3] *zêmia* (ζημία): Förster, *WB*, 316.

man belonging to you, because you have repaid me what I was to receive. And we have come to an agreement with each other over gold and silver and every shape and form[4] of article appertaining to our business except for the matter of our guarantee with each other, and the payment in full.[5]

We swear by God Almighty and the well-being of our lords who rule over us by the command of God[6] that we will observe the force of this written document that is untransgressable. And the one who transgresses it is to pay a pound of gold. For your security I have drawn up this written document which is valid.

[Greek] Written in the month of Phaophi, indiction four.

+ I George son of the late Matthew, I assent to the written document with all matters written therein, with my hand.

+ I Daniel son of the late Zacharias, I bear witness.—+ I Senouthios son of Elias, I wrote for him.

I Mena son of Abraham, I bear witness.—I Sergius, I wrote for him.

---

[4] *eidos* (εἶδος): Förster, *WB*, 227–28.

[5] ⲧⲉⲕⲧⲓⲥ: Till reads ⲧ- + ἔκτισις (*t-ektisis*). Or possibly with *ktisis* (κτῖσις), "the setting-up", since according to George (re)payment in full for the expenditures he paid out has already been made.

[6] Seidl, "Eid," 143.

P.KRU 66 AND 76

TESTAMENT

DATE: before 722[1]

PLACE: Jeme

PARTIES: Susanna, daughter of the late Moses and Tsia, testatrix; the St Patermouthios monastery, and her five grandchildren, Shenoute, Hemai, Stephen, Tsône, and Victorine (children of her late son Germanos), heirs designate

OBJECT: Arable and grazing land; house property; personal possessions

SUM [fine]: 6 oz. gold = 36 solidi

WITNESSES: 6

SCRIBE: Komes, priest[2] of St Patermouthios's

PUBLICATION: Till, *Erb*, 159–69

The testament of Susanna[3] is preserved in two parallel copies, apparently written by the same scribe (though he explicitly signs off on only one). Of neither copy is the beginning preserved. *P.KRU* 66 is in the British Library; 76, in Berlin. On the other side of 76 is written *P.KRU* 10, dated to 8 December 722: it is a sale of land by five siblings, children of the late Psate, to Shenoute, Hemai, and Stephen, all children of the late Germanos, whom we meet also in *P.KRU* 21; in this document we find out that they are Susanna's three grandsons, and that Germanos was her son. (The scribe of that text was the well-known Aristophanes son of John; the second scribe, Komes, wrote a copy of Susanna's will on the back of his predecessor's work.) Till prints the translated texts of 66 and 76 in two parallel columns. For readability I give a conflation: text from 66 is in roman type, text from 76 in italic.

Susanna owns a great deal of property of various kinds (see the discussion in Wilfong, *Women*, 135, cf.84 n.7; also Wickham, *Framing the Early Middle Ages*, 425). She owned a fifth share of the monastery church of St Patermouthios's (see Schmelz, *Kirchliche Amtsträger*, 35) and specifies that her granddaughters are not

---

[1] See the recent redating and reconsideration by J. Cromwell, "Another Family Archive from Jeme" (forthcoming).

[2] Also the scribe of *P.KRU* 35.

[3] See S. Schaten, "Ein weiteres Familienarchiv aus Djeme: KRU 66 und KRU 76, die Testamente der Susanna," in *Akten des 21. Internationalen Papyrologenkongresses*, ed. B. Kramer et al. (Stuttgart, 1997), 902–13.

to be kept away from the festivals held there. She apportions personal belongings by gender,[4] to women and men, and forcefully proclaims that no one is to doubt her *nous* (on account of her age and gender?). In both copies there is an inserted extra clause about a missing deed to one of the house properties—in one version, the deed was possibly stolen by Susanna's siblings or one of their children—and how the aggrieved parties are, in the other version, to be placated by a property exchange, land for the disputed house.

[(Invocation, etc.) I, Susanna,] am setting down my will and testament,[5] with my heart and my reasoning established, perceiving[6] the world as every human being does (and) walking upon the earth,[7] and I have set down this testamentary agreement, immovable and untransgressable, not to be set aside and indestructible by law, with the subscription of those who will subscribe for me and those who will represent credible witnesses who will also subscribe for me willingly at my very own request and by my free choice, as follows:

It is not revealed to me, my going out of the body, and (as for) the hour of my death, when it will be. For the rest, looking toward death, it passes before me daily; I was afraid lest death suddenly surprise me and I not know my end,[8] and I go the way that my fathers went, *and leave this place of temporary sojourning behind, going the way of all the earth,* again in the way that God defined for our first father Adam His first-created, (saying,) "You are earth and will sleep in earth [Genesis 3:19]"; and the Psalmist David, ancestor of Christ after the flesh,[9] said, "I am a sojourner upon the earth, as all my fathers were [Psalm 38:12 LXX]," and again, "Man is like a shadow that passes away [Psalm 108:23 LXX];"[10] and again, "Before I go hence and am no more seen [Psalm 38:13 LXX];" and yet again, "Man walketh in a vain show, (. . .) and heapeth up riches, and cannot tell who will gather them [Psalm 38:6 LXX]." As I heard all these witnesses *from being written in Scripture* coming to me about man being of earth and ashes [Genesis 18:27; Job 30:19], I was afraid.

Now I have sought for this will and testament with my heart and my reasoning *established (and)* unchanged, with no necessity incumbent upon me, nor

---

[4] See T. Wilfong, "Gender and Society in Byzantine Egypt," in *Egypt*, ed. Bagnall, 309–27, and idem, "Women's Things and Men's Things." Males are not to inherit in females' place, nor females in males'.

[5] In actual word order "testament and will."

[6] Till restores a form of *prattein* (πράττειν) and renders "treating the things of this world as all people do"; but earlier formulary does not jibe with this. There is, true, similar yet subtly different phrasing below.

[7] Cf. *P.Lond.* I 77.12.

[8] Cf. Psalm 38:4 LXX.

[9] *katasarx* (ⲕⲁⲧⲁⲥⲁⲣⲝ).

[10] Cf. Psalms 101:11, 143:4 LXX.

compulsion nor deception nor seizure nor circumscription, but rather in full satisfaction of heart. Moreover, I am swearing by God Almighty *(the holy, consubstantial Trinity)* and the well-being *(the establishedness and continuance)*[11] of the lords, these kings who rule over the whole earth by the counsel of God Almighty,[12] and I am adjuring everyone—by a fearsome oath—who will read *or hear* this testament (which is a will) that no transgression happen to it *or that it be destroyed*.

Subsequently I reflected upon the uncertainty[13] of the human condition, because I am to make plain the entirety of my possessions and my offering, while I am still alive, walking with a stick, hale in my body without any lack of strength in my body, but acting as far as the world goes like every person walking on earth, and being concerned daily *about worldly matters*. Again subsequently, being alive, I have become and I am owner of all that belongs to me.

But when God *in Whose hand is the breath of everyone* [Job 12:10] orders to take away the spirit He gave me, and that I am to leave behind this place of temporary sojourning and go the way that every human being goes *(has to go)*, the way God defined the sentence[14] for *our father* Adam saying, "You are earth and will sleep in earth [Genesis 3:19]," I wish and order[15] in this way: that my beloved (grand)sons the sons of my late son Germanos, namely Hemai, Shenoute, and Stephen, are to enter upon the inheritance that came to me from my late mother Tsia, which came to her in her turn from *her father* Elisha, the archdeacon of this *topos* of the one who gives light among the saints, the holy Apa Patermouthios[16] of Kastron Jeme, *on account of the good things they have done for me during the sickness that God sent upon me by His will*.

---

[11] Here *moun ebol* (ⲘⲞⲨⲚ ⲈⲂⲞⲖ), not *dianomê* (διανομή). It is noteworthy that the oath clauses vary from one instrument to the other, though they are engrossed by the same notary.

[12] Seidl, "Eid," 142–43.

[13] Förster, *WB*, 737, following Till, *Erb*, 161, insists on reading *skepsis* (σκέψις) and rendering "in human intent"; but clearly it is a formation from *kleptein* (κλέπτειν) and means "something that can easily be snatched away", so "transitoriness".

[14] *apophasis* (ἀπόφασις); Till (*Erb*, 161) preferred to read *prophasis* (πρόφασις), "allegation", but parallel phraseology to this in other documents (Förster, *WB*, 92) favors the clear reading.

[15] Again the Byzantine-law phrase *boulomai kai keleuô* (βούλομαι καὶ κελεύω).

[16] Papaconstantinou, *Saints*, 168–70, esp. here 169.

I give and define the entire fifth portion (of my property) to the church, together with its fields, meadows, its tax burden,[17] and its entire yield[18] *that comes from it, which is to go to the holy* topos. But my (grand)daughter is not to hinder her female siblings from going to the publically designated festivals, the feasts of the *topos and the great, obvious feasts,* to eat and drink: not to hinder them from going there in good order [Greek];[19] *only they are not to buy or sell on its behalf.*

Again, concerning my portion of the house that I bought from *the children of* Kalê son of Kalêl, *except for the* topos *of Apa Patermouthios,* and my portion up to the awning[20] *(i.e., the dining-room),* which is the fourth portion, and the house in Rope-Makers' Lane (?), that came to me from my grandfather the archdeacon Elisha *through my late mother Tsia, I define that all* is to belong to my three (grand)sons, Hemai, Shenoute, and Stephen. *But as far as my church*[21] *is concerned,* no female (grand)child of mine is to buy or sell on its behalf, ever, as defined above.

Again, concerning the houses that came to me from my late father Moses, my female (grand)children are to get them, shared by the two of them; and again, the house that my mother gave to me alone *and my father defined as being for me,* namely the house of Kanênê, *my female (grand)children are to get it. But if the children of my brother produce a document drawn up for them, my female (grand)children are to have nothing to do with them, for ever: for it is to belong to my female (grand) children Tsône and Victorine.*

---

[17] *dêmosion* (δημόσιον): important evidence that the Islamic government was beginning to tax Christian church property (cf. also Schmelz, *Kirchliche Amtsträger,* 217). See T. Wilfong, "Agriculture among the Christian Population of Early Islamic Egypt," in *Agriculture in Egypt,* ed. Bowman and Rogan, 217–35, here 226; idem, "Christian Communities," 181–83; and Frantz-Murphy, "Land-Tenure," 243–45; cf. Sijpesteijn, "Beginning of Muslim Rule," and Papaconstantinou, "Donation d'enfants," 102–5. For a thorough treatment see *P.Mon.Apoll.* pp. 23–26 and nos. 28–32; and S.J. Clackson, "Archimandrites and *Andrismos*: A Preliminary Survey of Taxation at Bawit," in *Akten des 23. Internationalen Papyrologen-Kongresses,* ed. Palme, 103–7.

[18] Equivalent not to *prosphora* (προσφορά), "offering" (Till, *Erb,* 162 n. 106) but to *eulogia* (εὐλογία).

[19] Christian monastic festivals continued strong (see Wilfong, "Christian Communities"), and perhaps keeping "good order" began to be a concern, over and above simple considerations of appropriate behavior by young women in public.—Till misread a form of *kôluein* (κωλύειν) here.

[20] Cf. below, *P.KRU* 18, n. 6.

[21] The feminine possessive prefix *ta-* (ⲧⲁ-), "my," is indeed used before the noun *ekklêsia*; while the monastery church is a beneficiary, Susanna's family may have been involved in its founding (cf. Schmelz, *Kirchliche Amtsträger,* 216–17). Cf. J.P. Thomas, *Private Religious Foundations in the Byzantine Empire* (Washington, DC, 1987); and, for western comparanda, S. Wood, *The Proprietary Church in the Medieval West* (Oxford, 2006).

My female (grand)children *Tsône and Victorine* are to get a woman's garment, a *colored* cloak, all my women's things,[22] *dyed women's dresses, a* mijke *(plain dress?), my headscarves, a kettle;* my (grand)sons, *Hemai, Shenoute, and Stephen,* are to get three silver necklaces, three silver pectorals *for wedding presents*, three lamps,[23] two water basins, a bronze basin,[24] a copper vessel, all my necessary bedclothes, three fringed blankets, three wooden chests, and all men's things *that I will name*, on account of the good things they have done for me in my old age *and in the severe sickness that God has brought upon me by His will*. And after my death they are to bury me[25] and bring my offering,[26] a year's (worth of) offering for each (grand)child, male and female, making five years' worth.

Concerning all the contents of my house, except for what I have (already) defined for each (grand)child severally, they are to be *equally* distributed among my five (grand)children, as each wishes. But none of my (grand)children is to be able to go to law with any of their other siblings in any way, shape or form, nor are they to swear oaths with one another, ever, *from today on*, because I have made them come to an agreement with one another. But should one of my (grand)children die—for all people must *die*—as far as this matter is concerned, should it be a *childless* male, his brothers are to inherit for him; should it be a female, her sisters are to inherit for her. *No male is to inherit in a female's place, and no female in a male's. And concerning my death: my male (grand)children are to bury me, according to the* ethos *of the village, and my five (grand)children are to give the five years' worth of offerings on my behalf, once a year.*

All these things I have defined for my (grand)children. They are, each of them, to enter in and be owner in all ownership over what I have defined for them above, for all time. And no transgression is to happen to this testament that I have drawn up while still alive, walking around, before any sickness had come upon me. And again, no man is to be able to destroy it, neither magistrate nor *hegemon* nor eparch nor *lashane* nor bishop nor ecclesiastic; neither brother nor sister nor relative in the first or in the second degree, neither kin nor kin of kin, neither from my family nor from outside my family, no man at all appertaining to me. *And no man is to doubt*[27] *my mind, but rather I wrote it* (the testament) *with a contented heart. No man is to be able to contravene*[28] *me in my desire, nor is he to be able to undo this testament that I have drawn up for my (grand)children.* Anyone who

---

[22] See Wilfong, "Women's Things and Men's Things," 213–15, for this and the following.

[23] Cf. Schmelz, *Kirchliche Amtsträger*, 123.

[24] *lakané* (ⲗⲁⲕⲁⲛⲏ).

[25] See F. Dunand, "Between Tradition and Innovation: Egyptian Funerary Practices in Late Antiquity," in *Egypt*, ed. Bagnall, 163–84.

[26] Presumably to the St Patermouthios monastery.

[27] *korpizein* (*κορπίζειν): Förster, *WB*, 435.

[28] From *paralogon* (παράλογον): Förster, *WB*, 619.

dares transgress my testament or mess with[29] it or legally tamper with it or move against it or slander[30] it, *should it be one of my (grand)children, he/she is not to be able to buy or sell anything ever. And should it be someone else,* chiefly before all else he will have no profit of it, nor will the matter do good for him, for he is to become and be a stranger to the holy, venerated oath of Christians by the Father, the Son and the Holy Ghost. Subsequently he is to pay the fine that the just kings (!) have defined, namely six ounces of pure gold, = [AV oz. 6] = *(3)6 solidi*[31] to the magistrate or *lashane* bearing rule at that time. Subsequently he is to provide it out of his own property—the fine, thusly—into the hand of the honored magistrate. He is to furnish it and appear and acknowledge the force of this testament, which is a will, the testament being drawn up so as to be secure and having force and validity and being warranted in every place where it may be produced in evidence.

They read it aloud to me in Egyptian; I rejoiced greatly; I was pleased with it. *They asked me, I agreed.* I walked on my feet and went and requested some credible, *respectable*[32] witnesses to witness it: they witnessed it with their hands: those who knew how to write wrote with their very own hands, while those who did not know how requested people to write for them.

I Susanna, daughter of the late Moses and of *the late* Tsia daughter of Elisha, the archdeacon, the aforewritten above, I assent to this testament, with the oath and the fine, and with all things written therein, as it stands above. +

Subsequently: God be witness for my soul that they drew up the document for the house of Kanênê in my youth. I put it in the house of my father. My siblings took it—or their children did. So if the children of Paul my brother find the document, it is to belong to my female (grand)children, as I said above. And my female (grand)children are not to be able to go to law with my male (grand)children, for I have given them what is theirs, as it stands above.

+ I Pshêre, by the mercy of God most humble priest and hegoumenos[33] of the holy church of *Kastron* Jeme, I bear witness *at the request of Susanna*. +++

+ I Zacharias, *by the mercy of God* most humble archpriest of the holy church of Kastron Jeme, I bear witness *at the request of Susanna.*

+ I Papnoute, by the mercy of God most humble priest of the holy church of Kastron Jeme, I bear witness.—+ I Zacharias, most humble archpriest, I wrote for him. +

---

[29] Either from *jôh* (ϫⲱϩ) "touch" (so Till, *Erb*, 166) or from *jôh* (ϫⲱϩ) "smear."

[30] Till, *Erb*, 166 prefers to read *parallassein* (παραλλάσσειν), "set it aside," but I follow Crum/Steindorff's text with a form of *paralalein* (παραλαλεῖν), "speak against, 'bad-mouth'."

[31] Here we are once again at the ratio of 1 oz. = 6 sol., 1 lb. gold = 96 sol. Cf. *P.KRU* 35 above.

[32] *eleutheros* (ἐλεύθερος).

[33] Cf. *P.CLT* 1, *P.KRU* 35, 38.

– It is clear that[34] if the sons of Paul my brother produce in evidence the document for the house aforewritten above, for my (grand)daughters, which is the house of Kanênê, and my (grand)daughters have a legal case with the sons of Paul, as to whether it is to be theirs, moreover God is the witness for my soul before the judgement-seat of God where my soul will appear that I sought to draw up the document to that house; I put it in the house of my father: so subsequently my female (grand)children are not to have a legal case with my male (grand)children over what I have made over to them in writing above; but rather they are to get my portion of the sown land by the share[35] of the Apostles'[36] (church) and the gate of Sourous the camelherd, in exchange for the house of Kanênê, as their own portion.

I Papas, most humble + deacon of the church of Jeme, I bear witness.

+ *I Psaiô son of the late Athanasius, of Kastron Jeme, I bear witness.*+

+ Shenetom son of the late Menas, I bear witness *at the request of Susanna.*—Komes, most humble priest, I wrote for him as he, *Shenetom,* who did not know how to write, *asked me to, in accordance with the* ethos *of Kastron Jeme.* +—*I Komes, most humble priest of the holy Apa Patermouthios of Kastron Jeme, Susanna asked me, I drew up this testament with my hand, and also I bear witness.* +++

---

[34] *dêlonhoutos* (ⲇⲏⲗⲟⲛ2ⲟⲩⲧⲟⲥ) (not -*ôs/ⲱⲥ*) for *dêlon(h)oti* (δῆλον ὅτι).

[35] Reading a form from *pôsh* (ⲡⲱϣ) rather than *pake* (ⲡⲁⲕⲉ) which Till thought a proper noun (*Erb,* 169).

[36] Papaconstantinou, *Saints,* 56–58, esp. here 57.

P.KRU 10

Sale of Landed Property

DATE: 8 December 722

PLACE: Jeme

PARTIES: Zacharias, Ephraim, Sophia, Mary, and Takoum, children of the late Psate; Shenoute, Hemai, and Stephen, sons of the late Germanos

OBJECT: Landed property

SUM: 7 1/3 solidi (original purchase price)

3 2/3 solidi (price of half-portion)

[fine]: 36 sol.

WITNESSES: 7

SCRIBE: Aristophanes son of John[1]

PUBLICATION: Till, *KRUTheb*, 102–4; *SB Kopt.* II 946

Here we follow the property affairs of two (possibly interrelated) extended families of Jeme: the children of Psate, and those of Germanos (cf. Wickham, *Framing the Early Middle Ages*, 424–25). From one family, five siblings, two brothers and their three sisters, all jointly sell back to another set of siblings (three brothers) a piece of land that they, the original parties, had earlier on sold to those three brothers' late father. In the past, a dispute seems to have arisen, and the original sellers went downriver to the provincial governor, who nullified the sale, telling the five to return the money and reassume their land. Back home in Jeme, the town authorities then found that part of that land was not the five's at all but actually belonged to someone else, one Pesyntheus son of Paul, who came forward with a deed to prove it. The five bought him out of half, while he for his part sold the other half of what he had owned to the three brothers. In an attempt to straighten all this out, the five are now selling the rest of the land to the three brothers.

On the back of this document, which the family preserved in their archive, is written *P.KRU* 76, the second copy of the testament of Susanna (see the previ-

---

[1] Another well-known and productive Jeme notary: Till, *D&P*, 61–62; and now J. Cromwell, "Aristophanes Son of Johannes," paper at the 25th International Congress of Papyrology, Ann Arbor, 2007; and eadem, "Individual Scribal Practice at Jeme: The Papyri Documents of Aristophanes Son of Johannes," Ph.D. diss., University of Liverpool, 2008.

ous document). Susanna was the late Germanos's mother and the grandmother of the five siblings we encounter here.

+ In the name of the holy and life-giving, consubstantial Trinity, Father, Son and Holy Ghost.[2]
 Written month of Choiak 12, indiction 6.[Greek]
 In the presence of the most illustrious Athanasius son of David and Menas son of the late Paam, *meizoteroi*[3] of Kastron Memnonion.
 We, Zacharias and Ephraim and Sophia and Mary and Takoum, children of the late Psate, and representing other siblings and acting on their behalf in all matters, all of us reckoned[4] to Kastron Jeme in the nome of the city of Hermonthis, subsequently putting in place a subscriber who will subscribe for us to this written document of sale, which is to be untransgressable and unshakable by law, and further establishing it through these other trustworthy witnesses who will witness it for us at our very own mutual request and by our intention: we are writing to Shenoute and Hemai and Stephen, sons of the late Germanos, men of the same *kastron*:[5] Greetings.
 WHEREAS: In these times past we sold the whole piece of land to you, this one east of the holy *topos* of Apa Patermoute in Kastron Jeme, to Germanos your late father [. . .] and Shenoute and Hemai and Stephen, you the aforewritten. He gave seven solidi [and a third] for that whole piece of land. We drew up a written document of sale, securing [it so that] your father was to be owner of that whole piece of land according to the force of the sale we drew up. After a long time we went to Antinoë; we approached our lord the most renowned duke[6] about that whole piece of land. He, our lord the duke, ordered us to give these 7 1/3 sol. of Germanos your late father back and reassume our land. After we came back south and approached your late father Germanos, subsequently being responsible for a lawsuit with your father over that whole piece of land, the authorities of the *kastron* found that a half portion of that piece of land belonged to Pesyntheus son of Paul, according to the force of the ancient sale that he, Pesyntheus son of Paul,

---

 [2] Invocation formula Type **2E**: *CSBE 2*, 100, 104–5, 293.
 [3] The Greek-language equivalent for *lashane*s: Förster, *WB*, 509.
 [4] From ὀπ (ⲱⲡ), "to number."
 [5] See Wilfong, *Women*, 142.
 [6] In the period of Byzantine rule the *dux* was the chief of the province: cf. J. Gascou, "*Ducs, praesides*, poètes et rhéteurs au Bas-Empire," *Antiquité tardive* 6 (1998): 61–64; idem, "L'Egypte byzantine," 416–17; Sarris, *Economy*, 109–13. By now he was most likely a Muslim official. See Sijpesteijn, "Landholding Patterns in Early Islamic Egypt," 121–22. The Thebaid duke's seat continued to be Antinoë (Antinoöpolis), capital (metropolis) of the Byzantine Antinoite nome.

brought forward.[7] Then we gave three solidi and two trimesia[8] to Pesyntheus son of Paul, out of the 7 1/3 sol., for the half-portion of land. He (then) sold (his) half of the land to you, Shenoute and Hemai and Stephen the aforewritten. So we also, Zacharias and Ephraim and Sophia and Takoum,[9] children of the late Psate, are unable to furnish and give you (Shenoute et al.) the other 3 2/3 sol. We wished to sell you, the aforenamed above, our half-portion.

But now we agree, swearing by God Almighty and the well-being of our lords who rule over us by command,[10] that we have sold to you, you, Shenoute and Hemai and Stephen, sons of the late Germanos, the buyers, the aforewritten, in all ownership, justice, and law, in a complete sale written for you from today and from now on for ever, for all time and forever coming after you, our whole portion of land east of the august *topos* of the holy Apa Patermouthios, which is the half-portion of that land, from its foundations[11] up to the air space, together with all the other possessions belonging to us in that land. And as far as its boundaries round about go, they are: south, the street; north, the threshing-floor of the *topos*; east, [unstated]; west, the holy *topos* of the holy Apa Patermouthios; and these are the boundaries of the half-portion of that land from its foundations [sic] up to the air space, together with the other utensils[12] belonging thereto.

And this price, that we have agreed upon with one another and with which we are satisfied on both sides, is three solidi and two trimesia by the standard of Kastron Jeme, = sol. 3 2/3, pure, by the standard of Kastron Memnonion [Greek]. The price aforesaid has come from your hands into our hands[13] as was made clear above, from-hand-to-hand [Greek], domestic, tried, and capital[14] gold.

And from now on you, Shenoute and Hemai and Stephen, the buyers, you are to enter in upon and have power over and dominion[15] over and ownership over the half-portion of that whole piece of land that we previously made clear, because its price came from your hands to our hands according to the ordinance that we first made plain above, it being acquired by you: acquired by you to administer, manage, make improvements to, dwell on, rent out, donate, cede, exchange, sell, give away, confer, make over to your children, bequeath to your

---

[7] From *saphênizein* (σαφηνίζειν).
[8] Half the original purchase price.
[9] Mary seems to have been omitted by the scribe.
[10] "God's" seems to have dropped out. Seidl, "Eid," 143.
[11] More for a building; *recte* "from the land surface" as we have seen earlier.
[12] *chrêstêria* (χρηστήρια): Förster, *WB*, 884.
[13] Cf. G. Frantz-Murphy, "A Comparison of the Arabic and Earlier Egyptian Contract Formularies," *Journal of Near Eastern Studies* 47 (1988): 105–12, 269–80.
[14] *oikothen* (οἴκοθεν), *dokimon* (δόκιμον), *kephalaion* (κεφάλαιον). For the first two terms see Förster, *WB*, 562, 207–8.
[15] From *kyrieuein* (κυριεύειν), "have (Roman-law) *dominium*" (*kyrios* [κύριος] = *dominus*).

heirs, or deal with after any fashion you like,[16] [Greek] in full possession and mastership,[17] and perpetual retention,[18] dominially[19] and without hindrance[20] at any time at all.

Anyone who proceeds against you or goes to law with you, whether brother or sister or relative in the first or second degree, on my [sic; for "our"] father's side or on my mother's side, suing you in court or out of court, within the nome or outside, or if we draw up any prosecution against you before any exalted and glorious authority, first off such a person is to have no profit of it at all, for in the first place he is to be a stranger[21] to the Father and the Son and the Holy Ghost,[22] and is to pay to the authority then in office 36 sol. apart from the penalty that the laws define for one who dares to transgress. And on top of all these things he is to recognize this sale, secured for you.

We have drawn it up, secure and having validity in every place where it may be produced in evidence before any and every rule or authority, upon being asked.

+ We, Zacharias and Ephraim and Mary and Takoum,[23] we assent to this sale in all matters written therein.—I Aristophanes son of John, I represented them; they asked me, I wrote for them at their request.

+ I Zacharias, most humble priest,[24] I bear witness. ++

+ I Papnouthios son of Cyriac, I bear witness.

+ I Constantine son of the late Solomon, I bear witness.[25]

+ I John son of the late Solomon,[26] I bear witness.—+ I Pesate son of the late Constantine, I wrote representing them as they did not know how to write, and I bear witness.

+ I Pmai son of the late Hllô, with Pesynte, we bear witness.—+ I George son of Phêu, I wrote for them. +

[Greek] Brought about (i.e., written) by me, Aristophanes son of John. +

---

[16] For just one (Byzantine) parallel cf. *P.Bingen* 130.8–10 (property division, Aphrodito, 526–545): "to possess and be master of and administer and dwell in and inhabit and assign to heirs and successors, and deal with in whatever fashion you please, unhindered."

[17] *despoteia* (δεσποτεία): Förster, *WB*, 165.

[18] *katochê* (κατοχή): Förster, *WB*, 398–99.

[19] *kyriôs* (κυρίως): Förster, *WB*, 454–55.

[20] Here *anepikôlytôs* (ἀνεπικωλύτως): Förster, *WB*, 56.

[21] This introduces the typical penalty clause.

[22] Under Islamic rule this was a weighty formulation: the contract-breaker was to be "a stranger" to the Trinity, deprived of his/her very identity. See Richter, *Sprache*, 311.

[23] Sophia appears to have been omitted here.

[24] The same as in *P.CLT* 1 above?

[25] Probably the illiterate former *lashane* who was a witness to *P.KRU* 35 above; also in *P.CLT* 1.

[26] Presumably brother of the preceding.

P.KRU 25

Sale of Half of a House

DATE: 722/23

PLACE: Jeme

PARTIES: Abessa daughter of the late Zacharias, seller; N., buyer

OBJECT: Part of house

SUM: 12 solidi (original purchase price); 6 5/6 solidi (selling price)

[fine] 15 solidi

WITNESSES: 3

SCRIBE: Aristophanes son of John

PUBLICATION: Till, *KRUTheb*, 123–24; Schiller, "Family Archive," 343–50

With this document we are introduced to the family and the property affairs of Abessa of Jeme. This instrument, and complex transactions related to it and its parties, are discussed, with stemma, by Wilfong, *Women*, 66–68. Decades later, on 29 June 763 (or perhaps 748), apportionment of the inherited portions of this house was made by the heirs in the settlement recorded in *P.KRU* 24 (Till, *Erb*, 105–9). Here, Abessa, dissatisfied with the arrangement of selling her late father's house that she has already made, has gone to the Muslim official and succeeded in getting him to render a judgement that she is to get half of it back. So the buyer here, saying "enough lawsuit!", agrees to take almost seven gold pieces for that half. So we see Christians having recourse to the Muslim rulers over their property, a practice that long persisted.

[I N. son of N., man of Kastron Jeme] in the name of the city of Hermonthis, subsequently putting in place a subscriber to subscribe for me to this written document of sale that is untransgressable and unshakable by law, making it still more established by some trustworthy witnesses who will witness it for me at my very own request and under my direction: I am writing to you, Abessa daughter of the late Zacharias, woman of this same Kastron Jeme in the name of the same city of Hermonthis.

WHEREAS: Acting at this present time now, the sixth (indiction) year, I bought the house of your late father Zacharias and the courtyard that lies below the house of Constantine's children and the workshop¹ of Antony son of Paul.² I paid twelve gold solidi, pure, for them. And now you have sued³ me before our most glorious lord 'Amr⁴ the representative of our lord the most renowned *amir*,⁵ concerning the half of the house and the room north of the half of the courtyard.⁶ And subsequently, there having been enough lawsuit carried on with each other, the most glorious lord *amir*⁷ has ordered that I give the half of the house to you, Abessa, the one (the half) to the north, and the half of the courtyard that it inside it.

Now I agree that, look, seven solidi less half a trimesion have come into my hand from you, Abessa, for the north half of the house and the half of the courtyard, just as you have given them to me, from-hand-to-hand [Greek].

And from now on you, Abessa daughter of Zacharias the aforewritten, are to enter upon it and have power and dominion⁸ over it and be owner of the half of the house and the northern room, from its foundations up to the air space, together with all the other utensils appertaining thereto, with the half of the courtyard, because that price has come from your hand into my hand, in the way that I, the first owner⁹ above, according to the ordinance that I made plain above, (authorize you) to acquire it, in acquisition, to administer it, manage it, leave it to a son or a daughter, bequeath it to your heirs, deal with it in any way you wish at any time at all.

Anyone who may ever proceed against you, whether myself or my sons or my daughters or my heirs, and go to law against you whether in court or out of court, or draw up any prosecution against you before any authority concerning this sale, first off he is to be a stranger to the Father and the Son and the Holy Ghost; and then he is to pay to account of fine fifteen solidi to the authority. Subsequently he

---

¹ *ergastêrion* (ἐργαστήριον: Förster, *WB*, 294): a workshop (textile? ceramic?) neither monastic nor (expressly) female.

² Seemingly the same Antony son of Paul whose house appears above in *P.KRU* 35.

³ From *proselthein* (προσελθεῖν) (*proserchomai*, προσέρχομαι: Förster, *WB*, 688).

⁴ After 717–720 Christian town officials were being replaced by Muslims—or was 'Amr a Christian Arab? See G. Frantz-Murphy, *Arabic Agricultural Leases and Tax Receipts from Egypt*, CPR 21 (Vienna, 2001), 24, 26; eadem, "Land-Tenure," 244–45; Sijpesteijn, "Landholding Patterns in Early Islamic Egypt," 126–27, 129–30.

⁵ See T.S. Richter, "O.Crum Ad.15 and the Emergence of Arabic Words in Coptic Legal Documents," in *Papyrology and the History of Early Islamic Egypt*, ed. Sijpesteijn and Sundelin, 97–114.

⁶ Till persists in using a transliteration of the Coptic *anh*; but it simply means "courtyard."

⁷ Till reads a proper name for him here; but it is probably traces of a separable causative form.

⁸ From *kyrieuein* (κυριεύειν) (again).

⁹ Crum/Steindorff write [sic], thinking it a scribal blunder, and Till (124) simply understands "as above", but "the original owner" makes perfect sense.

is to appear and acknowledge this secure sale. Accordingly I have drawn it up, secure and having validity in every place where it may be produced in evidence.[10]

    + I John, most humble priest, I bear witness.

    + I Isaac son of Constantine, I bear witness.

    + I Phoibammon, most humble priest, I bear witness.

    + [Greek] Brought about by me, Aristophanes son of John.

---

[10] Note that no clause stating the name of the framer and recording his assent is preserved.

P.KRU 47

Division of Sold House Property

DATE: 722/23 (Wilfong, *Women*, 67: 737/38)

PLACE: Jeme

PARTIES: Daniel son of the late Isidore; Takoum daughter of the late Zacharias, Abessa's sister

OBJECT: House property with courtyard

SUM [original selling price]: 12 (6 + 6) solidi

[fine]: 36 solidi

WITNESSES: 5

SCRIBE: Aristophanes son of John

PUBLICATION: Till, *KRUTheb*, 133–35

Here we follow more of Abessa's family saga. One Daniel, having been paid a money consideration, is agreeing to divide a house and courtyard with Abessa's sister Takoum. Since she is getting the southern half, he apparently is to close up the south-side door of his half, to separate the properties.

[In the name of the Fa]ther and of the Son and of the Holy Ghost [Greek].[1]

I Daniel son of the late Isidore, man of Kastron Jeme in the nome of the city of Hermonthis, and subsequently putting in place a subscriber to subscribe for me and some other faithful witnesses to witness this written document of property division[2] written in two copies, to be untransgressable and unshakable by law: I am writing to Takoum daughter of the late Zacharias, woman of the same Kastron Jeme in the nome of the city of [Hermonthis]. *** [damage]

. . . representing our lord the most renowned *amir* . . . the house and that courtyard, with the legal decision[3] having come about in this way such that we came to an agreement with each other, so that you become the owner of half of the house and half of the courtyard, you, Takoum the aforenamed,[4] to be the

---

[1] Invocation Type **2J**: *CSBE 2*, 100, 104–5, 293.

[2] *merismos* (μερισμός): Förster, *WB*, 513–14.

[3] *doxon* (ⲇⲟⲍⲟⲛ): Till (133) renders "agreement", but Förster *WB* 209 (with n. 26) s.v. δόξον more sensibly gives "decision, legal opinion."

[4] *-onomaze* (-ⲟⲛⲟⲙⲁⲍⲉ).

owner of half of the whole house and of half of that courtyard, from its foundations up to the air space. And look, the half of the price of the house and courtyard has come from your hand to my hand . . . *** [damage]

. . . [I am] taking the half of that house, the one to the north, I, Daniel the aforewritten, with the half of the courtyard lying within it, and every place I wish in that courtyard. Taking half of that house are you, Takoum, (viz.) the one to the south, (and) taking half of the courtyard. If they value[5] the portion to the north and that to the south, I shall set down the effective (?) . . . price . . . and the price in this way. [The boundaries] of that courtyard are, as of now: south, the children of the late Antony and the principal gate; north, Constantine; east, the heirs of Epiphanius; west, our courtyard, both portions, and the street going by. These are its boundaries on all sides round about, from its foundations up to the air space, together with their utensils appertaining to them.

But from now on you, Takoum daughter of Zacharias the aforenamed, are to enter upon and have power and dominion over the half of the courtyard and the half of the whole house as was made plain above, acquiring them in acquisition, to administer them, manage them, make improvements to them, dwell therein, rent them out, donate them, cede them, exchange them, sell them, give them away, confer them, leave them to your children, bequeath them to your heirs, dealing with them in any way at all you may wish, (enjoying complete) mastership . . . *** [damage]

Anyone who may ever proceed against you, myself or a brother or son or daughter or any person at all . . . concerning the half of the house and of the whole courtyard . . . in court or out of court, concerning the half-portion of the house and courtyard, first of all that person is to have no profit of it at all, and chiefly he is to be a stranger to the Father and the Son and the Holy Ghost, and is to pay to account of fine to the authority in place at the time thirty-six gold solidi. Subsequently he is to appear and acknowledge this written document of property division, which is secure. I drew it up, it being secure and having validity in every place where it may be produced in evidence. They asked me, I agreed.

It is clear that concerning the (previous) sale that I had drawn up for myself and siblings, should I bring it out to you, it is to be null and void, because you have satisfied me with the entire half of that sale, namely the six solidi.

It is clear that I am to [close up?] the door on the south side up to the street on the south.

+ I John, most humble priest,[6] I bear witness.

+ I Phil. . ., most humble deacon, I bear witness.

+ I Isaac son of Constantine, I bear witness.[7]

---

[5] *syntimazein* (συντιμάζειν).

[6] Probably the same one who witnesses *P.KRU* 25 above.

[7] Again probably the same as the witness in 25 above.

+ I Psmo son of Patermoute, I bear witness.—+ I Phibammon, most humble priest,[8] I wrote for him as he did not know how to write, and I bear witness.

[Greek] + Brought about (i.e., written) by me, Aristophanes son of John.

---

[8] Same as Phoibammon in 25 above?

P.KRU 68

Testament of Elizabeth

DATE: May-June 723

PLACE: Jeme

PARTIES: Elizabeth, now married to Abraham son of Theodore, testatrix; Abraham, her husband, heir designate

SUM [debt]: 10 solidi + 1 trimesion

[fine]: 4 oz. gold = 24 solidi

WITNESSES: 7 (including the notary)

SCRIBE: Abraham son of the late David

PUBLICATION: Till, *Erb*, 177–83

With this instrument we return to the affairs of the family of Elizabeth, Abigaia, and their relatives, as first documented in *P.KRU* 35 above. Wilfong, *Women*, 58–62 discusses this document in detail and translates many passages. Elizabeth, a widow, is now remarried, to Abraham from Aswan, to whom she wishes to leave her property, especially that which she herself had inherited from her late parents. Abraham for his part has sold his late parents' house, and they have put the cash to various uses, including making provision for other family members. Elizabeth, who possesses and controls her own funds, nonetheless freely shares both economic information and property and financial resources with her spouse; each has "hand-work" of his/her own which yields revenue. In *P.KRU* 68 Elizabeth sets up the provisions she intends to be obeyed after she is gone, especially that Abraham will be undisputed owner of her property and that her funeral expenses will be met. We will not have seen the last of the hapless black sheep of the family, George (Elizabeth's first-born son, by her first husband, the late Loule), and his "many troubles" (cf. *P.KRU* 37 and 38). George is a problem figure here, and Elizabeth does not want him to try to wrest property away from Abraham when his mother is no longer around to restrain his behavior.

[In the name of] the holy and life-giving, consubstantial Trinity, Father, Son and Holy Ghost.[1] Written in the month of Payni [. . .] in the sixth indiction.

---

[1] Invocation Type **2E**: *CSBE 2*, 100, 104, 293.

+ I Elizabeth, daughter of the late Epiphanius and of Mary, woman of Kastron Jeme in the nome of the city of Hermonthis: Greetings.

Gladly agreeing subsequently to put in place a subscriber to subscribe for me, and requesting some witnesses to witness for me to this written document of will and testament of my final decision, written to be untransgressable and unshakable and indestructible by law, I am making it further established through some trustworthy witnesses who will witness for me at my very own request and according to my intention.

+ I am writing to my husband Abraham son of Theodore, man of the city of Aswan, who took me to wife in Jeme: Greetings.

I am now intent upon this present written document of will and final counsel and testament; I am willing and persuaded and joyful, without any trickery or intimidation or compulsion or deception, with no seizure or circumscription, with no necessity incumbent upon me, being alive, ambulatory,[2] concerned, and behaving in my customary fashion, being owner in all ownership, so that the testament and all matters written therein may now have power and validity and be complete. And I adjure every magistrate and holy bishop[3] and God-fearing judge and every *lashane* who will read this written testamentary document and read out what is written in the testament, by the holy, consubstantial Trinity, Father, Son and Holy Ghost, and the fearsome judgement-seat of Christ that will judge all creation according to what they have done, whether good or evil, and the great sentence that God the Word defined with our father Adam, "From earth, you shall sleep in earth [Genesis 3:19]," to observe all that is written in the testament that I have laid down, as follows:

WHEREAS: In those years of dearth that are past,[4] you, Abraham, my husband, went south to Aswan, your city. You sold your house, the one that had come to you from your parents. You received fifty-seven gold solidi, = 57 sol., pure. You brought them to me, together with all the property[5] of your parents, including iron implements and bronze, in a word, from the most valuable down to the least. And a quantity of the division[6] you sold to John (son of?) Kalearios[7] in Nê;[8] you received another five trimesia for it. All these together make

---

[2] Cf. *P.Lond.* I 77.12.

[3] Cf. Schmelz, *Kirchliche Amtsträger*, 273.

[4] Possibly the plague of 689–690: see Kennedy, "Egypt as a Province in the Islamic Caliphate, 641–868," 71.

[5] *hypostasis* (ὑπόστασις).

[6] So Wilfong, *Women*, 59, solving Till's (*Erb*, 179 n. 142) conundrum.

[7] Or possibly "John the shoemaker" (Förster, *WB*, 368)—or (my suggestion) "John the *galearius*" (Daris, *Lessico latino*, 38), a kind of lower-ranking military man—possibly involved with shipping, as there are business doings in the port of Clysma recorded below.

[8] Timm, *Ägypten*, 4: 1762–63.

fifty-nine solidi less one trimesion. For the rest, a necessity occurred, and you gave six solidi therefrom for your father, for his offering.

And now I swear by God, the great King[9] of the great, fearsome judgement-seat that will judge all severally according to what they have done, whether good or evil, that except for the six solidi that you gave for your father, for his needful necessity, you have hidden nothing of them from me, up to and including the sum[10] of one trimesion. But rather we gave them to one another, I and the late Mary my mother, since she was old, and George whom I had with Loule my first husband. And as for him, George, I paid his tax[11] out of that money, and I hired a smith for him in Clysma.[12] In a word, we spent them (the solidi) in support,[13] until they were gone, with no division amongst ourselves, except for what came to us from our own hand-work. And now with God's help I (know) it is the right thing[14] so far as possible to (apportion?) your household goods[15] amongst one another, also lest God seek me suddenly, because man does not know the time of his lifetime, and (lest) I be wasteful and weak[16] and God judge me by placing me on His left hand,[17] away from you.

And now, look, I am writing to you, you, Abraham, my husband, so you may be owner in all ownership over this my house that came to me from my late parents Epiphanius and Mary, and my landholdings in the village and in the countryside, (property) movable and immovable, be it in every (kind of) property, house and courtyard and workshop, in iron and bronze[18] and wooden material and ceramic material, from small to large, from most valuable to least, from a ... to a nail, in a word: you are to be owner of everything in the way I spoke of it above, and no man is to be able to counterclaim[19] against you, neither any of my children that I have had with you nor George whom I had with Loule;[20] they are not to proceed against you with any allegation. {that is mine}[21]

---

[9] Seidl, "Eid," 145; alluding to Psalm 94:3 LXX.

[10] *analogia* (ἀναλογία): Förster, *WB*, 50.

[11] *dêmosion* (δημόσιον): Förster, *WB*, 171–73. For post-conquest taxation see *P.Mon. Apoll.*, pp. 23–26, and above, *P. KRU* 66 and 76, n. 17.

[12] Timm, *Ägypten*, 5: 2164–71; P. Mayerson, "The Port of Clysma (Suez) in Transition from Roman to Arab Rule," *Journal of Near Eastern Studies* 55 (1996): 119–26.

[13] From *dapanê* (δαπανή).

[14] *dikaion* (δίκαιον).

[15] *skeuê* (σκευή): Förster, *WB*, 735–37.

[16] Correcting Till here.

[17] Matthew 25:31–46 esp. 33, 41 (the form is from *aristera* [ἀριστερά]). This Last Judgement scene is often recounted in Coptic manuscript colophons.

[18] So in Crum/Steindorff's restoration; Till (*Erb*, 180) restored "clothing" (less likely).

[19] From *antilegein* (ἀντιλέγειν): Förster, *WB*, 62–63.

[20] Further on George's difficulties is recorded in *P.KRU* 37 and 38 (Wilfong, *Women*, 64–66).

[21] Apparently a scribal slip: see Till, *Erb*, 180 n. 145.

Again concerning this I am intent on this written document of wish and testament, which is legal and indestructible for ever, but rather you are to observe it, secure and untransgressed for ever, you and those who come after you, unto all time.

First of all, you are to be owner of all that belongs to me, and my house and my workshop and all my property that came to me from my parents aforenamed above. They (properties) are all to be under your authority, from small to large, up to and including a ceramic pot and a useless item: in a word, movable and immovable, owed by me or owed to me, while I am still alive and after I depart.

And when I shall depart from the body, first you are to take care for the clothing of my body[22] and my holy offering, as for every Christian woman; only (take care) lest my children be disobedient to you and argue with you over anything that was mine. But concerning George whom I had with Loule, because I agreed before God above that we had had the support money with one another, with no division amongst us, and I paid the tax for him and the workman that I hired for him, and all the rest of his troubles, apart from the bride whom I found for him—and God knows that from the day when I fulfilled matters with him over his late father Loule, up to and including the sum of a copper keration, from that day God knows that he entrusted another ten solidi and one trimesion to me—, I and my husband and my little children, look, I owe them, and God knows that I gave enough goods to him (George) until he came of age and went away from me and left me in debt. He is not to be able to dare, now or at any time or occasion, whether I am dead or alive, to proceed against my husband Abraham, nor anyone else at all, neither son nor wife nor anyone else nor any representative nor anyone on his side. But one who seeks to represent him, first of all he is to have no profit of it, but rather is to pay to account of fine to the magistrates four ounces of pure gold, = 24 sol.,[23] out of his very own property, and is to appear and acknowledge this written testamentary document, because he has quite[24] enough without needing the property of Abraham my husband.

Concerning Abraham my husband: because I have made him owner over all that belongs to me, so that he receives income and makes expenditure on my behalf, if he should for his part undertake to take him (George) in and grant him an inheritance, as though he were our son, that George is to repay[25] the ten gold solidi less [sic] one trimesion, because he was assured and supported from them as I made clear above. But the entire advance valuation[26] I gave to Abraham my husband, and he is to be its owner, he, Abraham, in all ownership over all things

---

[22] On funeral customs and clothing the dead see Dunand, "Funerary Practices."
[23] A very different ratio from that found earlier on, where 1 oz. AV = 4 1/2 sol. This would give 1 oz. AV = 6 sol.
[24] From *certum* (my suggestion, though it is not in Daris, *Lessico latino*).
[25] From *apologizomai* (ἀπολογίζομαι): Förster, *WB*, 84–85.
[26] *protimêsis* (προτίμησις): Förster, *WB*, 698.

belonging to me, to retain them, give them to his children, give them away, donate them, alienate them, rent them out, give them in commerce[27] or exchange with anyone, dealing with them in any fashion he may wish. And no son of mine or ours is to counterclaim against him, nor is any man at all representing me to go to law with him in any way or form at any time, nor your [sic] children either.

I Elizabeth daughter of the late Epiphanius and of Mary, the aforewritten above, I assent; and they read it out to me in Egyptian, I heard it, and I assent thereto: I have laid it down as it stands above.

+ I Komes son of the late Hatre,[28] I bear witness at the request of Elizabeth.

+ I Patermoute, most humble archpriest, I bear witness. +

+ I Shenoute, most humble priest[29] of the holy church of Jeme, I bear witness at the request of Elizabeth.

+ I Zacharias, most humble priest of St Cyriac's[30] in Jeme, I bear witness at the request of Elizabeth. +

+ I Athanasius son of George, most honorable *lashane*, I bear witness.—I Patermoute, most humble archpriest, I wrote for him as he did not know how to write.[31] +

+ I Theodore son of the late David, I bear witness with my hand at the request of Elizabeth, as it stands above. +

− + I Abraham son of the late David,[32] Elizabeth asked me, I drew up this written testamentary document the way she requested me to, and I bear witness. +

---

[27] *synallagê* (συναλλαγή).

[28] In *P.KRU* 9, 35.

[29] Same as in *P.CLT* 1 above?

[30] Papaconstantinou, *Saints*, 132–34; this is probably the same man as in *P.CLT* 1, *P. KRU* 10.

[31] Another illiterate *lashane*. Is this the same Athanasius as in *P.CLT* 5 above?

[32] Probably Theodore's brother.

P.CLT 6

Service Agreement

DATE: 9–10 February 724 (or 739?)

PLACE: Jeme

PARTIES: 17 men of Jeme acting in concert

WITNESSES: the same 17

SCRIBE: [not named]

PUBLICATION: Till, *KRUTheb*, 34–37

This interesting document records the collective declaration by a group of men from Jeme with regard to the terms under which they can be conscripted to serve in the Muslim rulers' military and/or public-works services, most often shipbuilding and the fleet.[1] Their primary concern seems to be equality of assessment. Some of the men are literate in Coptic, and some are not; but different kinds and degrees of literacy are allowed for.

+ In the name of the Father and of the Son and of the Holy Ghost.[2] [Greek] Written in the month of Mecheir, indiction 7.

+ Through us, we who are going to subscribe below to this common agreement,[3] those on the one hand who know how to write subscribing with their own hand, those who do not know how to write asking subscribers to subscribe for them, and among ourselves agreeing with the things that will be set in order in writing below, in unanimity,[4] out of our common opinion[5] and consent[6] and approval:[7] Greetings. As follows:

---

[1] And it seems that Byzantium then took a leaf from their book in developing its fleet: see C. Zuckerman, "Learning from the Enemy and More: Studies in 'Dark Centuries' Byzantium," *Millennium* 2 (2005): 79–135, here 107–25.

[2] Invocation Type **2J**: *CSBE 2*, 100, 104–5, 294.

[3] *koinê homologia* (κοινὴ ὁμολογία): not retaining the Greek accusative in loan-form. On this type of instrumental use see T.S. Richter, review of Förster, *WB*, *Byzantinische Zeitschrift* 96 (2003): 730–36, here 733; and idem, *Sprache*, 123–25.

[4] *homonoia* (ὁμόνοια): Förster, *WB*, 582.

[5] *koinê gnômê* (κοινὴ γνώμη: Förster, *WB*, 424–25, 151)—but here governed by *ek* (ἐκ) with both in the genitive.

[6] Here *synainesis* (συναίνεσις): Förster, *WB*, 773.

[7] *synkatathesis* (συνκατάθεσις): Förster, *WB*, 763.

WHEREAS: This very day today we have gathered together with one another with one accord: we have drawn up a convention with one another not in any fashion to reject the *cursus*[8] imposed upon the *kastron*, or any (such) work assignment[9] at all, with a great upset[10] being upon each and every one of us, and again as we thus consider that one man by himself is not able to measure up to the weight of that situation,[11] but rather we said, "It is a satisfactory thing for us to continue meeting together, with no work assignment incumbent upon us, so that we may measure up to that weight together. Let us find the way to look after ourselves in our *kastron* without upset." So with satisfaction we have proceeded to this community agreement, without any trickery or intimidation or compulsion or deception or seizure or circumscription, with no necessity being upon us, but rather out of our very own free choice; we agree, swearing by God Almighty and the well-being of our lords, that we, we the undersigned (including those who have had someone sign for them), are going to become and be in common with one another in all matters received in the compulsory public service[12] and the public tax register,[13] whether it be the *cursus* or any work assignment at all. We will be subject[14] at our own common risk,[15] shared by each one of us, to our not acquiescing[16] in one of us being made to pay[17] more than another one, whether being pressed into service as sailors or as anything else. And again it seemed right in this way, that, if it should happen to be the lot of one of us to appear before the presence of our lords to be sent to the *cursus* or any other work assignment at all incumbent upon us, we should enter in and compare matters with one another as far as being free[18] for it is concerned, so as not to acquiesce in giving anything at all more than the rest of us, in any manner at all whatsoever [Greek]. And if the lot should fall upon one or two or three of us and one of us should wish to

---

[8] Conscription into the fleet of the Muslim rulers: see Sijpesteijn, "The Arab Conquest of Egypt and the Beginning of Muslim Rule," 448. For a recently-studied example of the documentation, see L.S.B. MacCoull, "*P.Lond.* IV 1494 Revisited," *Aegyptus* 77 (1997): 125–35.

[9] *allagê* (ἀλλαγή): Förster, *WB*, 32 (with implication of its fungible nature).

[10] *tarachê* (ταραχή): Förster, *WB*, 794.

[11] *hypothesis* (ὑπόθεσις).

[12] *angareia* (ἀνγαρεία): Förster, *WB*, 5–6.

[13] *dêmosios logos* (δημόσιος λόγος): cf. Förster, *WB*, 173–74. See Wilfong, "The Non-Muslim Communities: Christian Communities," 181–83.

[14] *hypokeisthai* (ὑποκεῖσθαι): Förster, *WB*, 838–39.

[15] *kindynos* (κίνδυνος): Förster, *WB*, 414–15.

[16] *synchôrein* (συνχωρεῖν): Förster, *WB*, 763–64.

[17] *zêmia* (ζημία): Förster, *WB*, 316.

[18] *eleutheros* (ἐλεύθερος) here seems not to have its more usual connotation of "respectable," but to be used in a fashion closer to the root meaning.

delay,[19] he is not to be able to set this up in his own right [Greek],[20] nor claim not to know anything[21] out of opposition,[22] (but) first of all one who shall undertake the matter in this way shall be liable to the curse of the Scriptures,[23] and is to become and be a stranger to the Father and the Son and the Holy Ghost because he dared to transgress anything of this common agreement,[24] which is secured by us with one another.

We have drawn up this common agreement;[25] those who knew how to write subscribed it; those who did not know how to write asked subscribers and they subscribed it for them. We set it down.

+ I Phoibammon son of the late Pisês, I assent to this agreement as it is written.—David son of the late Severus,[26] he asked me, I wrote for him. +

+ I Samuel son of Philotheus, I assent.—David son of the late Severus, I wrote for him as he did not know how. +

+ I Athanasius son of Sanchêm, I assent to this agreement.+—+ I Aristophanes son of John,[27] man of Kastron Jeme, he asked me to represent him, I wrote for him as he did not know how. +

+ I Prêshe son of the late Jeremias, I assent to this agreement according to its force. +—+ I Zacharias son of the late Kalakôlf, I assent to this document according to [its force]; as Prêshe did not know how, I wrote for him.

I Abraham son of the late Psês, I assent to this document.

I Niharau son of Peha. . ., I assent to this document.—I Prêshe,[28] I wrote for them as they did not know how.

+ I Theophilus son of [N. assent to this document according to its] force.—Thomas son of the late [Victor], I wrote [for him].

+ I Peter son of Isaac, I assent to this agreement according to its force. +—+ Thomas son of the late Victor, I wrote for him at his request.+

+ I Ezekiel son of the late Matthias, I assent to this agreement according to its force.

+ I Daniel son of Phoibammon, I assent to his agreement according to its force.

I Zacharias son of the late Peter, I assent to this agreement according to its force. +

---

[19] *hysterein* (ὑστερεῖν): Förster, *WB*, 844.
[20] *tou dikaiou* (τοῦ δικαίου).
[21] *agnômonein* (ἀγνωμονεῖν): Förster, *WB*, 11.
[22] *antilogia* (ἀντιλογία): Förster, *WB*, 63.
[23] The Deuteronomic curses: cf. *P.CLT* 2 (above), n. 10.
[24] Here *symphônon koinonikon* (σύμφωνον κοινονικόν).
[25] Here *koinê homologia* (κοινὴ ὁμολογία) (no Greek case endings).
[26] Same as in *P.CLT* 1?
[27] The well-known scribe.
[28] Obviously a different person, this one literate.

+ I Lala son of the late Matthew, I bear witness.[29] —Cyriac son of the late Peter, I wrote for him as he did not know how to write.

+ I Cyriac son of the late Peter, I assent.

+ I Elias son of Zacharias, I assent to this agreement according to its force.—Cyriac son of Peter,[30] he asked me, I wrote for him as he did not know how to write. +

+ I Constantine son of Philotheus, I assent to this agreement according to its force.—+ I Isaac son of the late Zacharias, he asked me, I wrote for him as he did now know how to write. +

+ I Agnatius son of the late Matthias,[31] I assent to this agreement according to its force. +

---

[29] This person seemingly has written the rote formula "I bear witness" instead of "I assent" as is usual in this document.

[30] "The late" inadvertently omitted here.

[31] Probably the brother of Ezekiel above.

P.KRU 51

Settlement Among Neighbors Over Wall-Building

DATE: 27 March 724

PLACE: Jeme

PARTIES: Philemon, Panachôre, and Prese, sons of Joseph; children of Athanasius, of Theodore, and of Daniel

OBJECT: Common wall

WITNESSES: 5

SCRIBE: John son of (the late) Lazarus[1]

PUBLICATION: Till, *KRUTheb*, 135–36

Neighbors plus adjoining walls equals legal trouble throughout history. In this document three Jeme brothers who have already built a wall on their property address three other sets of siblings concerning the latter's intention to build a further wall that may or may not create an inconvenience. They agree that at least one stretch of wall is to be in common, "without any grumbling."

+ The Holy Trinity, Amen.[2] Month of Pharmouthi 1, indiction 7.

We, Philemon and Panachôre and Prese, sons of Joseph, man of Kastron Jeme in the nome of the city of Hermonthis, we are writing to the children of Athanasius and the children of Theodore and the children of Daniel, men of Kastron Jeme, as follows:

Whereas: I [we] have built the wall outside Cistern Street to the south of the house of Stephen . . . [this construction having been approved by?] . . . Peter son of Komos the *dioicetes*.[3] But now, today, after more time (has passed) . . . [you have wished to enclose?] the exterior land of your parents. You have not located

---

[1] The same scribe as that of *P.KRU* 35 above (dated 719).

[2] Not a usual invocation formula; more reminiscent of earlier epistolary usage. Cf. MacCoull, "'The Holy Trinity' at Aphrodito."

[3] Though this title usually is taken to be an equivalent to *ape* (ⲁⲡⲉ), "village headman" (*prôtokômêtês* [πρωτοκωμήτης]; the Coptic word means "head") and/or "financial magistrate" (Förster, *WB*, 201–2 with n. 19), here it clearly equates to *lashane*, which Peter had been (cf. *P.CLT* 1, *P. KRU* 9, 35, 55). Cf. Schmelz, *Kirchliche Amtsträger*, 306.

the wall outside my wall that we built, we, Philemon and Panachôre and Prese sons of Joseph, from its foundations up to the air space . . . the wall outside the street, for the price you are paying, the half of your construction, to us, so that the wall outside the street is to be in common with one another, according to the order of Peter son of Komos, without any grumbling.

+ I Panachôre, with Philemon and Prese, sons of Joseph, assent. +++

+ I Zael son of the late Theodore, with Menas son of the late Abraham,[4] with Cosmas son of Victor, we bear witness.—John son of Lazarus wrote for them.

+ I Philotheus son of Komos and Souai son of Zacharias +[5]

+ John son of Lazarus, I executed it.

[Docket] The written document of the sons of Joseph . . . about the matter of the exterior wall.

---

[4] The same individual as in *P.KRU* 55 above?

[5] The usual phraseology for "bear witness" seems to have been carelessly omitted.

P.KRU 36

Settlement of Inheritance Dispute

DATE: 4 June 724[1] (or 5 May 723)

PLACE: Jeme

PARTIES: Stephen, Chareb, and Abigaia, siblings, with their father Samuel and Abigaia's husband Daniel; Elizabeth and her husband Abraham

OBJECT: Inherited property

SUM [paid]: 5/6 solidus

[fine]: 24 solidi

WITNESSES: 6

SCRIBE: Psate son of Pisrael, who has been active in these people's legal cases

PUBLICATION: Till, *Erb*, 115–17

Here we return to Abigaia and her family's doings. This document is discussed, with passages translated, in Wilfong, *Women*, 62–64. Abigaia and her relatives have been at odds with Elizabeth and her second husband Abraham over the property inherited from Elizabeth's late parents. The *lashane*s and other officials have been called in to try and resolve the dispute, but in vain; then the parties have gone to the church as well. It would seem that oaths not to sue one another—even oaths sworn in church with the "Great Men" of the town monitoring—did not have a very long-lasting effect among the people of Jeme.

[traces remain of an Arabic-language protocol reading 'there is no God save God alone; Muhammad is the messenger of God']

+ In the name of the holy and life-giving, consubstantial Trinity, Father, Son and Holy Ghost.[2] In the month of Payni, 10, seventh indiction ⲁⲣⲭⲏ,[3] in Kastron Memnonion in the nome of the city of Hermonthis. + [Greek]

+ We, Stephen and Chareb and Abigaia, together with Samuel son of the late Chareb, our father, consenting with us—our mother being Tshenoute—and with Daniel son of Komes, my husband, consenting with me, Abigaia, over all

---

[1] *CSBE* 2, 112 date: 5 May 723.
[2] Invocation Type **2E**: *CSBE* 2, 100, 104–5, 293.
[3] *CSBE* 2, 112.

matters written in this written document of warrant, which is a settlement of release, people of Kastron Jeme in the nome of the city of Hermonthis, subsequently putting in place a subscriber who will subscribe, and requesting some trustworthy witnesses to witness for us at our very own request and to our intention, and making it yet more established through some of these trustworthy witnesses who will witness it for us at our very own request, + we are writing to Elizabeth daughter of the late Epiphanius and Mary, and to Abraham her husband, son of Theodore, in this same *kastron*: Greetings.

WHEREAS: In this sixth (indiction) year just past, under[4] the most honorable Athanasius son of the late George[5] and Victor son of the late Joseph, *lashane*s of the *kastron*, we went to law with you over this inheritance of the late Epiphanius and the late Mary, (Elizabeth's) parents aforenamed above by name, we received a decision[6] affecting one another, with Psate son of the late Pisrael,[7] man of the same *kastron*. After we received the decision, the most honorable Athanasius and Victor, the *lashane*s, effected an agreement with one another (of us) over this inheritance of those late persons aforenamed above by name. We drew up a written document of settlement with one another, and you (pl.) came to an agreement with us over every shape and form of item, from large to small, up to and including a most humble ceramic object and a sewing-needle. And we drew up the settlement with one another through the notary[8] of the *kastron* in accordance with the law[9] of the *kastron*, not to go to law with one another over anything receivd from this inheritance of the late Epiphanius and the late Mary. And in the seventh (indiction) year that is now you went to law, saying: "We cannot finalize the oath with you (sg.), but rather you and your wife wish to fulfil the oath with us, according to the decision." After we approached you (pl.) over this allegation of this oath, thus, we repeated the case[10] in the presence of the most honorable Athanasius and Victor the *lashane*s, with some other "Great Men." You were willing to fulfil the oath with us, as we said, without any obstacle, in great joy, without any blame. Accordingly, when you were willing to be persuaded by us in this, as we aforesaid above, and when we saw you willing to lay down[11] the oath with us as we said, subsequently when you accordingly went into the holy Apa Victor's[12] (church) and began to swear, some "Great Men" came into our

---

[4] See Schmelz, *Kirchliche Amtsträger*, 303.

[5] Cf. *P.CLT* 5, *P.KRU* 68.

[6] *horos* (ὅρος: Förster, *WB*, 590); also "(legal) definition."

[7] The well-known notary (and scribe of the present instrument, at the bottom of which he does not designate his father as deceased), here recorded as acting in his jurist capacity.

[8] *nomikos* (νομικός): Förster, *WB*, 545–46.

[9] *nomos* (νόμος): see Steinwenter, "ΝΟΜΟC."

[10] *hypothesis* (ὑπόθεσις).

[11] *kataballein* (καταβάλλειν): Förster, *WB*, 385.

[12] Papaconstantinou, *Saints*, 62–68, esp. here 64.

midst and got us to be persuaded with one another. We finalized the oath with you. We requested you, you gave us half a gold solidus and a trimesion, = AV sol. 1/2 + 1/3, from-hand-to-hand [Greek]. After you had rendered[13] to us this 1/2 + 1/3 sol. satisfactorily,[14] you sought to receive from us this written document of release.

Accordingly we went for it, willingly and persuaded, without any trickery or intimidation or compulsion or deception, with no seizure or circumscription,[15] with no necessity incumbent upon us, but rather swearing by God Almighty and the well-being of our lords who have power over us from God[16] that we have received and have been satisfied by you with the oath according to the force of the legal decision: (viz.) you Abraham and Elizabeth your wife,[17] and we agree not to proceed against you hereafter over anything coming from this inheritance of the late Epiphanius and Mary, [neither against you nor] anyone coming after you, unto all time: neither ourselves, Stephen and Chareb and Abigaia, nor me, Samuel their father, nor Daniel, nor any man representing us. And if anyone should dare to, myself or any son or heir, first of all that person is to have no good of it, but rather chiefly he is to become and be a stranger to the holy, venerated oath by the Holy Trinity, and he is to pay to account of fine twenty-four solidi of pure gold, = AV sol. 24. And after the fine he is to acknowledge the force of this written document of release that we have drawn up for your security, it being secure and having validity in every place where it may be produced in evidence. They read it out to us, we heard it, we were satisfied. We requested a subscriber, he subscribed it for us. We got witnesses for it. We set it down, complete by the notary, in all its sequence. +

+ We, Stephen and Chareb and Abigaia, . . . and Samuel our father, consenting together, written above, we assent to this release, a *typos* (ⲧⲩⲡⲟⲥ) of settlement,[18] as it stands above.—I Abraham son of the late David, I wrote for them with my hand at their request. +

+ I Victor the *lashane*, son of the late Joseph, I bear witness. +—I Psate, I wrote for him.+[19]

+ Stephen son of the late Moses, I bear witness. + I Psate, I wrote for him.

+ I Antony son of the late Paul,[20] I bear witness.

---

[13] From *anadidōmi* (ἀναδίδωμι).

[14] *eulogôs* (εὐλόγως): Förster, *WB*, 308.

[15] Miswritten *paragraphē* (ⲡⲁⲣⲁⲅⲣⲁⲫⲏ).

[16] Seidl, "Eid," 142–43.

[17] The scribe has absent-mindedly reversed the order of the names Abraham and Elizabeth, resulting in "your wife" being in the wrong place.

[18] A formulation possibly chosen for its religious overtones, given the oath in church and all.

[19] Again noteworthy.

[20] Probably the same as the Antony son of Paul in *P.KRU* 35 and 25 above.

+ I Cyriac son of the late Andrew, I bear witness.—I Shenoute, most humble priest[21] of the holy church of Jeme, I wrote for him as he did not know how to write. +

+ I Hamôs son of the late Peter, I bear witness.—I Pshêre, most humble deacon of the Apostles',[22] I wrote for him as he did not know how to write. +

+ Athanasius son of the late George, I bear witness.

+ Written by me, Psate son of Pisrael [Greek]

---

[21] Probably the same as in *P.CLT* 1, *P.KRU* 68 above.

[22] Papaconstantinou, *Saints*, 56–58, esp. here 57.

P.KRU 37

Settlement of Division of Inheritance

DATE: 724

PLACE: Jeme

PARTIES: George, son of the late Loula (Elizabeth's first husband); and Elizabeth and her second husband Abraham (and her children by her second marriage, namely Isaac and Kyra, implied)

OBJECT: Inherited property

SUM [fine]: 32 solidi

[additional]: 1 1/3 solidi

WITNESSES: 9

SCRIBE: Psate son of Pisrael

PUBLICATION: Till, *Erb*, 118–21

We are still with Elizabeth's family. George, her feckless son by her first husband Loula, is worried because his mother's will (*P.KRU* 68 above, from the previous year) has designated as her sole heir her second husband Abraham, with whom she now has a son and a daughter. Will the never-satisfied George, who refused to accept the bride his mother had picked out for him, be able to get any property for the future household he himself may plan for?

See Wilfong, *Women*, 64–65, where the document is analyzed with passages translated, and 138–41 on the different kinds of bridal property and its partibility;[1] again the stemma (48) helps to clarify relationships. The problem at hand here is, as so often, that of inheritance in a family with two marriages that produced half-siblings. The son of the first marriage is concerned that the children of the second marriage are trying to diminish the portion that he will want to have for himself in anticipation of his own future marriage.

[invocation lost]

[I George son of the late Loula, man of Kastron Jeme, . . .] . . . and making it yet further established through some trustworthy witnesses who will witness it for me at my very own request by my intention, am writing to my beloved mother

---

[1] Cf. Beaucamp, *Statut de la femme*, 1: 229–37, 246–55, 2: 112–15, 295.

Elizabeth daughter of the late Epiphanius and Mary, and to Abraham her husband, son of Theodore, of this same *kastron*. Greetings.

WHEREAS: After the death of my late father Loula, and in this seventh [indiction] year ⲁⲣⲭⲏ² that is now present, I went to law with you, my beloved mother Elizabeth, and I brought the case before the most honorable Athanasius and Victor, the *lashane*s,³ in the precincts⁴ of the prize-bearing martyr Abba Cyriac⁵ of this same *kastron*, with the most God-loving Apa Victor the archpriest and *meizoteros* (being present) with them. On that day you fulfilled the oath with me before St Cyriac. After you fulfilled the oath with me, I received and came to an agreement between ourselves about the matter of dividing up⁶ this entire inheritance of my late father Loula, in gold and silver and clothing and bronze and every shape and form of gift for bride, gift for groom, year of sustenance, and everything received by me from my late father. And you (pl.)⁷ fulfilled the oath with me over everything I received from my late father that I previously named by name above.

Now I shall not be able to proceed against you (pl.) ever, over anything received from this entire inheritance from my late father Loula and my late grandparents Epiphanius and Mary, over no thing received from their entire inheritance, neither to assert that I have any allegation with regard to you (pl.) nor to acquire with regard to you (pl.) any shape or form of allegation: neither myself nor brother nor sister nor relative in the first or second degree, on my father's side or my mother's side, nor (an allegation) against you, Elizabeth, or a child of yours, a brother or sister or relative in the first or second degree, or kin or kin of kin, stranger or person of the house, nor anyone else appertaining to you, in any way, shape or form or (under any) allegation. Nor shall I be able to go to law with you, in court or out of court, in city or in nome, nor in any assembly⁸ of the city or the praetorium, nor by any glorious, venerated religious law⁹ or commandment

---

² *CSBE 2*, 110 n. 1.

³ See Till, *D&P*, 234.

⁴ This shows that churches were approved legal venues, endued with power and respect. As we see here, solemn oaths were taken in the presence of the church's dedicatory saint. See Schmelz, *Kirchliche Amtsträger*, 288.

⁵ Papaconstantinou, *Saints*, 132–34; already encountered in *P.CLT* 1 above (from 698).

⁶ Till (*Erb*, 119) prefers "the matter of what belongs to the inheritance. . ."; but surely shares are in question here, as George will have to be mindful of his younger half-siblings and what they are to get. Indeed the instrument is called a "division" (*merismos* [μερισμός]) below (line 87 of original text).

⁷ Now he must be addressing his half-siblings, Isaac and Kyra.

⁸ *koinêsis* (κοίνησις). Till (*Erb*, 119) thought it was *kinêsis* (κίνησις), "movement" (followed by Förster, *WB*, 424, 415–16) but that hardly seems to fit. It apparently means some sort of deliberative body of the city. The same phrase is found above in *P.CLT* 1.

⁹ MacCoull, "ⲧⲩⲡⲟⲥ."

or the great divine[10] constitution[11] or a great, valid, prevailing rank,[12] in a word: because I have received and have come to an agreement with you over this entire inheritance from my late father Loula and my grandparents and forebears whom I have made plain above, Epiphanius and Mary, over gold and silver, gift to bride, gift to groom, year of sustenance, paraphernalia,[13] over any matter about which I previously went to law with you.

But if I should dare, at any opportunity or time [Greek], (I) or any of my children or my heirs or my kin or my kin of kin or stranger or man of my house, to go to law against you over anything received of what I have previously named, any shape or form of thing, from a valuable sort to a mean, including even a ceramic object and a sandal-strap,[14] first of all that person is to get no good of it, but rather chiefly he is to become and be a stranger to the holy, venerable oath[15] by the Father, the Son, and the Holy Ghost. Subsequently he is to pay to account of fine thirty-two solidi of pure gold: he is to render[16] it (the fine) out of his very own property[17] into the hand of the honored magistrates. On top of that [Greek], after the paying-in[18] of the fine, he is to furnish it and appear and acknowledge the force of this written document of release and settlement, because I have received and have come to an agreement with you (pl.) over this inheritance from my forebears Loula and Epiphanius and Mary, in all matters of gift to bride and gift to groom and year of sustenance and paraphernalia, in every fashion and in totally complete discharge [Greek]. And we have settled with one another completely over all these things, swearing by the power of the holy, consubstantial Trinity[19] and the well-being of our lords to observe the power of this written document of division, which is this settlement.

I have drawn it up, securing it for you without any trickery or intimidation or compulsion or deception, with no seizure and circumscription, it being secure and having validity in every place where it may be produced in evidence. They read it out to me,[20] it was satisfying.

I requested a subscriber; he subscribed it; and I asked some trustworthy witnesses to witness it for me. I let it go, through the notary,[21] complete in its entire

---

[10] Calquing *theia* (θεῖα), with *diataxis* (διάταξις).
[11] *diataxis* (διάταξις), again an imperial law.
[12] *taxis* (τάξις).
[13] Crum, *CD*, 245a.
[14] Cf. Mark 1:7; Luke 3:16; John 1:27.
[15] A variant of the "stranger" type of penalty clause, as we have seen.
[16] *apaitein* (ἀπαιτεῖν): Förster, *WB*, 69–70.
[17] *hypothesis* (ὑπόθεσις).
[18] *katabolē* (καταβολή).
[19] Seidl, "Eid," 140.
[20] Again the open interplay of orality and literacy (in various languages).
[21] *nomikos* (νομικός).

ordering.²² And it is clear that [Greek] I am further making clear this capital matter,²³ as follows: over the place of the solidus and the trimesion [text damaged here] ... as defined ... my brothers ... I prosecuted you ... you gave me the solidus and the trimesion, from-hand-to-hand [Greek].

+ I Zebedee son of George,²⁴ I bear witness.—I Lole, most humble deacon of the principal church²⁵ of Jeme, I wrote for him as he did not know how to write. +

+ I Peter son of the late Patermouthios, I bear witness to this written document of settlement.—+ I N. son of the late Severus, he asked me, I wrote for him as he did not know how to write, and I bear witness. +

+ I Elias son of the late Zacharias,²⁶ I bear witness.

+ I George son of the late Loula, man of Jeme, the aforewritten above, I assented to this written document of settlement and release in all matters written therein, (with) the holy oath as above.—I Abraham son of the late David,²⁷ he asked me, I wrote for him as he did not know how.

+ Victor son of Joseph,²⁸ *lashane*, I bear witness.

I Stephen son of Moses,²⁹ I bear witness.—I Abraham son of the late David, I wrote representing him with my hand as he did not know how. +

+ I N. son of the late Basil, I bear witness.

I Abraham son of the late Constantine, I bear witness.

I Shenoute, most humble priest³⁰ of the holy church [of Jeme, I bear witness.]

[Greek] + Written by me, Psate son of Pisrael.

---

[22] Here *akolouthia* (ἀκολουθία).
[23] *kephalaion* (κεφάλαιον).
[24] Same as in *P.KRU* 9 above?
[25] *katholikê ekklêsia* (καθολικὴ ἐκκλησία); same as the "Holy Church" of Jeme.
[26] Same person as in *P.CLT* 6 above?
[27] Scribe of *P.KRU* 68 above.
[28] "The late" inadvertently omitted.
[29] Cf. *P.KRU* 36 above (also omitting "the late").
[30] Cf. *P.CLT* 1, *P.KRU* 68, 36.

P.KRU 50

DOCUMENT OF RELEASE IN LAND DISPUTE

DATE: 22 August 724

PLACE: Jeme

PARTIES: Anatolius son of the late Samuel and Rebecca; Tsherkah and Arsenios, children of the late George and Abessa

OBJECT: Area of landed property

SUM [fine]: 6 solidi

WITNESSES: 4

SCRIBE: Cyriac son of Peter

PUBLICATION: Till, *Erb*, 146–49

With this document we are back with Abessa's family: see Wilfong, *Women*, 67. A later phase of this ongoing set of transactions is embodied in *P.KRU* 48,[1] in which we find an alternate name: Tsherkah is there also called Thekla. In it three sets of parties, Leontius with his three siblings (Ananias, Charis, and Nymphe), Paul, and Mark, sell Thekla/Tsherkah and Arsenios house property in Kulol Street and a (further) half-portion of the land area by the house of the same Anatolius son of Samuel who appears here. He, Anatolius, had once donated a house to the St Psate monastery, but then bought it back (we have seen this kind of mutually beneficial transaction in the Byzantine period [cf. P.Mich. inv. 6898]). After a dispute, he has agreed to divide the house: three-quarters for himself, one-quarter for Abessa's daughter and son.

[Greek] [+ In] the name of the holy and life-giving, consubstantial Trinity, Father, Son and Holy Ghost.[2] Month of Mesore, 29, seventh indiction. In the

---

[1] Till, *Erb*, 144–46, gives Schiller's dating ("Family Archive," 353) as "around 740"; but Wilfong puts 48 at about a year later than 50. The scribe of 48 is the well-known Aristophanes son of John, who here in 50 calls his father "the late". One of 48's witnesses is the same as one who appears here, Isaac son of Constantine, though in 48 he does not call his father "the late". Should the datings be reversed?

[2] Invocation Type **2E**: *CSBE 2*, 100, 104, 293.

presence of Flavius Saul, most renowned *amir* from Diospolis, the most highly regarded[3] pagarch.[4]

[I] Anatolius son of the late Samuel and the late Rebecca, people of Kastron Jeme in the nome of the city of Hermonthis, subsequently putting in place a subscriber to subscribe for me to this written document of release that is set down untransgressable and unshakable by law, and making it yet more established through some trustworthy witnesses who will witness it for me at my very own request and at my direction, am writing to Tsherkah daughter of the late George and Abessa,[5] and to Arsenios, her legitimate brother, in this same *kastron* in the nome of this same city. Greetings. As follows:

WHEREAS: At this time, under[6] the most honorable Peter son of Komes[7] and John son of Mathias, *dioicetai* of our *kastron*, you went out and went to law against me over the matter of the area[8] that is near this house of mine, which I obtained by redemption[9] from the holy *topos* of the one shining with light among the saints, the holy Abba Psate,[10] in the mountain of our *kastron*, because I had donated it to that holy *topos* by the hand of the late Epiphanius his[11] brother while he was still alive. You established a sufficiency of quarrels[12] with us, since you wished to undo the sale which I had concluded with the *oikonomos* of the holy *topos* so you could manage it (the property). Thereupon subsequently a sufficiency of lawyering[13] with one another took place in our midst, such that the conflict came before the presence of John the *dioicetes*. They came to a judgement[14] among themselves with us about what was right,[15] together with some other respectable,[16] experienced people of the *kastron*. It seemed right[17] in this way:

---

[3] *ellogimôtatos* (ἐλλογιμώτατος), the Byzantine title (Förster, *WB*, 248–49). This is further evidence that the post-conquest pagarch was called *amir*: cf. Richter, "Emergence of Arabic Words." On pagarchs in this period see Sijpesteijn, "Landholding Patterns in Early Islamic Egypt," 121–23, 127–30.

[4] We encounter him again below in *P.KRU* 45.

[5] This is the Abessa we know: see the stemma in Wilfong, *Women*, 68.

[6] Cf. Schmelz, *Kirchliche Amtsträger*, 306.

[7] The *lashane* we have already met (cf. *P.CLT* 1, *P.KRU* 9, 35, 55, 51).

[8] *chôrêma* (χώρημα): Förster, *WB*, 891.

[9] *analytrôsis* (ἀναλύτρωσις): cf. Förster, *WB*, 50.

[10] Papaconstantinou, *Saints*, 217–19: the monastery existed already in the reign of Justinian, according to the attestation in *SB* XVIII 13777.

[11] A scribal error for "my"?

[12] Literally "skirmishes," *hapsimachia* (ἁψιμαχία): Förster, *WB*, 128.

[13] *dikasimon* (ⲇⲓⲕⲁⲥⲓⲙⲟⲛ): seemingly a *hapax* here: Förster, *WB*, 196.

[14] *anakrinein* (ἀνακρίνειν): Förster, *WB*, 49.

[15] *dikaion* (δίκαιον), "just."

[16] *eleutheros* (ἐλεύθερος).

[17] *dokei* (δοκεῖ): Förster, *WB*, 206–7.

I Anatolius, the aforewritten above, am to dwell in[18] three portions of that area, while you for your part are to be owners of the fourth portion, for your part, and are not to be able to go to law with one another for the rest. And this seems right in this way and satisfies us well.[19]

You sought for this written document of release from me, and I issued it of my own free will and being persuaded, without any trickery or intimidation or compulsion or deception or seizure or circumscription, with no necessity occurring to us, but by our very own free choice.

I agree, swearing by God Almighty and the well-being of our lords,[20] to renounce[21] to you, Arsenios and Tsherkah, children of the late George, the aforenamed above, the entire fourth portion of the area that lies by my house in this same *kastron*, according to the neighbors[22] that thus surround it: south, myself, Anatolius; north, Pake; east, myself again, Anatolius; west, the public street and the place where the gate opens onto. But the gate inwards (the interior gate) is to be common for us among ourselves, so that each one severally may go into his or her portion. These are its boundaries as a quadrilateral, such that accordingly you from now on, you, Arsenios and Tsherkah, are to enter in and have power and have ownership[23] over and be owners of the fourth portion of the area that I have made plain above according to its boundaries, the one that I got in return from the holy *topos*. You are its owners, yourselves and those who come after you, acquiring it for yourselves to administer it, manage it, make improvements to it, build on to it, dwell in it, donate it, cede it, exchange it, sell it, give it away, confer it, leave it to your children, bequeath it to your heirs and successors, dealing with it in any fashion you care to, without let or hindrance, acting upon it in all possession and all ownership and retention, for ever, as owners and without hindrance, because I have come to an agreement with you about that area.

And it is not possible[24] for me, me Anatolius the aforewritten above, to proceed against you in future on any pretext of taking back the fourth portion of that area: neither myself nor son of mine nor heir nor any man representing me. Nor is it to be possible to draw up any prosecution against you before any rule or authority, neither in court nor out of court, neither in the city nor outside of the nome, concerning this written document or any portion thereof at all.

---

[18] Here *oikeiousthai* (οἰκειοῦσθαι): Förster, *WB*, 561.
[19] *eulogôs* (εὐλόγως).
[20] Seidl, "Eid," 139.
[21] *apotassein* (ἀποτάσσειν): Förster, *WB*, 90–91.
[22] *geitoneia* (γειτονεία): Förster, *WB*, 145.
[23] *kyrieuein* (κυριεύειν).
[24] *ouk exesti* (οὐκ ἔξεστι).

But if it should happen—may it not! [Greek]²⁵—that anyone dares (as is likely²⁶) and wishes to go to law with you over the fourth portion of the area, which I articulated²⁷ above, first of all it shall be of no use to him, but rather he is to pay to account of fine six solidi. And so thusly this written document is to be secure²⁸ in every place where it may be produced in evidence. And we are compelled from now on to observe it according to its force.

+ I Isaac son of the late Constantine,²⁹ I bear witness.

+ I Ezekiel son of the late Mathios,³⁰ I bear witness.

+ I Peter son of the late Severus, I bear witness to this release according as it is written.—I Aristophanes son of the late John,³¹ I represent him; he asked me and I wrote for him at his request, and I bear witness.

+ Written by me, Cyriac son of Peter,³² from Kastron Memnonion. +

[Docket:] [Greek] Release that was brought about by Anatolius son of Samuel and by Tsherka and Arsenios likewise her brother, from Kastron Memnonion, on behalf of the fourth portion.

---

[25] The interjection *hoper mê eiê* (ὅπερ μὴ εἴη).
[26] *eikos* (εἰκός): Förster, *WB*, 229.
[27] *saphênizein* (σαφηνίζειν).
[28] The notary seems to have omitted "and valid".
[29] Same as in *P.KRU* 25, 47?
[30] Same person as in *P.CLT* 6? (spelling the patronymic differently).
[31] The scribe we know, now designating his father as deceased.
[32] Cf. *P.CLT* 6 above?

P.KRU 17

Donation of House Property to a Woman for Her Dowry

DATE: Early 725 (?)

PLACE: Jeme

PARTIES: Shenoute son of the late Phoibammon, donor; Nonne daughter of N., recipient

OBJECT: House property (dowry)

SUM [fine]: 36 solidi

WITNESSES: 3

SCRIBE: Aristophanes son of (the late?) John

PUBLICATION: Till, *Erb*, 102–3; idem, *KRUTheb*, 115–16

In this document a man named Shenoute is giving a woman named Nonne the house that had belonged to his late father, to become her bridal portion. No relationship between the two people can be inferred from the data preserved in this instrument, but they must have been associated in some way.

[fragmentary] [I Shenoute son of the late Phoibammon, man of Kastron] Jeme in the nome of the city of Hermonthis, . . . [subsequently putting in place a subscriber to] subscribe for me, and asking some other [trustworthy witnesses to] witness it for me . . . sale and . . . [that is to be untransgressable and] unshakable by law, am writing to Nonne daughter of N. of this same [Kastron] Jeme in the nome [of the city of Hermonthis], as follows:

WHEREAS: I received . . . (being) in straitened circumstances[1] . . . I agree, swear[ing by God Almighty and . . .,] [boundaries including the (*x*) of] N. daughter of Peter . . . from its foundations up to the air space, together with all its utensils belonging thereto, because I have received and have been satisfied from you about it according to the ordinance previously made plain above, so that you have acquired it in acquisition, treating it in any fashion you please at any time at all.

---

[1] *stenôsis* (στένωσις): Förster, *WB*, 749.

Anyone who may proceed against you over the house of my late father Phoibammon, this one that I have given you for your dowry,[2] whether myself or brother or sister or relative in the first or second degree, whether on my father's side or on my mother's, my male children or my female children whom I have begotten, or children of my sons or daughters, who may proceed against you, going to law with you over the house of my late father Phoibammon, summoning[3] you in court or out of court, or draw up any prosecution against you, be it myself or my children or any children who shall be begotten, first of all he is to have no profit of it, chiefly on the one hand being a stranger to the Father and the Son and the Holy Ghost, and is to receive the [apportionment] of Ananias and Sapphira his wife,[4] and is to pay to account of fine thirty-six solidi to the authority in office at the time; and apart from the penalty that the laws define, . . . on top of all these things he is to appear and acknowledge the validity of this [written document] that is secure for you. I drew it up, and it is [secure and has validity in every place where it may be] produced in evidence, before every rule and authority. They asked me, I agreed.+

+ I Shenoute son of Phoibammon, I assent.—+ I Mark son of Papnoute, deacon, I wrote for Shenoute, and I bear witness.

+ I George son of Daniel, I bear witness. +

+ I Chaêl son of Psmô, I bear witness. +—+ I Aristophanes son of the late John, Chaêl asked me, I wrote for him as he did not know how, at his request. +

+ Brought about (i.e., written) by me, Aristophanes son of John. + [Greek]

---

[2] See Wilfong, *Women*, 138–41.
[3] From *enkalein* (ἐνκαλεῖν): Förster, *WB*, 224.
[4] Acts 5:1–11; cf. above, *P.CLT* 1, written by Psate son of Pisrael.

P.KRU 45 and 46
Division of a House

DATE: 24 April 725 (or 740?)

PLACE: Jeme

PARTIES: Abessa and Takoum, sisters, daughters of the late Abigaia and the late Zacharias

OBJECT: House property divided between the sisters

SUM [fine]: 36 solidi

WITNESSES: (45) 6; (46) 6

SCRIBE: (45) unstated; (46) John son of John

PUBLICATION: Till, *Erb*, 140–44

With this document we return to the affairs of Abessa's family, specifically here the continuing story of what happened with Abessa herself and her sister Takoum when they had to divide up between them the house they had co-inherited from their late mother Abigaia (wife of Zacharias). They had to involve the "Great Men" of Jeme: see Wilfong, *Women*, 67–68. This is a pair of instruments, one drawn up in the first-person name of each sister. The witnesses are identical in both.

[initially following the text of 45 which preserves its opening]
+ In the name of the holy and life-giving, consubstantial Trinity, Father, Son and Holy Ghost.[1] Written in the month of Pharmouthi, 29, indiction 8. + In the presence of Flavius Saul son of 'Abdullah, the most glorious *amir*, former pagarch of Diospolis and Latopolis.[2]
+ I Abessa daughter of the late Zacharias and of Abigaia, woman of Kastron Jeme in the nome of the city of Hermonthis, subsequently putting in place a subscriber who will subscribe for me to this written document of settlement of property division[3] and release, untransgressable and unshakable by law, and moreover making it still more established through some of these other trustworthy

---

[1] Invocation Type **2E**: *CSBE 2*, 100, 104–5, 293.

[2] This individual could have been either a Muslim or a Christian Arab—or possibly a Christian Egyptian. Cf. above, *P.KRU* 50, nn. 3 and 4.

[3] *merismos* (μερισμός).

witnesses who will witness it for me at my very own request, + I am writing to Takoum my legitimate sister, (born) from the same father and the same mother, in the nome of this same city: Greetings. As follows: I agree that,

WHEREAS: in this very time that obtains for us now, in the eighth indiction, we went to law with each other concerning the house of our late father Zacharias, this one that is above (the house of) Andrew son of Secundinus, so as to divide it up between ourselves, each one being owner of her portion, subsequently a renewed lawsuit was made between us. We chose some "Great Men" and the builder of the *kastron*. We had them enter that house. They divided it up, and they assigned lots to us over that whole house. The lot fell to you, you, Takoum my legitimate sister, to be owner of the entire portion of that house from the half of the room on the south (Takoum's document has "room on the north", the corresponding part) up to the wall of that house, from its foundations up to the air space, with all its utensils appertaining thereto. And again you, my sister Takoum, may extend the door of your portion out to the street by the room. The door of your portion opens to the north because you have got the whole south portion, from the half of the room on the south up to the wall of that house. Thusly I (Abessa) am going to make clear its boundaries, which are these: south, Hêu son of Antony; north, myself, Abessa the aforewritten (telling you, Takoum, that you can extend through to the south); east, the house of the sons of Andrew son of Secundinus; west, the house of Aristophanes son of John.[4] These are the boundaries of that house and of the portion that you, Takoum my sister, have got.

(46.10–14: Takoum for her part declares her boundaries: "south, myself, Takoum the aforewritten; north, the sons of Antony; east, the courtyard of Epiphanius our father's brother; west, the public street and the place where the principal gate opens on to. These are the boundaries of the portion of the house that Abessa has got.")

From now on you, Takoum, are to enter in and be owner of the half of that entire house, from its foundations up to the air space, with all its utensils appertaining thereto as I am going to make plain in the settlement of property division according to the ordinance above, acquiring it in acquisition, to administer it, manage it, make improvements to it, build on it, rent it out, donate it, cede it, leave it to your sons and daughters, bequeath it to your heirs, dealing with it in any way or form at all.

(46.16–25: Takoum has most of the same clauses, with κυριεύειν added before "owner" and "property division" omitted after "settlement"; also just "sons", omitting "and daughters".)

Anyone who shall dare at any time to proceed against you ever, whether myself or my son or brother or sister or relative in the first or second degree, either

---

[4] The well-known scribe; he is also a witness here below, to both instruments.

on my father's side or on my mother's, or go to law with you before any exalted, honored authority concerning the portion of the house you have got or another portion, first of all that person is to have no profit of it, being chiefly on the one hand a stranger to the Father and the Son and the Holy Ghost. Subsequently he is to pay to account of fine thirty-six gold solidi to the authority exercising office[5] over us at that time. Subsequently he is to appear and acknowledge this settlement of property division and release, that is secure in every place where it may be produced in evidence. They asked me, I agreed. +

(46.25.-36: Takoum's instrument omits "dare" and does not list herself; the religious penalty clause is the same, and the fine is the same amount, 36 sol.; her validity clause has "valid" while Abessa's seems to omit it.)

45: + I Abessa daughter of the late Zacharias, the aforewritten above, I assent to it.—+ I Philochristos, most humble deacon, son of N., I wrote for her. +

+ I Aristophanes son of the late John, I bear witness. +

+ I Ezekiel son of the late Mathias,[6] I bear witness. + I Peshate son of Joseph, I bear witness.—Thomas son of the late Victor,[7] they asked me, I wrote for them as they did not know how, and I bear witness. +

+ I Noah, priest and hegoumenos, I bear witness at the request of Abessa. +++

46: [I Takoum][8] + I Takoum daughter of Zacharias, the aforewritten above, I assent.—+ I Philochristos, most humble deacon, I wrote for her, and I bear witness. +

+ I Aristophanes son of John,[9] I bear witness. +

+ I Ezekiel son of the late Mathias, I bear witness. + I Peshate son of Daniel [sic!], I bear witness.—Thomas son of Victor, I wrote for them as they did not know how, and I bear witness. +

+ I Noah, priest and hegoumenos, I bear witness at the request of Takoum. +++

---

[5] Here *prattesthai* (πράττεσθαι): Förster, *WB*, 670–71.
[6] As in *P.CLT* 6, *P. KRU* 50 above.
[7] Probably the same as in *P.CLT* 6.
[8] Erased and then rewritten in the manuscript.
[9] His designations do not seem reliable or consistent.

P.KRU 21

Sale of Half a House, With its Land

DATE: 12 June 725

PLACE: Jeme

PARTIES: Pesyntheus son of the late Paul, seller; Hemai and Shenoute sons of the late Germanos, buyers

OBJECT: Half of a house property with the land it stands on

SUM [price]: 4 1/3 solidi

[fine]: 4 oz. gold

WITNESSES: 10

SCRIBE: John son of Lazarus

PUBLICATION: Till, *KRUTheb*, 120–23

We return to the affairs of Shenoute and Hemai, sons of the late Germanos, on the one hand, and Pesyntheus son of Paul, on the other, known from *P.KRU* 10 above. They are named heirs to their grandmother Susanna (above, *P.KRU* 66 and 76). Here we find out that Shenoute is a priest. Pesyntheus is selling the two brothers half of his house property together with its land; he reminds the buyers of the earlier transaction he had with their late father, already cause of an earlier dispute (now seemingly resolved).

+ In the name of the Father and of the Son and of the Holy Ghost, consubstantial Trinity [in Coptic],[1] and the rule[2] and establishedness and continuance of our lords, these kings who have power over the whole earth by the command of God Almighty.[3] + Today, this day being the eighteenth of the month of Phaophi, in the eighth indiction year, in the presence of the most illustrious, honorable Peter

---

[1] Invocation Type **2L**: *CSBE 2*, 101, 104–5.

[2] This scribe, who also wrote *P.KRU* 10 above (from 722) and will write *P.KRU* 38 below (from 738), has a strange habit of confusing invocation phraseology ("In the name of . . .") with oath-clause phraseology that uses such rulership concepts to swear by. Compare the oath clause below in this document.

[3] Cf. Seidl, "Eid," 142–43.

son of the late Komos[4] and John son of Mathias,[5] *dioicetai* of Kastron Jeme[6] in the nome of the city of Hermonthis.

+ I Pesyntheus son of the late Paul, man of Kastron Jeme in the nome of the city of Hermonthis, subsequently putting in place a subscription[7] of the one who will subscribe for me, and some believable and trustworthy witnesses who will witness for me to this written document of sale, willingly and being persuaded, without any trickery or intimidation or compulsion,[8] (the sale being) untransgressable and unshakable, but rather established and not to be disregarded, and making it (the sale) yet more established through some trustworthy witnesses who will witness for me to this written document of sale according to my very own request and the wish of my heart:

I am writing to Hemai and Shenoute the priest, sons of the late Germanos, people of Kastron Jeme in the nome of the city of Hermonthis, willingly and being persuaded, without any trickery or intimidation or compulsion or deception, with no seizure or circumscription, but acting upon my very own persuasion, and moreover swearing by the name of God Almighty and the well-being of the lords who have power over us from God.[9]

I am giving to you, you, Hemai and Shenoute the priest, sons of the late Germanos, people of Kastron Jeme in the nome of the city of Hermonthis, in all masterly[10] ownership by sale, in an ownership unhindered and unimpeded ("without let or hindrance"), the half of my entire house that lies outside (the precincts of) the great bishop, the holy Apa Patermouthios of Kastron Jeme,[11] according to its old-time location, and according to its four corners round about: north, the threshing-floor; east, the house; west, St Patermouthios's; south, the public street and the old gate on to which the door opens. And the price of the house is solidi 4 1/3, four and a trimesion.[12] The other half of the house is for you, Hemai and Shenoute, sons of the late Germanos, viz., you have been in charge of[13] that whole house, but from now on you are to be in charge of the half of the house that I have sold to you. You have given me the price from your hands; and that other half of the house is for you to be in charge of, for ever, for your times and your children and your children's

---

[4] Already known from *P.CLT* 1, *P.KRU* 9, 35, 55, 51, and 50, above.

[5] In *P.KRU* 50 above.

[6] Cf. Schmelz, *Kirchliche Amtsträger*, 307.

[7] Here the feminine abstract noun *hypographê* (ὑπογραφή): cf. Förster, *WB*, 835.

[8] Such a clause usually applies to a document's framer, as here just below, but here seems to be applied to the witnesses, who are to bear their witness without any of those constraints. Or did the scribe just get carried away?

[9] Seidl, "Eid," 140; for "name" added cf. above, P.Mich.inv. 6898.

[10] *despotikon* (δεσποτικόν): Förster, *WB*, 166.

[11] Papaconstantinou, *Saints*, 168–70, esp. here 169.

[12] This seems low.

[13] Literally "give orders concerning," *keleuein* (κελεύειν).

children and all those who shall come after you, because I bought that land[14] from your father Germanos before those times were past.[15] And additionally there is no legal encumbrance[16] remaining upon me over that land. I have sold it to you, you, Hemai and Shenoute, sons of the late Germanos, so you may be in charge of it in every mastership matter. You can build on it, add on to it upwards up to the sky, pull it down, add on to it upwards up to the sky [sic]; and no man on either my father's side or my mother's is ever, ever to proceed against you: neither myself nor my son or brother or sister, relative in the first or in the second degree, neither from my clan[17] nor outside my clan, no man at all representing me, is to go to law with you, you, Hemai and Shenoute, sons of the late Germanos, over the matter of the half of the land that I sold—I have received its price—in court or out of court, in city or in nome, in any place.

Anyone who may dare to proceed against you and go to law with you over the matter of the half of the land that I sold to you, he is to pay four ounces of gold as fine to the magistrate exercising office at that time. But you will (possess) it for yourselves and your children and your children's children and all those who will come after you. First of all that person is to have no profit from (his attempt) at all, but rather he is to be a stranger to the Father and the Son and the Holy Ghost; and he is to acknowledge the force of the sale, with the oath and the fine, in all matters written therein; and on top of all these things he is to swear by the name of God Almighty and the well-being of our lords the kings[18] not to stray from[19] what I said above many times in the sale.

Accordingly, for your security I have had drawn up for you this sale, which is to be secure and valid and warranted in every place where it may be produced in evidence, before every rule and every authority, having validity. Subsequently we acknowledge the force of this sale in all matters written therein, as it stands above. +

+ I Pesyntheus son of the late Paul, the aforewritten above, I agree to the sale in all matters written therein.—I Pcher son of the late Epiphanius, I wrote for him as he did not know how to write, and I bear witness. +

+ I Demetrius son of the late Leontius, I bear witness.

I Sanagapê son of the late Menas, I bear witness.—I Demetrius wrote for him as he did not know how. +

+ I Psêre son of the late Peter, by the mercy of God priest and hegoumenos of the holy church of Jeme, I bear witness to the sale of Pesyntheus. +

---

[14] Presumably the land the house stands on.

[15] On the Roman-law *longissimi temporis praescriptio* documented in postclassical practice see *P.Col.* VII 175 with commentary.

[16] *dikaion* (δίκαιον): cf. Förster, *WB*, 194.

[17] *genos* (γένος): Förster, *WB*, 147–48.

[18] Seidl, "Eid," 141.

[19] *planan* (πλανᾶν): Förster, *WB*, 649.

+ I George son of the late Daniel,[20] I bear witness.

+ I Aroou son of the late Daniel,[21] and Patermoute son of the late Constantine, we bear witness.—John son of Lazarus,[22] I wrote for them. +

+ I Noah, priest and hegoumenos,[23] I bear witness at the request of the framer.

+ I Philotheos son of the late Solomon, I bear witness.—(I) Noah, he asked me, I wrote for him.+

+ I David son of the late Victor, I bear witness.—John son of Lazarus, I wrote for him. +

IC XC   IC XC

---

[20] Cf. *P.KRU* 17?
[21] Brother of the preceding.
[22] The scribe; cf. *P.CLT* 1, *P.KRU* 35, 51 above.
[23] He witnessed *P.KRU* 45 and 46 above.

P.KRU 67
Testament of Paham, Monk and Priest

DATE: 2 November 725 (by inference)

PLACE: Jeme

PARTIES: Paham (son of Epiphanius and Thatre), monk and priest (widower), testator; Jacob, his second-born son by his late wife Susanna, heir designate

OBJECT: House property

SUM: [debt owing] 2 ½ solidi

WITNESSES: 5

SCRIBE: Paham, the testator, himself

PUBLICATION: Till, *Erb*, 169–77; cf. O'Connell, "Monastic Dwellings," 265

With this document we eavesdrop on a really gripping family drama. Paham, widower and hieromonk, is with his own hand drawing up a will to arrange for the disposal of his goods; he narrates the sad story of his troubled son's life and death. For his part Paham is bound and determined that his (unnamed) disreputable former daughter-in-law, widow of his deceased elder son Papnoute and mother of Papnoute's deceased children, is not going to get her hands on any of his, Paham's, property. The property is considerable, and the family complex. The testator hedges round his specifics with strong religious phraseology.

[In the name of the holy, life-giving,] consubstantial Trinity, [Father, Son and Holy Ghost. Written in] the month of Hathyr, 6, in the ninth, 9, indiction year.

[I Paham] the monk, son of Epiphanius, [priest of St Colluthus's[1] of] Psenantonius[2] which is in the nome of the city of Coptos . . . [. . .], with my whole heart and my entire wish un[constrained], with no necessity incumbent upon me nor compulsion nor seizure, but rather of my very own wish and free choice unregretted, with good and unshakable counsel, in my right mind, with my reasoning established and my heart fixed, and . . . with my whole heart and my unregretted choice I am writing to you, you, my beloved son Jacob, writing to you in an established and un-undoable written and eternal testament for you and

---

[1] Papaconstantinou, *Saints*, 122–28, esp. here 124.
[2] Timm, *Ägypten*, 4: 2027–28.

your children and your children's children and all those your heart wishes well, that they will listen [to you] according to your word:

I Paham, I am writing this testament with my very own hand, dwelling upon the mountain of Jeme and being a monk. It could be seen that there was no blood relation[3] at my side in that place. I remembered that man does not know his way [Proverbs 20:24].[4] I said, "Do not let a sickness come upon me so that I die suddenly, with no one with me to whom I may convey my word concerning the small, quite humble property which came to me from my father and mother, and their dwelling-places."[5]

WHEREAS: I had three children. I went and became a monk;[6] I left them behind while they were still alive. They lived in the world, the three of them. As far as the eldest son, Papnoute, is concerned, he took a wife against my wishes. I grieved very, very much. But his path did not go straight from the time he married her. Fights and disturbances occurred in their situation. They went south to me; they told me the reason: her virginity was not intact. I said that this was his problem because he had not obeyed me. I yielded to God, the true Judge, and the prayers of my holy father.[7] Subsequently he (Papnoute) went away, and his mind was deceived by talk of flattery. She was placed with him. He engendered children with her, though his heart was troubled. And when he came and conveyed his heart's sorrow to me, many times, so that my heart was greatly saddened, I still did not want to throw him out, on account of God and my own compassion. I gave him a little place to live in my house, with his household goods,[8] silver and gold and bronze and clothing: in short, what I gave him will be found written in another place. Then, God came for him as He does for every man: he died, together with his children, all at once,[9] without his leaving any living seed.[10] Now, as God has made him and his children strangers to this world, I for my part make him a stranger[11] to all my dwelling-places that came to me from my parents, and

---

[3] *katasarx* (ⲕⲁⲧⲁⲥⲁⲣⲝ), "according to the flesh."

[4] Cf. also Proverbs 14:8, 16:25, 19:3.

[5] Again the technical term for a monastic dwelling (*ma-n-shôpe*), literally "place-to-be": cf. Brooks-Hedstrom, "Divine Architects." If Paham's late father Epiphanius had also been a priest, perhaps he was a monastic priest, bequeathing his dwelling in the time-honored way; cf. O'Connell, "Monastic Dwellings."

[6] After the death of his wife Susanna.

[7] Paham's superior.

[8] *skeuê* (σκευή).

[9] Perhaps in the plague of 724? (Kennedy, "Province," 74).

[10] *sperma* (σπέρμα): Förster, *WB*, 743.

[11] Slightly different from the more usual "stranger" type of clause, which is a penalty for breaking a contract, as occurs also here below.

his wife too. And (as for) my inheritance that belongs to me now, no one representing him is to take from it.

And concerning the house I gave him that he lived in until his death, his wife is not to inherit it or live in it as though she were its owner, nor is anyone representing her (to do so): but Jacob is to get it and inherit it, with his children, forever and ever.

Concerning the household goods that I gave him, Papnoute, while he was alive: when he died I looked for them; I found that none of them, of any kind, had been destroyed while he had been alive, but I found that he had two solidi and a half owed. Look now, I am giving you the authority, you, Jacob, my beloved son whom I wish well,[12] to be (their) owner and to look for every kind of object that I gave Papnoute and acquire it, every single shape and form of object, from precious to ordinary. Subsequently you are to satisfy his moneylender about the two and a half solidi. And, being owner, you are to require of his wife an oath about every item that has gone missing, up to and including a ceramic object, because I am the one who gave orders about it while I was alive. And moreover again he gave me the authority (to do this) through those who were sitting beside him at the time of his death. His wife for her part is to swear as to what she brought with her, and take it as her portion. You too, Jacob, are to treat her like the widows in your village that are childless, and get her to go to her house in good order, back to her village that she came from.

Concerning Thatre my daughter: I have decided her portion in everything I own, as God has put it into my heart, whether what has come to me from my parents or from her mother; she is to have no quarrel[13] with Jacob her brother about any shape or form of item from today on, as far as I, Paham, her father, am concerned. But if they have anything coming to them from their mother—Jacob and Thatre, that is—they are to divide it up into thirds: one for Jacob, one for Thatre, and the remaining third they are to give as an *agapē* for the souls of the departed, namely Papnoute and Susanna his mother and Martyria,[14] Susanna's mother.

But if after my death you, Jacob and Thatre, find occasion to go to law against the brothers of your mother Susanna, namely John and those representing the deceased[15] Pesyntheus, if they should say "Your mother and father took their share, and we came to an agreement with them while they were alive": look, I here lay down my holy oath, swearing by God Almighty Who does great

---

[12] Allusion to the phraseology of Matthew 3:17 and 17:5, Mark 1:11, Luke 3:22.

[13] *enklēma* (ἔνκλημα): Förster, *WB*, 225.

[14] The Martyria daughter of Victor who sold her silver and was alive in 713? (*P.KRU* 34 above).

[15] Here not *makarios*, "the late", but the Coptic ⲚⲦⲀϤⲚⲔⲞⲦⲔ, "who has fallen asleep."

wonders [Psalm 135:4][16] that when Susanna your sister came to me she brought nothing at all with her, as is clearly apparent in my memory, neither anything your parents might have given her as paraphernalia nor anything else she might have taken and brought to me.

Concerning the articles that we divided up—myself, Paham, and Gera and John and Pesyntheus: we put the other things aside without dividing them up at the time when we did the dividing up, but rather we agreed—myself, Paham, and Gera—that Tsible[17] should swear an oath with us about the other kinds of articles. Concerning the gold objects that are being adjudicated,[18] they have not given any of them at all to us, Paham and Gera, but rather John and Tsible have subsequently taken them. Any time you may wish to go to law with them concerning the gold objects or any other shape or form of item, you can give orders about that according to our wish. Look, I have satisfied them with the oath by the Lord that they are not to produce any excuses (along the lines of) "we came to an agreement with your father while he was still alive."

I Paham, who have previously written the above[19] with my very own hand, and am writing this testament with my hand alone, am writing to Jacob my son as follows: the place of the house that came to Epiphanius the priest from his father Paham, because he had built it, it came to me, me the son of Epiphanius the priest. Look, I for my part am giving it to you only and your children, so that you inherit it, with those who come after you, obeying you. No man is ever to proceed against you, neither son nor daughter nor grandchild, over that house that lies east of St Colluthus's, with one wall being in St Colluthus Street, the other wall (where my room is) being the boundary of the House of the Blind,[20] the third wall being in the lane (?), with the door leading in, and the fourth wall being, on the south, the house of "the Ox," namely Samuel, and the house of Abraham son of Tobias. I have named the old-time names that are still on those houses, up to today.

Concerning the wall that Isaac built under compulsion, there being no freedom[21] at that time as we were abroad, lest—if God gives you the means to build—they go to law against you since they do not want to let you build on it, seek out architects who will inform you as to the entire wall matter, because my wall is in the way and my parents never permitted them to build on it at all.

---

[16] Here in this Coptic with *eire* (ⲉⲓⲣⲉ) instead of *tamio* (ⲧⲁⲙⲓⲟ): cf. Psalm 76:14 that also omits "great" (as here).

[17] See Till, *D&P*, 224. A testatrix of this name makes her will in *P.KRU* 69 below.

[18] *dikazein* (δικάζειν): Förster, *WB*, 192.

[19] Here *shrpshai* (ϣⲣⲡⲥϩⲁⲓ)—"first-write"—is active in meaning, not passive.

[20] A charitable establishment?

[21] *parrhêsia* (παρρησία): Förster, *WB*, 626–27.

Only because this is my wall alone—but all the others round about belong to my house.

Concerning the courtyard that is inside the constructed place of the waterwheel machinery (?), it is all to belong to you, up to its boundary. If you wish to build on to it, you are its owner in all respects, so you can.

Accordingly, concerning the third of a house that I got from my mother, to the south of the village, which is by the gate, and the third of the courtyard in that place that came to Thatre my mother from Sara her mother, look: I, Paham, am giving them to you, Jacob, my son, and no man is ever to go to law with you over them, ever.

And concerning Thatre, my daughter and your sister too: you are not to be able to throw her out of the place where she lives in the days while she is alive. May her son not take a wife with whom her heart is not content, who might come and live there—for man does not know what is coming to meet him. But if she dies, either while you are alive or after you are dead, she is not to leave orders that say "I am giving it to my son or to whoever I want." If she says that, she is to be a stranger to God, and so is the "Great One" of that time to be if he condones her doing that: he is to be a stranger to God, because I saw my father treating his sister thus until his death. And she is not to be with any stranger, not even someone she requests, so that no scandal occur. As for you, she is not to hinder you from living there, for it belongs to you alone; but do not allow any stranger to live there. I have done this with no digging being done above up to that place.[22]

I, Paham, am writing to Jacob: that all things that came to me from my parents, whether house or courtyard or any kind of household goods from precious to common, are all to belong to you and your children and those who come after you, up to and including one single *nummus*.[23] No man is to be able to go to law with you over anything [even if] not written down or not intended to be written down or not remembered to be written down. But of all these, I am owner of them, I, as long as I live, I Paham the most humble. I said: "Lest while I am alive it happens that I get a sickness and you forget me, if you do what I wish in my lifetime you will inherit everything that is mine after my death."

Look, I have accordingly drawn up this testament with my own hand, establishing it for you and those who will come after you. And no man is to approach you over the testament wishing to go to law with you, neither kin nor kin of kin nor a man not remembered. And anyone who will proceed against you is to become a stranger to the Father and the Son and the Holy Ghost, the perfect

---

[22] I.e., for enlarging the house?

[23] Cf. *P.Lond.* I 77.22: "up to and including one *assarion* and one obol." However, *nummi* had been Byzantine currency not too long before Paham's lifetime; Roman asses and Greek obols were history.

Trinity that is worshipped at all times. The testament is to be established and indestructible, because this is the way I have made it. And willingly I drew it up according to what God put into my heart, with my very own hand, dwelling upon the mountain of Jeme at the time when I drew up the testament. But if, either while I am alive or after I shall have laid down the body according to the limit of all men, someone should go to law with you, Jacob, over the testament, wishing to destroy it, either brother or sister <u>or brother's wife</u>[24] or heir, or anyone at all, they are to become strangers to the Father and the Son and the Holy Ghost and to every community[25] of Christians.[26] Subsequently they are to pay a large fine[27] to the magistrate who is in office at that time, accordingly as God may put it into the heart of that magistrate.[28] For they entirely wished, in the design of their heart,[29] to undo this testament with the name of God written on it and with the fearsome oath that we also put in it. And the bishop appointed at that time, if he should wish to disregard[30] and destroy the testament saying in such a way that it is not established, wishing to undo it, whether through words of flattery or through some heartless men or through some bribery,[31] or any person whosoever in the rank[32] of priesthood, whether bishop or priest or deacon or lector, or layman, whoever wishes to undo the testament is to be a stranger to the Father and the Son and the Holy Ghost, and will have to appear and be judged at the fearsome judgement-seat of God. Subsequently again the magistrate in office at the time, whether supervisor[33] or village *lashane* or any man at all, if anyone acts to undo the testament he is to be a stranger to the Father and the Son and the Holy Ghost, consubstantial and life-giving.

I, Paham, have drawn up this testament with my very own hand; it is secure and has validity in every place where it may be brought forward.[34] +++

---

[24] Emphasis added.

[25] *koinônia* (κοινωνία).

[26] Note this even more explicit and emphatic extension. This bore heavy weight in the Egypt of 725. Paham repeats it at the end of his document.

[27] Here not *prostimon* (πρόστιμον) but the Coptic *ose* (ⲟⲥⲉ), "forfeit."

[28] Cf. Schmelz, *Kirchliche Amtsträger*, 303.

[29] Allusion to Luke 1:51.

[30] *amelein* (ἀμελεῖν): Förster, *WB*, 36–37.

[31] *spondarion* (σπονδάριον): Förster, *WB*, 744.

[32] *taxis* (τάξις).

[33] *pronoêtês* (προνοητής).

[34] Here not the usual *emphanizein* (ἐμφανίζειν) but the Coptic *eine ebol*, "come forth."

+ I Theophanes son of the late Joannake, man of the city of Côs,[35] Father Paham overseeing[36] me, I witnessed the testament at his request. +

+ I Nabernoukios, most humble priest of the principal church of Pi-Sinai,[37] I bear witness to the testament at the request of Apa Paham the monk. +

+ I Cyril son of the late Phoibammon, hegoumenos, I bear witness. +++

+ I Isaac son of the late Phoibammon,[38] of Pi-Sinai, I bear witness. +

+ I Philotheus son of Meus, of Pi-Sinai, I bear witness to the testament as it is written.

+ I Paham, most humble monk, son of Epiphanius, priest of St Colluthus's in Psenantonius, I Paham wrote this testament with my very own hand and I assent in all matters written therein. And subsequently I requested some other trustworthy men; they witnessed it: and anyone who may undo it in contravention of my directive is to be a stranger to every community of Christians. +++

---

[35] Qus: Timm, *Ägypten*, 5: 2173–80.
[36] *epitrepein* (ἐπιτρέπειν): Förster, *WB*, 289–90.
[37] Timm, *Ägypten*, 1: 410–13 (s.v. 'Bišināy').
[38] Brother of the preceding?

P.KRU 42

Settlement of Division of House Property

DATE: 725/26

PLACE: Jeme

PARTIES: Moses and Pesate, sons of the late Joseph, brothers

OBJECT: House property

SUM [fine]: 3 oz. gold

WITNESSES: 8 [or 9?]

SCRIBE: John son of Lazarus[1]

PUBLICATION: Till, *Erb*, 131–33

A property division has been effected in Jeme, with the help of the *lashane*s, the *amir*, the "Great Men," and a relative of a security official. It has taken all this authority, along with a procedure of casting lots, to get one brother to agree with another brother about who is to get which bits of one of those characteristically complex Jeme town houses—not to mention which areas are to be in common.

[I Moses son of the late Joseph, man of Kastron Jeme, . . . , having requested some] trustworthy witnesses [who will witness for me,] am writing to Pesate son of the late Joseph, my brother, man of Kastron Jeme, subsequently putting in place the subscription[2] of the one who will subscribe for me and credible and trustworthy witnesses: Greetings.

WHEREAS: in this year, the ninth indiction ⲁⲣⲭⲏ[3] that it is now, under Samuel son of Mena and George son of Chmntsnêu and Theodore son of Anatole and Abraham son of Pses, *lashane*s,[4] with Samuel son of Enoch being headman[5] of

---

[1] Also the scribe of *P.KRU* 35 and 21 above; cf. also *P.CLT* 1, *P.KRU* 51.

[2] Here the feminine abstract noun *hypographê* (ὑπογραφή).

[3] Cf. *CSBE 2*, 110–15.

[4] Seemingly an outgoing pair and an incoming pair. For the last-named (before he held office) cf. also *P.CLT* 6 above.

[5] *ape* (ⲁⲡⲉ), "head": alone it can mean *lashane/protocometes*, but in this phrase it seems to indicate the "chief"—here, of town security.

the guardians,[6] in the presence of our most glorious lord Pahal the *amir* ruling over our Kastron Jeme, we brought our matter before our most glorious *amir* 'Abd al-Homar, representing ... the *amir*.[7] He ordered Apa Kyri, the brother of Samuel son of Enoch the headman of the guardians, to appear. He sent the "Great Men," who are Noah the hegoumenos[8] and Thomas son of Victor[9] and Aaron son of Andrew and Pesyntheus son of Psyrus the builder. They entered into the new house that they had built. They set the price for the building. They received half its price, according to the order of the *amir*. Likewise again they divided up that house in the interior portion. And they cast lots for the exterior, they did, namely the "Great Men" together with Apa Kyri son of Enoch, the brother of Samuel son of Enoch the headman of the guardians. Each one severally got his lot, as God has appointed to you.

But you, my brother Pesate son of the late Joseph, man of Kastron Jeme, are to have command of[10] the three dining-rooms, and likewise of the storeroom above the exedra,[11] up to the air space. And the air-shaft[12] is to be closed off. Likewise you are to take pains to see about the space outside the door of the lower exedra. And open up your door to the north, taking pains (about it). The hall, the water-stand,[13] and the exterior door and the up staircase are to be in common, up to the air space.

Look, this is your portion assigned to you, you my brother Pesate son of my late father Joseph, man of Kastron Jeme. These are the boundaries of the new house: north, is our courtyard; west, is Victor son of Joseph;[14] south, the courtyard of Victor son of Thomas;[15] east, the public street and the old gate on to which the door opens.

Bur from now on you, you my brother Pesate, are to have command of them for ever and ever. Nor shall I ever be able to go to law with you, ever, ever, neither myself nor brother nor sister nor child, nor relative in the first or second degree, neither kin nor kin of kin, no man at all, nor anyone representing me. We shall not be able to go to law {go to law} against each other, in court or out of court, in

---

[6] See Torallas Tovar, "Police."

[7] The proper name might be read as 'Ayub'.

[8] We will encounter him as a witness here below. Known from *P.KRU* 21 and elsewhere; see Till, *D&P*, 147.

[9] Same as in *P.CLT* 6, *P.KRU* 45/46?

[10] Literally "give orders for", *keleuein* (κελεύειν).

[11] See above, *P.KRU* 35; also Wilfong, *Women*, 51.

[12] Crum, *CD*, 106a; Vycichl, *Dictionnaire étymologique*, 78b.

[13] See Wilfong, *Women*, 51.

[14] The *lashane* of *P.KRU* 36 and 37?

[15] The *lashane* of *P.KRU* 35?

city or in nome, in the praetorium or with any honored, venerated religious law,[16] to make a long story short. And if any one of us dares to, now or after some time, first of all he is to have no profit of it, but rather chiefly he is to be a stranger to the Father and the Son and the Holy Ghost. Subsequently he is to pay to the account three ounces of gold as fine, out of his very own property, into the hand of the honorable magistrate. After the paying-in[17] of the fine he is to appear and furnish me an acknowledgment of the validity of this settlement in all matters written therein.

Thereupon I swear by the name of God Almighty and the well-being of our lords who rule over us by God[18] not to depart from[19] what I said in all matters written therein, it being secure and having validity in every place where it may be produced in evidence.

They asked me, I agreed to this settlement in all matters written therein, as it stands above. [Greek]

+++ I Moses son of Joseph, [I assent to] the force of this sale [sic] in all matters written therein.

+ I Thomas son of the late Mark, I bear witness.

+ I Phoibammon son of the late George, I bear witness.

+ I Peter son of the late Severus,[20] I bear witness.—Thomas son of the late Mark, I wrote for him as he did not know how, and I bear witness.

+ I Pisrael son of Paul, I bear witness.

+ I Faustus son of the late Andrew,[21] I bear witness.

+ I Noah, priest and hegoumenos of the holy church of Jeme, I bear witness at the request of the framer. +++

+ I Isaac son of the late Constantine,[22] I bear witness.

+ I John son of Lazarus, I drew it up. + IC XC

[Docket] I Moses son of the late Joseph, the aforewritten above, I assent to this settlement in all matters written therein.—I N.[23] wrote for him, and I bear witness.

---

[16] See MacCoull, "ⲧⲩⲡⲟⲥ."
[17] *katabolê* (καταβολή).
[18] Seidl, "Eid," 140–43.
[19] *planan* (πλανᾶν).
[20] Appears also in *P.KRU* 50.
[21] Also a witness in *P.KRU* 27 below.
[22] Cf. *P.KRU* 25, 47, 50.
[23] *nim* (ⲛⲓⲙ): probably indicating that this was written after the fact and the name was to be supplied.

P.KRU 49

Surrender of Collateral Against Money Loan

DATE: 17 January 728

PLACE: Jeme

PARTIES: Philemon son of the late Joseph, debtor; Premnhot son of Athanasius, creditor

OBJECT: 1 solidus (loan); parcel of land (collateral)

WITNESSES: 3

SCRIBE: Philemon son of Joseph, the framer, himself

PUBLICATION: Till, *KRU Theb*, 135

Another short business document. In it the framer/scribe/debtor agrees that he is surrendering to his creditor some of his, the debtor's, own land that has been pledged as collateral for a loan of one solidus, which he has apparently been unable to repay in cash.

+ Drawn up Tybi 21, eleventh indiction.—I Philemon son of the late Joseph[1] am writing to you, Premnhot son of Athanasius, as follows: Pursuant to the guarantee about the solidus that you had drawn up with me, I have divided the land outside my gate and my . . . with you as collateral. Look, I have no more claim to it (the land) from you, nor would I dare to, either myself or any man at all. Anyone who brings it up against you will find it (such a claim) null and void.

Philemon the aforewritten above, I assent to this as it is written, and I wrote (it) with my hand.

+ I Elias son of Zacharias,[2] I bear witness.
[I N.,] I bear witness.
I Shenoute, most humble priest,[3] I bear witness.+

---

[1] Probably the same individual as in *P.KRU* 51 above, the wall dispute.
[2] Also in *P.CLT* 6, *P.KRU* 37.
[3] As in *P.CLT* 1, *P.KRU* 68, 36, 37.

P.KRU 44

Settlement of Inherited House Property and Dowry

DATE: 10 September 728

PLACE: Jeme

PARTIES: Mary daughter of the late Theodore, and her husband Peter son of Pheu; her (Mary's) sister Sophia and Sophia's husband Phoibammon son of the late George

OBJECT: Half of an inherited house, as dowry

SUM [fine]: 12 solidi

WITNESSES: 5

SCRIBE: Psate son of Pisrael

PUBLICATION: Till, *Erb*, 136–40

In this document we look in on the family affairs of two married sisters of Jeme (together with their husbands). The sisters have gone to the St Phoibammon monastic sanctuary in company with the town *lashane* to arbitrate the matter of dividing up their inheritance from their late father and determining the house portion that should go to one sister's husband. That man has sworn to his late father-in-law's ante-mortem intent to make over half of the house to his wife. Other property and buildings are to be in common. On the dowry practices here see Wilfong, *Women*, 138–39.

[. . . requesting trustworthy witnesses who will] witness it [for us at our ve]ry own request, we, [Mary daughter of the late Theodore and Peter son of Pheu her husband, people of Kastron Jeme,] are writing to Phoibammon son of the late

George[1] and to Sophia daughter of the late Theodore, my sister and your wife, you, Phoibammon, people of this same Kastron Jeme: Greetings.

WHEREAS: In the years past we agreed among ourselves on a definition[2] of this inheritance from the late Theodore, our [sic: *rectius* 'your' addressing Phoibammon] father-in-law, according to the order of the lord Justin, the pagarch of the city of Hermonthis, and in this twelfth indiction year that is now, under the most honorable Abraham[3] and Souros, *lashane*s, we wish to come to an agreement with one another according to the force[4] of the arbitration[5] that we arranged with one another. We have brought the equivocated matter before the most honorable Abraham the *lashane*; he has adduced the arbitration.

You have fulfilled it for us, you, Phoibammon, in the precincts of the combatant fair in victory, the holy Abba Victor,[6] of this same *kastron*, according to the force[7] of the arbitration that was defined for us. You (Phoibammon) fulfilled it for us in this way, (saying): "By the power of the sanctuary,[8] I know surely that the late Theodore, my father-in-law, made half of the house of Baruch, the one that he built with David son of Shoi, over in writing to Sophia my wife." After you had fulfilled the oath for us, the legal decision[9] took place, such that we drew up a release with one another. And now we, the aforewritten above, Peter and Mary, agree that the half of the house of Baruch has devolved upon you, you Phoibammon and Sophia your wife, according to the force of the arbitration and according to the force of the oath that you swore[10] for us.

Accordingly, the result for you is that you, Phoibammon and Sophia, are to enter in and have power over and be owners of and have dominion over[11] the entire half of the house of Baruch, according to the force of the arbitration and according to the force of the oath. You can acquire it for yourselves, administer it, make improvements to it, give it away, confer it, cede it, exchange it, build on it, make additions to it, rent it out, give it in pledge as collateral, lease it out to any person or their representative you wish, give it to your children as an inheritance, and your children can in their turn give it as an inheritance to their children, to

---

[1] The one we have already met in *P.KRU* 42 above, it seems.

[2] *horos* (ὅρος): Förster, *WB*, 590.

[3] Probably the same one as in *P.KRU* 42.

[4] Here *dynamis* (δύναμις).

[5] *mesiteia* (μεσιτεία). Cf. above, *P.Lond.* V 1709.

[6] Papaconstantinou, *Saints*, 62–68, esp. here 64.

[7] Here *chom* (ϭⲟⲙ).

[8] *thysiastêrion* (θυσιαστήριον): Förster, *WB*, 341–42; the term for the part of a church structure in which the eucharist was consecrated. Cf. Seidl, "Eid," 145, and the "copy of the oath" here below.

[9] *doxon* (ⲇⲟⲝⲟⲛ): again Förster, *WB*, 209.

[10] *kataballein* (καταβάλλειν), literally "laid down" or "entered."

[11] *kyrieuesthai* (κυριεύεσθαι).

make a long story short. And those who come after you up to any time are to enjoy all ownership and law.

And again, we make clear this capital matter:[12] we have received and we have come to an agreement with one another about all things belonging to the late Theodore, according to the force of the definition: the gold, the dowry, the bride's-side gift to the husband, the year of sustenance,[13] according to the force of the definition that we received amongst ourselves. The house of Theodore and the courtyard of Temenoute and the little house of Taue and the oil-press are to be in common among us, according to our half-and-half arrangement.

From now on we will not be able to proceed against you, you, Phoibammon and Sophia, over the half of the house of Baruch that has devolved upon you, nor over anything belonging to the late Theodore, neither the gold nor the silver nor the dowry nor the gift to the husband nor the year of sustenance nor the paraphernalia,[14] up to and including the house of Theodore and the little house of Taue and the oil-press that we have laid down as being in common, nor over the half of the house of Baruch:[15] neither myself nor son nor daughter nor brother nor sister nor relative in the first or the second degree, neither kin nor kin of kin, neither stranger nor person of (our) house, nor anyone else for us, according to any shape or form or allegation: not against you, you, Phoibammon and Sophia, nor your children nor your heirs nor your kin nor your kin's kin, nor any man representing you and/or your children and/or heirs. And we shall not be able to go to law with you in court or out of court, neither in city nor in nome, nor (before) any body[16] of this city or another city or praetorium or by any honored, venerated religious law,[17] all told: because we have received and we have come to an agreement with one another so as to lay down what is common, in every form and in every perfect legal relief[18] [all Greek].

And over and above all these things we swear by the power of the holy, consubstantial Trinity, the Father, the Son and the Holy Ghost,[19] that we will observe the force of this written document of settlement, which is valid.

And if anyone should dare to (proceed thus), either now or at any time, first of all that person is to have no profit of it, but chiefly he is to become and be a

---

[12] *kephalaion* (κεφάλαιον).
[13] In addition to Wilfong, *Women*, 138–41, see also Richter, *Sprache*, 272, 310, 251.
[14] Crum, *CD*, 245a.
[15] The notary seems to have just repeated this.
[16] Again Till, *Erb*, 138 read *koinêsis* (ⲕⲟⲓⲛⲏⲥⲓⲥ) as *kinêsis* (ⲕⲓⲛⲏⲥⲓⲥ/κίνησις), "(legal) motion," but in this context it ought indeed to be κοίνησις, a common body, perhaps an assembly of town magistrates if such survived, or the "Great Men" of Jeme assembled. Cf. above, *P.CLT* 1 and *P.KRU* 37.
[17] See MacCoull, "ⲧⲩⲡⲟⲥ."
[18] *apallagê* (ἀπαλλαγή): Förster, *WB*, 70.
[19] Seidl, "Eid," 140.

stranger to the holy venerable oath. Subsequently he is to pay to account of fine twelve solidi of pure gold that will be required of him out of his very own property, to the hand of the honorable magistrates. Thereupon, after the paying-in of the fine, he is to furnish your matter of law in this way, appearing and acknowledging the validity of this valid settlement, which we have drawn up for you without any trickery or intimidation or compulsion or deception, with no seizure or circumscription: it is secure and valid in every place where it may be produced in evidence. They asked us, we agreed.

+ I Peter son of Pheu, and Mary his wife, the aforewritten above, we assent to this sale [sic] in all matters written therein.—I George, archdeacon[20] of St Victor's of Jeme, I wrote for them as they did not know how to write.

+ I Abraham son of Theodore,[21] I bear witness.

+ I Theodore son of the late David,[22] I bear witness to the settlement as it is written.

+ Patermoute, most humble priest of the holy church of Jeme, I bear witness.

+ I Cyriac son of the late Abraham, I bear witness.

I Plêin son of Patermoute, I bear witness.—I Cyriac, I wrote for him as he did not know how to write, bearing witness to the settlement as it is written.

— + Copy of the oath: "By the holy *topos*, by its power,[23] in this oath I give my soul. I know surely that the late Theodore my father-in-law made over in writing the half of the house of Baruch, this one that he built with David son of Shoi, to Sophia my wife. And again that he granted that the house be added on to for you, Mary, and without revealing it to me he wrote in his testament that he was making an addition to the house. And this is the way he read that testament aloud to me many times, to the effect that Sophia was going to get the half of the house of Baruch that he built with David son of Shoi, and that Mary was to get the addition to the house." This is the oath that Phoibammon swore for Peter and Mary.—Thoth 13, indiction 12.

+ Brought about (i.e., written) by me, Psate son of Pisrael.[24]+ [Greek]

---

[20] On this rank see Schmelz, *Kirchliche Amtsträger*, 37, and Wipszycka, "Les ordres mineurs."

[21] Probably not the same person as in *P.CLT* 5.

[22] Cf. *P.KRU* 68.

[23] Seidl, "Eid," 145.

[24] As in *P.CLT* 1, 5, *P.KRU* 35, 36, 37.

P.KRU 3

Sale of Inherited Landed Property

DATE: 728/29

PLACE: Jeme region

PARTIES: Daniel son of Saul, Koloje daughter of Paham (?), and Tachel daughter of Martha, co-sellers; Solomon son of the late Moses, buyer

OBJECT: Inherited land with courtyards

SUM [price]: 3 1/3 solidi

[fine] 10 solidi

WITNESSES: 6

SCRIBE: Moses (son of the archpriest Shenoute), deacon

PUBLICATION: Till, *KRUTheb*, 90–92

With this document we enter the world of Koloje, female moneylender of Jeme, as laid out by Wilfong, *Women*, 116–33 (also 142 for this text). Koloje and another woman, together with a man, Daniel son of Saul, are selling to Solomon son of the late Moses some land they inherited, discontinuous parcels of urban land in Jeme town near the principal gate.

[Invocation; month, day, indiction year] [We, (parties named,) having drawn up] . . . this written document of sale, un(alterable?)[25] and eternal, written so as to be untransgressable and unshakable by law, and making it yet more established through some of these other trustworthy witnesses who will witness the sale for us at our very own request and under our supervision,[26] we are writing to the most admirable[27] Solomon son of the late Moses of Tsei,[28] to the south of this same village: Greetings. + As follows:

WHEREAS: In this year which is now, which is the twelfth (indiction), willingly and well persuaded, without any trickery or intimidation or compulsion or deception or seizure or circumscription, with no necessity incumbent upon us,

---

[25] Förster, *WB*, 526 does not aid in interpreting this.
[26] *epitropê* (ἐπιτροπή): Förster, *WB*, 290.
[27] *thaumasiôtatos* (θαυμασιώτατος), the Byzantine title.
[28] Timm, *Ägypten*, 3: 1205–6 (s.v. 'Itsā').

but rather by our very own free choice, we agree, swearing by the salvation[1] of the holy, consubstantial Trinity, Father, Son and Holy Ghost, Unity in Trinity,[2] that we have given our consent[3] in writing to you, you, Solomon son of Moses, (for) our portions of land that came to us from our parents and came to them also from their parents, those lands being called Cabbage Land (?) of the holy bishop Apa Germanos:[4] so that you are to give orders over them for ever, at all times that come after you. And the boundaries are these of those lands of ours, their four boundaries round about on four sides: the first piece of land and the second, these are their boundaries: south, Shenoute son of Phoibammon;[5] north, Anatole son of Samuel;[6] west, Kos the butcher, son of David; east, the main gate. Look, these are the boundaries of one piece of land on its four surrounding sides. Likewise, to the east the boundaries of the other piece of land are these: west, Jacob son of Andrew; east, the main gate; south, Isidore son of Tribunus;[7] north, Solomon son of Moses, the buyer. Look, these are the boundaries of the two pieces of land on all four sides. No other legal claim or liability[8] is left remaining upon them that we have not transferred over to you.

And the price that we have agreed upon on both sides is three gold solidi and a trimesion, = 3 1/3, three-and-a-third. The price accordingly we have received, from hand to hand, by the standard of the *kastron* and the evaluation[9] of the "Great Men" and the builder.

We, Daniel son of Saul and Kouloje daughter of Paham (?) and Tachel daughter of Martha, we establish with you, you, Solomon, such that you are to enter upon and have power of and give orders for and manage the two courtyards located in Cistern Lane (?), to build on them, add on to them upwards, dwell in them, sell them, give them to your children and your heirs, in short, dealing with them in any way, shape and form you please.

Anyone who will dare (as is likely [Greek]) to proceed against you over the two courtyards is to pay ten solidi, and is to have no profit of it. But if it should happen that anyone so dare, whether son or brother or heir or any man representing us or a stranger, he shall be fined and will have no profit of it.[10] Securing this for you in every security in Christ Jesus our Lord, in every place, we assent and

---

[1] *oujai* (ⲟⲩϫⲁⲓ), the same word used for the "well-being" of rulers sworn by.
[2] Compare the phraseology of invocation formulas **2F, 2G, 2K, 2N** in *CSBE 2*, 100–1: more usually "Trinity in Unity". This oath is not discussed in Seidl, "Eid."
[3] Literally "our 'Yes'."
[4] See Timm, *Ägypten*, 1: 165.
[5] Cf. *P.KRU* 17?
[6] Probably the same individual as in *P.KRU* 50.
[7] Or "Isidore the tribune"?
[8] *dikaion* (δίκαιον).
[9] *dokimasia* (δοκιμασία): Förster, *WB*, 207.
[10] Note the variant phraseology here.

we agree (that it is) secure and valid. They read it aloud to us; we heard it, and it is complete according to all possession[11] and order of clauses.[12] + IC XC +

+ I Koloje daughter of the late Paham (?), I assent to this sale as it is written.—I George son of the late Cosmas, Koloje asked me, I wrote for her at her request.

+ I Daniel son of Saul, I assent to the sale as it is written.—I David son of Peter, I wrote for him as he did not know how to write.

+ I Menas son of Philotheus, I assent to the sale.

+ I Psêre son of the late Peter, by the mercy of God priest and hegoumenos[13] of the holy church of Jeme, I bear witness. +

+ I Papnouthios son of the late Peter,[14] most humble archdeacon of the holy church of Jeme, I bear witness. +

+ I Phoibammon son of Stephen, most humble priest of Apa Victor's,[15] I bear witness.

+ I George son of the late Cosmas,[16] I bear witness.

+ I David son of Peter, I bear witness.

+ Pesyntheus son of Stephen,[17] I bear witness. [Greek]

+ I Moses, most humble deacon, son of Shenoute the archpriest,[18] of Kastron Jeme, I wrote this sale with my hand at the request of the framers.

---

[11] *nomê* (νομή) (cf. Förster, *WB*, 544–45); can also be "according to every legal norm."
[12] *akolouthia* (ἀκολουθία).
[13] We met him above in *P.KRU* 21.
[14] Brother of the foregoing? (Both are clerics at the same establishment.)
[15] Papaconstantinou, *Saints*, 62–68, esp. here 64.
[16] Koloje's signer above.
[17] As in *P.KRU* 35.
[18] Could this be the Jeme priest Shenoute of *P.CLT* 1, *P.KRU* 68, 36, 37, 49, now in a higher clerical rank?

P.KRU 69

Testament

DATE: 18 August 729

PLACE: Jeme

PARTIES: Tsible daughter of Hypatius, testatrix; unnamed, probably a religious house, heir designate[1]

OBJECT: Offering for prayers for the soul of the deceased

SUM [property]: 4 trimesia plus price from house and land sale

  [fine]: 3 oz. gold

WITNESSES: 3

SCRIBE: Severus son of the late Samuel

PUBLICATION: Till, *Erb*, 183–85

Here we find a married woman concerned about both her afterlife and her property. Tsible has been moved by a recent bout of illness, during which her husband has cared for her, to direct him to donate both money and inherited house and landed property to a religious foundation, for the repose of her soul. She insists explicitly on her own right to dispose of what is her own (phraseology noted in another context by Richter, "Donation Documents," 242).—Is this Tsible the Tsible related to Paham the monk's family in *P.KRU* 67 above? (That one bears no patronymic.)

+ In the name of the Father and of the Son and of the Holy Ghost. Today being the twenty-fifth of Mesore in the twelfth indiction year, in the presence of the most honorable Leontius and Mena, *lashane*s of Kastron Jeme: I Tsible daughter of Hypatius (state) as follows:

WHEREAS: I fell into a severe illness, and I was afraid lest God should come for me and I go out of this life, to my destruction, with my work left undone[2] and my final offering as well, I sought (to make) this testament, untransgressable and indestructible, making it yet more established through some trustworthy

---

[1] Till, *Erb*, 183 thinks the heir is to be her husband, but this is erroneous.

[2] *apoiêton* (ἀποίητον; to be added to Förster, *WB*) (*pace* Till, *Erb*, 183, who misunderstands).

witnesses and with a scribe who would write for them, with my heart firm, sitting in the place where I sleep, with my mind firm and my reasoning established. I was afraid lest the judgement[3] come upon me as it does upon all people in the way that God the Word defined it for the father of us all, Adam, saying: "You are earth and you shall sleep in earth [Genesis 3:19]." I sought (to make) this testament because I saw that my husband was taking care of me in all my pains and was making improvements for me, looking after me in every way with all his might. I said, "Do not let God bring me before His fearsome judgement-seat [negatively], on account of his trouble and my offering." So now I am giving orders in this way:

Concerning the four trimesia: let my husband take them and give them as an offering on my behalf. And again, my portion of the house which came to me from my father, and my portion of the field . . ., my husband is to become and be owner of them, and he is to receive their price from my brothers and give it as an offering on my behalf. And again concerning the household goods[4] that came to me from my father: I swear by God Almighty that I am not giving any of them to my husband, nor is any other man to be able to proceed against you[5] ever, on any allegation at all, thus: neither brother nor sister nor anyone at all on my side or on yours, nor all those coming after you, now or at any other time.

The one who shall dare to transgress this testament, whether stranger or person on my side, concerning my offering and my oath that I swore,[6] (is to have no good of it,) but my husband is to become and be owner of my entire offering; in the fear of God he is to administer it. No man is to be able to administer it except him; and I adjure by God Almighty every magistrate and *lashane*, and (according to) every honored, venerated religious law written in a book,[7] that as for this testament, they are to observe it as it is written. (And it is possible for me to do what I like with what is mine.[8]) The one who dares to transgress it, first of all he is to have no profit of it, but rather chiefly he will become and be a stranger to the holy oath by the Father and the Son and the Holy Ghost; and then he will pay on account three ounces of gold, that he will give out of his own property. Subsequently, after furnishing that, he is to appear and acknowledge the validity of this testament and the penalty payment[9] to the *lashane* at that time. Accordingly the testament is to be established.

---

[3] *apophasis* (ἀπόφασις): Förster, *WB*, 92.

[4] *skeuê* (σκευή).

[5] The heir designate, probably a monastery. Cf. Wilfong, *Women*, 7, 136.

[6] The word *prosphora* (ⲡⲣⲟⲥⲫⲟⲣⲁ) here was misunderstood by Seidl, "Eid," 158. Meaning "offering" (see Glossary), it signifies Tsible's bequest, not a feature of her oath.

[7] See MacCoull, "ⲧⲩⲡⲟⲥ."

[8] Cf. Beaucamp, *Statut de la femme*, 1: 323–35, 2: 301–2.

[9] *zêmia* (ζημία).

I Tsible, the aforewritten above, I assent to this testament in all matters written therein, because they read it aloud to me and I heard it in (the) Egyptian (language); and again I asked a scribe and some other witnesses to witness for me. I had it set down, as it stands above. [Greek] +

+ I Andrew son of the late Phoibammon, I bear witness.

+ I George son of the late Samuel, I bear witness.

+ I [N.] son of the late Psan, I bear witness.—I Theopistos, lector of St Cyriac's,[10] I wrote for them as they did not know how to write.

+ I Severus son of the late Samuel, I wrote the testament with my hand at the request of the framer. +

---

[10] Papaconstantinou, *Saints*, 132–34, esp. here 133.

P.KRU 27

Sale of Textile Works

DATE: c. 730 (?)

PLACE: Jeme

PARTIES: Ananias son of the late Psês, seller; Peter son of Zacharias, buyer

OBJECT: Loom installation

SUM [price]: 1 solidus

      [fine]: 6 solidi

WITNESSES: 3

SCRIBE: Aristophanes son of John

PUBLICATION: Till, *KRUTheb*, 124–26

In this document a man sells to another man a weaving installation that he, the seller, has inherited from his late mother: the apparatus and structure are located in his own courtyard. The illiterate seller has requested a subscriber to sign for him. Textile crafts were indeed practiced in Jeme throughout its known history.

+ In the name of the holy and life-giving, consubstantial Trinity, Father, Son and Holy Ghost.[1] [month, day, indiction] Under our master, through Flavius Cyrus son of Colluthus, magistrate[2] from the Three Kastra[3] and that of Memnonion. + [Greek]
    + I Ananias son of the late Psês and Tmanna, man of Kastron Jeme in the nome of the city of Hermonthis, subsequently putting in place some subscribers who will subscribe for me and some witnesses who will witness to this written document of sale, untransgressable and unshakable by law, + I am writing to Peter son of Zacharias son of Petale, man of this same *kastron*, as follows:
    I agree, I Ananias son of Psês the aforewritten, (that I have made a sale) to you, you, Peter son of Zacharias, the buyer and the aforewritten, according to this sale that is written (so as to be) warranted and straight in each and every

---

[1] Invocation Type **2E**: *CSBE 2*, 100, 104–5, 293 (=*SB* I 5570).
[2] I expand as reading *archôn* (ⲁⲣⲭⲱⲛ); Till (*KRUTheb*, 124) did not discern the title "Flavius" and thought the name was "Colluthus son of Ars(enius)."
[3] Is this a way of designating Jeme, Thebes, and Hermonthis all together? Cf. Wilfong, *Women*, 8.

matter in it. I have proceeded to it willingly and well persuaded, without any trickery or intimidation or compulsion or deception, with not one single necessity incumbent upon me, but rather by my very own free choice, subsequently swearing by God Almighty and the well-being of our lords who rule over us by God's counsel,[4] that I have sold to you, you, Peter son of Zacharias son of Petale, the buyer, the one I have clearly indicated[5] above many times, in all ownership and justice and law,[6] by a complete sale,—and I have written (it) for you from this day today and from now on for ever until all times ever to come after you,—my entire loom installation[7] that is in the courtyard of Tsacho[8] the daughter of Blind Jacob. That loom is located within the street to the west of the men of Pshoumane;[9] this is below the west of the house of Zacharias son of Psês,[10] over by its surrounding boundary. That loom came to me, me, Zacharias son of Psês [sic],[11] from my late mother Tmanna, and you are to become and be owner of that loom installation from its foundations up to the air space, with its utensils belonging thereto, according to the old-time arrangement[12] and as it appeared from old times.[13] Thus obtaining:[14]

The price that we agreed upon for it between ourselves and were satisfied with on both sides is: a solidus, pure gold, = 1 sol., one, obr., such that you are to enter upon it and have power over it and be owner of that entire loom installation, the one that is inside the door of my courtyard of/with Tsacho daughter of Blind Jacob, (you) being its owner from its foundations up to the air space, together with all its utensils belonging thereto, because its price has come to my hand from your hand, from hand to hand, in tried gold and a capital sum, according to the ordinance made plain above. You have acquired it in acquisition for yourself, to administer it, manage it, make improvements to it, dwell in it, rent

---

[4] Seidl, "Eid," 143.

[5] *saphênizein* (σαφηνίζειν).

[6] See Steinwenter, "ⲚⲞⲘⲞⲤ."

[7] On textile crafts at Jeme see Wickham, *Framing the Early Middle Ages*, 764–65, as well as Wilfong, *Women*, 17, 143. Here a man owns the loom setup / workshop, which he inherited from his mother and is located in property owned by a woman; he sells it to another man.

[8] This can also be a designation for a female craft worker: Wilfong, *Women*, 89.

[9] Crum, *CD*, 567a (for parallels). Still attested in post-Umayyad times, e.g., in *P.KRU* 6 (dated 14 August 758), in which Aaron son of the late Shenoute, the property entrepreneur we are about to meet in the next document, buys a courtyard in this street, just to the east of "the house of Peter son of Zacharias", i.e., this structure.

[10] The seller's brother?

[11] Clearly a mistake by the scribe.

[12] *thesis* (θέσις): Förster, *WB*, 338.

[13] Reading *palaiopsis* (παλαιόψις) with Förster, *WB*, 602 (apparently an inner-Coptic neologism).

[14] From *periechein* (περιέχειν), "circumstantial": Förster, *WB*, 639.

it out, donate it, cede it, give it in exchange, sell it, give it away, confer it, leave it to your sons and daughters, bequeath it to your heirs, treating it in any way or form at all, according to all possession and mastership [Greek], with eternal retention, unto all time.

Anyone who may ever proceed against you, whether myself or brother or sister, relative in the first or in the second degree, on my father's [or my mother's] side, going to law with you in court or out of court, or who may bring any prosecution against you before any authority, first of all he is to be a stranger to the Father and the Son and the Holy Ghost, and is to pay to account of fine six solidi to that authority. Subsequently he is to appear and acknowledge this sale, which is secured to you. I drew up this purchase,[15] secure and having validity in every place where it may be produced in evidence, before any magistrate or authority. They asked me, I agreed.

+ I Ananias son of Psês assent to this sale.—+ I Mark son of Papnoute,[16] (myself) representing this person, he asked me, I wrote for him as he did not know how, and I bear witness.

+ I George son of Daniel,[17] I bear witness.

+ I Faustus son of Andrew,[18] I bear witness.

+ Written by me, Aristophanes son of John,[19] from Kastron Memnonion. [Greek]

---

[15] ônê (ὠνή): Förster, *WB*, 898.
[16] Could this be the deacon of *P.KRU* 17? Here no clerical title is given.
[17] Cf. *P.KRU* 17.
[18] Seemingly the same witness as in *P.KRU* 42 above, where however he designates his father as deceased.
[19] The scribe of *P.KRU* 10, 25, 47, *P.CLT* 6, *P.KRU* 17, 45/46; see Cromwell, "Aristophanes" and "Papyri Manuscripts."

P.KRU 5

Sale of Inherited Land

DATE: 24 March 733

PLACE: Jeme

PARTIES: Victor and Pelotare, sons of the late Shenoute, sellers; Aaron son of the late Shenoute, their brother, buyer

OBJECT: Landed property

SUM [price]: 1/3 solidus

[fine]: 6 solidi

WITNESSES: 4

SCRIBE: David son of Psate[1]

PUBLICATION: Till, *KRU Theb*, 94–96

With this document we come to know the ongoing story of Aaron son of the late Shenoute, the property entrepreneur (see Wickham, *Framing the Early Middle Ages*, 424). Here he buys from his two brothers Victor and Pelotare an urban landholding in the town of Jeme. Interestingly, one of the penalty clauses specifies that ecclesiastical court authority is not to be resorted to in case of a dispute (see Schmelz, *Kirchliche Amtsträger*, 273).

[In the name of the ho]ly and life-giving, consubstantial Trinity, Father, Son and Holy Ghost.[2] Written in the month of Phamenoth, 28, first indiction. + [Greek]
 + We, Victor and Pelotare sons of the late Shenoute, men of Kastron Jeme in the nome of the city of Hermonthis, subsequently putting in place a subscriber to subscribe for him [sic] and some trustworthy witnesses to witness to this written document of sale, untransgressable and unshakable by law, and making it yet more established by some of these other trustworthy witnesses who will witness it for us at our very own request and under our direction: Greetings.[3] As follows:
 We agree, we, Victor and Pelotare sons of the late Shenoute the aforewritten above, with you, Aaron son of the late Shenoute, man of the same Kastron Jeme,

---

[1] See T.S. Richter, "Zwei Urkunden des koptischen Notars David, des Sohnes des Psate," *Archiv für Papyrusforschung* 44 (1998): 69–85.

[2] Invocation Type **2E**: *CSBE 2*, 100, 104–5, 294 (=*SB* I 5558).

[3] Addressee not named here, as would be usual ("we are writing to . . .").

the buyer aforewritten above,[4] according to this sale written so as to be warranted and straight in every single matter therein, which we have sought, willingly and well persuaded, without any trickery or intimidation or compulsion or deception, with no seizure or circumscription, with no necessity incumbent upon us, but of our very own free choice, without any ill will[5] or evil character,[6] without one single necessity incumbent upon us, but in every good intention [Greek], and subsequently swearing by God Almighty and the well-being of (those who) rule over us now by God's command,[7] that we have sold to you today, to you, Aaron son of Shenoute, the buyer, the one with whom we have come to an agreement by name many times, in all ownership and justice and law,[8] in a sale that is complete, and we are making over in writing to you from now on until all times for ever that come after you, our portion of the landholding[9] belonging to us in Kastron Jeme, in Ermoudet Street: so that you may become and be its owner on all four sides, from its foundations up to the air space,[10] together with all the utensils appertaining thereto, which came to us by name from our late (father) Shenoute, in the way we are about to make clear for you now according to its old-time arrangement: in a quadrilateral: north, Stephen son of {son of}[11] Pchol; south, Tbêk; east, the parcel of land;[12] west, Ananias.[13]

This price, upon which we have agreed among ourselves on both sides, is a trimesion, pure gold, by the standard of Jeme, = pure by Memnonion standard 1/3 sol. The complete price has come to our hand from your hand, hand to hand, full, measured, good, from-hand-to-hand [Greek], tried, a capital sum.

And from now on you, you, Aaron son of the late Shenoute, the buyer, the aforenamed[14] above many times according to the ordinance that I [sic] made plain before above, having acquired it (the property) for yourself in acquisition, may administer it, manage it, make improvements to it, dwell in it, donate it, cede it, give it in exchange, sell it, give it away, confer it, leave it to your children, bequeath it to your heirs, treating it in any way you please, in possession for ever, in timely fashion and without any let or hindrance at any time at all.

Anyone who will ever proceed against you, you, Aaron, previously made plain above, be it ourselves or our children or brother or sister or kin or kin of

---

[4] Actually not: see previous note.
[5] *kakonoia* (κακόνοια): Förster, *WB*, 366.
[6] *kakoêtheia* (κακοήθεια): Förster, *WB*, 366.
[7] Seidl, "Eid," 143.
[8] Steinwenter, "ⲚⲞⲘⲞⲤ."
[9] *chôra* (χώρα): Förster, *WB*, 890.
[10] Seemingly more applicable to a building.
[11] Mistakenly repeated by the scribe.
[12] *chôrêma* (χώρημα): Förster, *WB*, 891.
[13] The seller in the previous document?
[14] *-onomaze* (-ⲞⲚⲞⲘⲀⲌⲈ).

kin, stranger or man of the house, on our father's side or on our mother's, going to law with you in court or our of court, within the nome or outside of the nome, in the praetorium or outside the praetorium, or will bring any prosecution against you before any exalted, glorious authority, whether we summon[15] you or not, concerning this sale, either a portion thereof or the whole, before magistrate or church (authority),[16] first that person will have no profit of it, but chiefly he is to be a stranger to the Father and the Son and the Holy Ghost, and is to pay to account of fine, to the authority in being at present, six gold solidi, over and above the penalty that the laws have defined for one who dares to transgress it. And on top of all these things he is to appear and acknowledge the clean purchase[17] in all matters written therein.

Accordingly for your security I have drawn it up, secure and valid and warranted in every place where it may be produced in evidence. They asked us, we agreed. They read it aloud to us, we heard it, we established it with subscribers and witnesses. We gave it forth according to the order[18] of the laws.

+ John son of the late Papnouthios and Chaêl son of Severus and Peêu son of the late Thomas, we bear witness. +—+ I Shenoute son of the late Chmntsnêu,[19] most humble deacon, as representative: they asked me, I wrote for them as they did not know how to write, and I bear witness at the request of Pelotare and Victor.

+ Written by me, David son of Psate. [Greek]

[Docket] Victor and Pelotare, sons of Shenoute . . .

. . . north: Stephen; south, Tbêk, Ermoude Street; west: Ananias.[20]

---

[15] *enkalein* (ἐνκαλεῖν).

[16] Cf. Schmelz, *Kirchliche Amtsträger*, 273.

[17] *kathara ônê* (καθαρὰ ὠνή) (not preserving the Greek accusative endings in the loan-form).

[18] *akolouthia* (ἀκολουθία).

[19] Probably the father of the priest, hegoumenos, and scribe of *P.KRU* 13, 12, 106 below.

[20] The rest of the other side of this document was later used for the accounts recorded as *P.Lond.Copt.* I 459, bearing a date of 4 Choiak, indiction 1. They are financial accounts apparently being sent to Fustat ('Babylon').

P.KRU 13

Sale of House Property

DATE: 30 November 733

PLACE: Jeme

PARTIES: Cyriac son of Demetrius, superior of St Phoibammon's, seller; Aaron son of the late Shenoute, buyer

OBJECT: Fourth portions of two houses in Jeme

SUM [price]: 1 solidus

[fine]: 12 solidi

WITNESSES: 4

SCRIBE: Chmntsnêu son of Shenoute, priest and hegoumenos[1]

PUBLICATION: Till, *KRU Theb*, 108–10

In this document we follow more of Aaron's property dealings. Here he is buying house shares from the current superior of the St Phoibammon monastery (cf. Godlewski, *Phoibammon*, 73, 86), properties part of which he, the superior, has himself co-owned after they had initially been donated to the monastery as pious *prosphorai*. The superior, Cyriac, is going to use the solidus Aaron has paid him for the properties to benefit the poor (see Schmelz, *Kirchliche Amtsträger*, 170). This document is one of a pair engrossed by the same scribe; its counterpart is *P.KRU* 12 just below, the instrument framed by Patermoute, Cyriac's co-owner. It also has connections to *P.KRU* 18 below.

[Traces of an Arabic-language protocol are preserved, with the end of the Bismillah and the name of the governor and head of taxation 'Ubayd Allah (724–734).]
  + In the name of the holy and life-giving, consubstantial Trinity, Father, Son and Holy Ghost.[2] Written in the month of Choiak, 4, second indiction. [Greek]

---

[1] Also the scribe of the next document and of *P.KRU* 106 below; probably the son of a witness to the previous document, reasoning from papponymy.

[2] Invocation Type **2E**: *CSBE* 2, 100, 104–5, 293 (= *SB* I 5562).

(Before?) our master Argama ibn Ered,[3] most renowned *amir* of the city of Hermonthis, (in) Kastron Memnonion, Jeme, Chaêl son of Psmô (being) *dioikêtês*.[4]

I Cyriac son of Demetrius, most God-loving priest and hegoumenos and superior of (the monastery of) the prize-bearing, crown-wearing combatant fair in victory, the holy Apa Phoibammon,[5] in the mountain of Jeme in the nome of the city of Hermonthis, subsequently putting in place for subscription a subscriber so he will subscribe for me, and some credible witnesses who will witness to this our sale, written so as to be untransgressable and unshakable by law, it rather being established at my very own request and by my intention, am writing to Aaron son of Shenoute, man of the same Kastron Jeme in the nome of the city of Hermonthis: Greetings. As follows:

I agree, I Cyriac the monk, son of the late Demetrius, the aforewritten, with you, you, Aaron, the buyer, whom I have clearly indicated[6] above, [by] this written document of sale, written so as to be warranted and straight in every single matter that is in this agreement, that I have sold to you, Aaron son of Shenoute, the fourth (part) of these two houses that now (have) belonged to me, (actually) half to Patermoute[7] and half to myself, lying in Kastron Jeme, as I am about to make plain, in Leek-Sellers' Street. (Boundaries are:) south, Lasan son of Paman (?); west, up to the wing (of the building [?]); north, Aaron son of Shoumara; east, the lane going in. And these are their boundaries round about, the two houses portions of which the sons of the late Pe{i}shate son of Pestine had given to the holy Apa Phoibammon in the mountain of Jeme as an offering for their poor souls, and lest I be condemned[8] at the [fearsome judgement-seat] of Christ and so that the holy martyr will not find fault with me[9] for having disbursed, whether for good or for ill [Greek], an offering (made) to him for the salvation of souls.

Accordingly, the result is that you, Aaron son of Shenoute, are to be owner of the portions of these houses of Peshate, because you have given their price to me, from hand to hand, in gold, as I came to an agreement about with you, namely, one gold solidus, = 1 sol. I have put it into the bank[10] for the poor and needy in the holy *topos*, for the repose of the soul of the late Peshate. And you,

---

[3] Listed in Till, *D&P*, 61.

[4] See Wickham, *Framing the Early Middle Ages*, 422 with n. 99; Till, *D&P*, 68; cf. *P.KRU* 17.

[5] See Godlewski, *Phoibammon*, 73.

[6] *saphênizein* (σαφηνίζειν).

[7] See below, *P.KRU* 12.

[8] *katakrinein* (κατακρίνειν): Förster, *WB*, 390.

[9] The titular saint of a monastery or church was regarded as the property owner/recipient: cf. Biedenkopf-Ziehner, *Schenkungsurkunden*, 95.

[10] *trapeza* (τράπεζα): as per R. Bogaert, "La banque en Égypte byzantine," *Zeitschrift für Papyrologie und Epigraphik* 116 (1997): 85–140: possibly also at this time (Förster, *WB*, 816) literally "table" as here "table of the poor," i.e., a charity food operation.

Aaron son of Shenoute, are to be owner of the portions of those houses that are made plain above, complete with their boundaries as above; and you, Aaron son of Shenoute, may administer them, manage them, build on them, dwell in them, exchange them, leave them to your sons and daughters, rent them out, give them away, dealing with them in full possession.[11]

And no man is to be able to proceed against you over the portions of those houses, neither myself nor brother nor sister nor relative in the first or in the second degree, neither kin nor kin of kin, neither stranger nor man of the house, nor anyone on my side, under any shape or form or allegation whatsoever; nor is he to be able to go to law with you in court or out of court, in city or in nome, or by any honored religious law[12] or any valid, prevailing rank, to make a long story short.

But if anyone should dare to, either now or at any time, first of all that person is to have no profit of it, but chiefly he is to be a stranger to the holy, venerated oath of Christians,[13] and is to receive the apportionment of Ananias and Sapphira his wife.[14] Subsequently he is to pay to account of fine twelve gold solidi, furnishing them out of his very own property into the hand of the honorable *amir*. And after the paying-in of the fine he is to appear and acknowledge this written document of sale that I have had drawn up, securing it for you, you, Aaron son of Shenoute, without any trickery or intimidation or compulsion or deception, with no seizure or circumscription,[15] with no necessity incumbent upon me, it being secure and having validity in every place where it may be produced in evidence.

They asked me, I agreed; they read it aloud to me, I heard it, I had it written down in this same Egyptian language, and I gave it forth.

+ I Patermoute son of the late Pestinos,[16] man of Kastron Jeme, I assent to this sale as it has been established, namely about the fourth (portion).—+ I Joannake son of John, I wrote for him and I bear witness. +

+ I Noah, priest and hegoumenos of the holy church of Jeme,[17] I bear witness. +++

+ I Samuel son of the late Enoch,[18] I bear witness at the request of Cyriac the hegoumenos and superior of the holy Apa Phoibammon in the mountain of Jeme. +

+ I Senouthios son of the late Apa Dios, I bear witness. +

---

[11] *nomê* (νομή).

[12] MacCoull, "ⲧⲩⲡⲟⲥ."

[13] Cf. Seidl, "Eid," 147, and *P.KRU* 12 just below (the counterpart of this document).

[14] Again Acts 5:1–10, so often invoked to intimidate would-be transgressors.

[15] Miswritten *paragraphê* (ⲡⲁⲣⲁⲅⲣⲁⲫⲏ).

[16] Not the (former) co-owner, whose document is the next one, but seemingly a person related to the original donors.

[17] Also a witness above in *P.KRU* 45/46, 21, and 42, and below in the counterpart piece, *P.KRU* 12 from eight days later.

[18] Also a witness in *P.KRU* 12 just below. Could he be the (former) chief of police of *P.KRU* 42, now retired from that post?

I Cyriac the aforewritten, I assent.

+ I Chmntsnêu, most humble priest and hegoumenos, son of Shenoute, I wrote with my hand at the request of Cyriac.[19] +

---

[19] Does this indicate that Abbot Cyriac could not do it himself, or just that he commissioned a scribe for this instrument?

P.KRU 12

Sale of House Property

DATE: 8 December 733

PLACE: Jeme

PARTIES: Patermouthios son of the late Constantine, seller; Aaron son of Shenoute, buyer

OBJECT: Fourth portions of two houses in Jeme

SUM [price]: 1 solidus

[fine]: 16 solidi

WITNESSES: 5

SCRIBE: Chmntsnêu, priest and hegoumenos (same scribe as of preceding)

PUBLICATION: Till, *KRUTheb*, 106–8

This piece is the counterpart to the preceding document: an instrument here drawn up by Abbot Cyriac's co-owner, a layman. It was written by the same scribe, eight days after the first piece of the pair.

+ In the na[me of the holy and life-giving, consubstantial Trinity,] Father, Son and Holy Ghost.[1] Written in the month of Choiak, [12, second indiction.] [Greek] Under our master Argama ibn Ered, most renowned *amir* of the city of Hermonthis; Chaêl being *dioikêtês* of Kastron Memnonion and *meizoteros*.[2]

I Patermouthios son of the late Constantine, man of Kastron Jeme in the nome of the city of Hermonthis, subsequently putting in place a subscriber so he will subscribe for me at the bottom of this written document of sale, written, laid down and untransgressable and un-undoable and indestructible by law, and making it yet more established through some other trustworthy witnesses who will witness it for me at my very own request and by my intention, am writing to Aaron son of Shenoute, man of the same Kastron Jeme in the nome of this city of Hermonthis: Greetings. As follows:

---

[1] Invocation Type **2E**: *CSBE 2*, 100, 104–5, 293 (= *SB* I 5561).

[2] Again, here = *lashane*; but cf. also Sarris, *Economy*, 76, 107 for earlier background. This is the Chaêl son of Psmô of *P.KRU* 17 and 13 above.

I agree, I Patermouthios son of the late Constantine, according to a written document of sale, written and straight in every single matter, this one that I have sought willingly and well persuaded, without any trickery or intimidation or compulsion or deception or seizure or circumscription, but rather of my very own free choice, swearing by God Almighty and the well-being of the lords who rule over us,[3] that I have sold to you, you, Aaron son of Shenoute, the buyer aforewritten, from now on for ever until all time to come, my portion of those houses in the "House of the Leek-Sellers" Street, lying in Kastron Jeme, namely one-fourth of those houses that came to me from my parents, from their foundations up to the air space, with all of their utensils appertaining thereto. And these are the boundaries of those houses: south, Lasan (son of) Paman; west, Palêu; ea[st, Pa]ul; north, the main gate and the lane going out. These are the boundaries of those houses.

[Patermouthios goes on to specify the same details as Cyriac had done in the preceding document: the price, one gold solidus by the standard of Kastron Jeme; Aaron's ownership rights; enumeration of persons who will not be allowed to sue him and of prohibited venues; a penalty clause making any future bringer of suit "a stranger to the holy, venerated oath of Christians, [here adding] the Father, the Son and the Holy Ghost" (and omitting Ananias and Sapphira). Here, though, the fine called for is sixteen solidi, not twelve.]

I have drawn up this written document of sale, secure and valid in every place. Subsequently I have asked some trustworthy witnesses to witness it for me. They read it aloud to me, I heard it, and I gave orders, they wrote it down in this same Egyptian language. I gave it forth according to the order[4] of the laws.

+ I Psêre son of the late Peter, by the mercy of God priest and hegoumenos of the holy church of Jeme,[5] I bear witness at the request of Patermouthios. +

+ I Demetrius son of the late Leontius,[6] I bear witness. +

+ I Noah son of Jeremias, priest and hegoumenos of the holy church of Jeme,[7] I bear witness at the request of Patermouthios. +++

+ I Samuel son of the late Enoch,[8] I bear witness at the request of Patermouthios son of Constantine. +

+ I Colluthus son of the late John, I bear witness at the request of the framer. +

+ I Chmntsnêu, most humble priest and hegoumenos, son of Shenoute, of the holy church of Jeme, I wrote it with my hand at the request of Patermouthios.

Written in the month of Choiak, 12, second indiction. [Greek]

---

[3] Seidl, "Eid," 141.
[4] *akolouthia* (ἀκολουθία).
[5] Known from *P.KRU* 21 and 3 above. See Till, *D&P*, 190.
[6] Known from *P.KRU* 21 above.
[7] Same as in *P.KRU* 45/46, 21, 42, and 13 above.
[8] Same as in *P.KRU* 13 above.

P.KRU 74

Testament

DATE: 28 December 733

PLACE: Jeme

PARTIES: Paul son of Ananias, testator; his wife Sarra, heiress designate, along with their daughter Susana and son David; also the St Phoibammon monastery

OBJECT: Money and house properties

SUM: [donation]: [lost]

[fine]: 4 oz. gold

WITNESSES: 3

SCRIBE: Elias son of Moses, priest

PUBLICATION: Till, *Erb*, 193–98; *SB Kopt.* II 954

In this will Paul of Jeme names his wife as heiress to all his property provided she continues to live in their house and does not remarry. He also leaves money to the St Phoibammon monastery as a pious offering. In addition, his daughter is to receive both money and a portion of the house he, Paul, inherited from his late mother; and his son gets a house for himself plus another house and a courtyard.

[In the name of the Father and of the Son and of the Holy] Ghost.[1] Today, the second [of the month of Tyb]i, in the sec[ond] indiction year. In the presence of the most honorable Elisha son of Elias and Peter son of N., *lashane*s of Kastron Jeme: Greetings.

I Paul, son of Ananias and Sarra, man of Kastron Jeme in the nome of the city of Hermonthis, am writing in this way, putting forth this donative testament which is a thing put forth,[2] immovable and untransgressable by law, putting in place the subscription of the one who will subscribe it and trustworthy witnesses for me who will witness for me to this will and testament at my request and under my very own direction.

---

[1] Invocation Type **2J**: *CSBE 2*, 100, 104–5, 294.

[2] *blêsis* (βλῆσις): Förster, *WB*, 137 though he is influenced by Preisigke's (*WB*) notion of "account"); really "an issuance."

There has come round to me the last thing, what everyone will have required of him,[3] because this is an unrevealed thing upon the earth since power and dominion do not belong to a man for ever, nor is there [an enduring] generation, according to the saying of Ecclesiastes [Ecclesiastes 1:4], and so I do not know when the hour of death is going to come upon me, or at what time, according to the saying of our Lord, "Watch therefore, for ye know neither the day nor the hour" [Matthew 25:13];[4] so, for the rest, looking at the death of everyone who has gone on before me, I called to mind my very own death. I was afraid lest in a sudden departure[5] and contrary to my expectation I end this life and undo my work, leaving it unplanned for and neglected, concerning the capital matter[6] of my offering and my burial preparations,[7] and the affairs of my children and my wife, and everything that is mine, lest it be dispersed.

Because of this I have proceeded to this testament which is my will, with my heart and my reasoning established, without any wandering (of mind), acting in accordance with my customary behavior,[8] with no compulsion upon me, nor any necessity nor deception nor circumscription nor . . . nor seizure, with no falsehood, with not one single necessity incumbent upon me, but rather of my very own free choice, and moreover swearing by the holy, consubstantial Trinity, the holy oath of Christians, and by the power and establishedness and continuance of our lords who have power upon the earth at the command of God Almighty,[9] and adjuring by fearsome oaths everyone who will read this immovable testament that no transgression will happen to it, but rather it will be untransgressable and uncircumscribable by law.

Subsequently I considered, in observation[10] of the human condition, that I was to make plain the whole entirety of my affairs while I was still alive, sleeping in my bed without a wandering mind and a dazed condition coming upon me. As follows: being still alive I am to become and be owner of all of what is mine, according to just law,[11] such that a man who becomes and is owner of all that is his can give it to whomever he wishes and deal with it in any manner, according to the whole desire of his soul. For the rest, I considered it with upright reasoning, that it is a just and fitting thing to reveal my speech in an established way, in writing, for a testament that is pre-established does not get set aside[12] or

---

[3] Cf. Luke 12:20.
[4] Cf. Matthew 24:42, and Mark 13:33.
[5] Literally "separation."
[6] *kephalaion* (κεφάλαιον).
[7] Again see Dunand, "Funerary Practices."
[8] *synêtheia* (συνήθεια).
[9] Cf. Seidl, "Eid," 140, 142–43.
[10] *skepsis* (σκέψις).
[11] Steinwenter, "ⲚⲞⲘⲞⲤ."
[12] *athetein* (ἀθετεῖν): Förster, *WB*, 15–16.

have (counter-)commands given about it, and the testament is established by the deceased person . . .

So, when what happens to everyone happens to me as well, and I leave behind this place of sojourning[13] and go the way of all the world, as everyone before me has done, according to the command of God the good Master of the universe, Sarra my wife is to become and be owner of all that is mine, in all matters, until she goes out of the body, (provided) she dwells in my space and does not dwell with a husband. And I wish and order that [x] solidi be given to the holy *topos* of Apa Phoibammon the mighty martyr for the salvation of my soul.

Subsequently Susana my daughter [is to get x] solidi from my inheritance, along with my portion of the house that came to me from my mother, according to my portion as they were (apportioned) severally to my mother's heirs. And David, my son, as well, is to get my house, in which he alone lives. Look, these are its boundaries: west, Symeon son of Tbenê; north, again Symeon son of Tbenê; east, the bakery of . . .; south, the public street that the main gate opens on to. Subsequently he is to get my other house—again he alone—that one that I acquired as my very own. And look, these are its boundaries in a quadrilateral: east, Jacob son of Simon; west, Sina son of Thesê; south, again Jacob son of Simon; north, the public street on to which the door of that house opens. These are its boundaries on all sides. And again he is to get my courtyard, this one that came to me partly by inheritance and partly by purchase: in short, that courtyard of mine, all mine up to the portion of Soua and the portion of George, which is the courtyard of Daniel son of David and Tellole, according to its boundaries round about, and these are: north, the courtyard of N.; . . ., the public street on to which the door opens.

Accordingly, with the result that this testament is established as to matter, it is written (so as to be) established and no man is to destroy it. And it is not possible for [me] or a son of mine or an heir of mine, or a relative in the first or the second degree, or my kin or kin of my kin, or for any man at all coming after me or representing me at any time or occasion, to be able to change[14] or alter what I have made clear,[15] as I have made it clear in this testament which is a will, or to go to law with my wife in any way, shape or form so as to transgress what I have commanded, whether on their own or through others or representatives, or by a commandment or order or great, valid [rank],[16] contrary to this will and testament, whether in court or out of court. For this is what I have had set down. [. . .]

And the man who will dare to proceed against my children or my wife, or should one of my children wish to go to law with the others or with his/her mother at any time or occasion, first of all he is to have no profit of that daring

---

[13] Cf. Psalm 38:12 and 1 Peter 1:17.
[14] Here the Christological word *shibe* (ϣⲓⲃⲉ).
[15] Here *saphēnizein* (σαφηνίζειν).
[16] Formulaically restoring *taxis* [ⲧⲁⲝⲓⲥ] and not Crum/Steindorff's *etouaab* [ⲉⲧⲟⲩⲁⲁⲃ].

that he has done, but rather he is to pay to account of fine as damages,[17] as the just laws have defined for one who dares to transgress a written document that is secured in this way with validity, and into the hand of the honored magistrate and the authority in office[18] at that time, four ounces of gold [as fine].—Later on he will have to go before the judgement-seat of the God of the universe to be judged for this subterfuge,[19] because he wished to undo the word of (the document's framer).—Thereupon he is to be admonished by the magistrate of that time to agree not to transgress anything written in this will and testament, and he is to appear and acknowledge every matter written therein. And subsequently this testament is to be secure and warranted and valid [in every place where it may be produced in evidence,] before any rule or authority [of whatever kind at any time. And I have put in place] witnesses to witness for me at my very own request. I finalized it, I gave it forth [as it stands above,] and I am quit.

+ I Paul son of Ananias, the aforewritten above, I assent to this testament as it is written. — + I Abraham son of the late Cyriac, he asked me, I wrote for him at his request.

... [I N. son of N.,] they reported to me[20] the words of this testament.

+ I Zacharias son of John, I bear witness.

+ I Joseph son of Palêtheos, I bear witness.—I Peter son of Theophilus, I wrote for him as he did not know how to write.

+ I Jacob son of Pashêm, I bear witness.—I Samuel son of Menas, I wrote for him as he did now know how to write.

+ I Elias son of Moses, most humble priest and lector of St Mary's,[21] I executed it.

---

[17] *katadikê* (καταδίκη): Förster, *WB*, 389.
[18] *prattesthai* (πράττεσθαι): "acting." Cf. Förster, *WB*, 670–71.
[19] Here a different meaning for *hypothesis* (ὑπόθεσις)!
[20] *apangellein* (ἀπαγγέλλειν): Förster, *WB*, 69.
[21] Papaconstantinou, "Sanctuaires de la Vierge," 88–89 (no. 17).

P.KRU 88
Donation of a Child Oblate

DATE: 8 March 734

PLACE: St Phoibammon monastery, Jeme

PARTIES: Theodore son of Aaron and his wife Mary, parents, donors

OBJECT: Sonchêm, their son, donated child

WITNESSES: 4

SCRIBE: Job son of Alexander

PUBLICATION: Till, *KRUTheb*, 165–66

With this document begins the well-known, much-studied series of child oblate donations (cf. also Godlewski, *Phoibammon*, 73–74). After earlier analysis by jurists, they have recently been put into historical, social, and economic context especially by the work of Arietta Papaconstantinou.[1] She views these documents as manifestations of the interaction between locally rooted Christian devotion and the increasing financial pressures imposed on Egypt's Christians by the Muslim rulers. Even more recently, T.S. Richter has studied the corpus of twenty-six of these documents as "mini-narratives,"[2] emotionally weighted autobiographical stories that were based on known biblical and hagiographical models. The children donated may have been those suffering from birth deficits, physical and/or mental, who would in the monastery receive care their parents could not provide ("Donation Documents," 256–61). The St Phoibammon monastery, recipient of the donated individuals, was also the bishop's residence and thus a redoubled locus of Christian power as it transformed from a city-based to a monastery-based structural model. Donated children were, according to Richter, also safeguarded from the slave trade. The entire corpus of child donation documents ought to be the object of an up-to-date study by a culturally aware historian well versed in the matters, now so much in the forefront of scholarship, of gender and property.

[Traces remain of an Arabic-language protocol which mentions "year 4. . ." (Diocletian year? If so, the year in question was Diocletian year 450) and the "chair of

---

[1] Papaconstantinou, "Notes sur les actes de donation d'enfant au monastère thébain de Saint-Phoibammon;" eadem, "ΘΕΙΑ ΟΙΚΟΝΟΜΙΑ: les actes thébains de donation d'enfants ou la gestion monastique de la pénurie," *Travaux et mémoires* 14 (2002): 511–26.

[2] Richter, "Cultural Narratology and Coptic Child Donation Documents."

the church of Alexandria", i.e., the patriarchal throne; the patriarch at this date was Theodore (731–743).[3]]

+ In the name of the holy and life-giving, consubstantial Trinity, Father, Son and Holy Ghost.[4] Month of Phamenoth, 12, indiction 2. [Greek]

With God. I Theodore the builder, son of Aaron, am writing today for all time and eternity to you, you, Peter, superior of the holy Apa Phoibammon in the mountain of Jeme, Cyrus son of Chaêl and Psmô being *dioikêtai* of Kastron Jeme by the will of God Almighty.[5]

I Theodore am writing today to donate Sonchêm my son whom I engendered of my body[6] from his mother Mary, donating him and giving him by vow to the holy *topos* of the holy Apa Phoibammon in the mountain of Jeme, for all the days of his life, so that it (the *topos*) will become and be his lord[7] all the days of his life, he being a servant[8] to it and giving it his efforts all the days of his life: because God brought a sickness upon him, according to His will, since his childhood. I took him, I brought him to the *topos* of the holy Apa Phoibammon; I put him there, I asked him, and he asked God: He graced him with healing. I said in my very own agreement with his mother Mary that we should donate him as a donation to the holy *topos* of the holy Apa Phoibammon so that he would become its servant forever, so as to give all his effort, as God would assign for him, to the holy martyrion.

And no man is to dare to go to law with or proceed against this *topos*, nor proceed against it over Sonchêm my son, or dare to do so at all over this matter in (any) way, or before (any) authority, in village or in city, in the praetorium or outside the praetorium. First of all that man is to have no profit of it, but rather is

---

[3] Cf. L.S.B. MacCoull, "Redating the Inscription of El-Moallaqa," *Zeitschrift für Papyrologie und Epigraphik* 64 (1986): 230–34; repr. in eadem, *Coptic Perspectives on Late Antiquity*, no. XIV, and now J. van der Vliet, "Perennial Hellenism: László Török and the al-Mu'allaqa Lintel (Coptic Museum inv.no. 753)," *Eastern Christian Art* 4 (2007): 77–80.

[4] Invocation Type **2E**: *CSBE 2*, 100, 104–5, 294 (= *SB* I 5599).

[5] These data differ from what is recorded in Till's lists in *D&P* 234–36, esp. 235; he thought "κύριος" was a title here, and Psmô was Chaêl's patronymic.

[6] Literally "limb[s]," *melos* (μέλος).

[7] The same word as that used for "owner," *joeis* (ⲭⲟⲉⲓⲥ).

[8] *hmhal* (ϩⲙϩⲁⲗ): this word, coupled with the word *joeis* (ⲭⲟⲉⲓⲥ), has occasioned much discussion by jurists about the possibly 'unfree' status of the oblate: see now Papaconstantinou, "Donation d'enfants," 92–93, 96–99, and Richter, "Donation Documents," 243–44. There are two Coptic terms for "slave", *hmhal* (ϩⲙϩⲁⲗ), connoting a small or young servant, and *chaouon* (ϭⲁⲟⲩⲟⲛ), usually thought to be closer to "chattel slave". This probably goes back to the distinction in Roman law between categories of laborers (*CJ* 11.68.3). Cf. J. Banaji, "Aristocracies, Peasantries and the Framing of the Early Middle Ages," *Journal of Agrarian Change* 9 (2009): 59–91, here 74. However, compare the phraseology of the later *P.KRU* 104, below.

to become and be a stranger to the Father and the Son and the Holy Ghost, and is to receive the apportionment of Judas and the apportionment of Ananias and Sapphira his wife,⁹ and the God of the holy martyr Apa Phoibammon will wreak vengeance on him, because he so much as dared to enter the holy place.

Accordingly, for security, I Theodore, and Mary his [sic] wife, we have drawn up this donation document for you, you, the most pious Peter, the superior of the holy Apa Phoibammon, myself witnessing to it and assenting to it. +++

I Papas son of Stephen, I bear witness. +
+ I Umai son of Zaêl, I bear witness.
+ I Paul son of Kanah, man of Romoou,¹⁰ I bear witness.
+ I Souai son of George, man of Timeshor,¹¹ I bear witness.
+ I Job [son of Alexander, I wrote it at the request of Theodore.]
+ Written by me, Job son of Alexander [Greek].

---

⁹ Especially appropriate in this situation, the boy being in a sense "church property".
¹⁰ Unclear.
¹¹ Timm, *Ägypten*, 6: 2681.

P.KRU 78

Donation of a Child Oblate

DATE: 28 September–27 October, [early 8th century]

PLACE: St Phoibammon monastery, Jeme

PARTIES: John son of Victor, father, donor

OBJECT: Victor, his son, donated child

SUM: 1 solidus per year (from labor, to be paid to the monastery)

WITNESSES: 4

SCRIBE: [unnamed; the framer himself?]

PUBLICATION: Till, *KRUTheb*, 149–50

Another somewhat early child donation, included for example and comparison. As often in these cases, the child's parent is making the offering in gratitude for the child's miraculous healing by the saint. Victor, the donated son, is contracted to pay the monastery one solidus a year (on this provision see Papaconstantinou, "Donation d'enfants," 97). Further on the child's legal status see Richter, "Donation Documents," 243–44.

[beginning not preserved]
 + This donation document, untransgressable, un[shakable], eternal, un-undoable for [ever, I have drawn it] up with a pure heart, with a [mind] sure and an intent[1] [fixed] and reasoning unchanging, I John son of Victor, man of Kastron Jeme, this day today, being the month of Phaophi, [x, y] D.V. indiction,[2] and itself... [. . .]. In an orderly fashion and going through with it [Greek], I give and donate to the holy *topos* of Apa Phoibammon in the mountain of Jeme through its [oikonomos] at the time, so as to receive him by its holy *oikonomia*, Victor my legitimately-born son[3] whom I engendered in the manner of all men. After three years since he was born he fell into a great sickness; accordingly, when

---

[1] *skopos* (σκοπός): Förster, *WB*, 738.
[2] Till, *KRUTheb*, 149 read a form of *epinemêsis* (ἐπινέμησις), for which see *CSBE 2*, 11 n.36, 31–32.
[3] The practice of papponymy is still alive: the grandson Victor is named for his grandfather.

he continued in the sickness with no healing coming to him, I took thought,[4] I vowed him to the [holy] *topos* of Apa Phoibammon in the mountain of Jeme, saying, "If the God of the holy Apa Phoibammon graces him with healing, I shall donate him to it, and he will become a contributor[5] to it all his life, (at the rate of) a solidus per year, in perpetuity." Accordingly (for) the feeding and the mastery[6] of Victor my son, the aforewritten, I donate (him) to the aforedesignated *topos*, to be there from today, accordingly, the aforewritten (day). The governing board[7] of the holy *topos* of the holy Apa Phoibammon in the mountain of Jeme through its oikonomos at the time will undertake by its holy *oikonomia* that Victor my son will be under the obedience of the holy *topos* for ever, and will be so as to give a solidus, the same each year, without any other (requirement) save this 1 sol. of full weight, not being disobedient . . . [break in manuscript]

It is not possible for me or my heirs or those related to me, or a man of my village or any other man at all, to overturn[8] this donation document or undo it or draw up a counsel of ingratitude against it on any occasion or at any time, or for us to say "We wish to undo it," or "We regret this written document," or "We give another opinion[9] against it, it is (to be) null and void," or for us to act against it by any means, in court or out of court, with church or lay help or (with the help of) some higher authority. Rather I agree that I and those who come after me for ever will not seek to take back[10] from the holy *topos* of the holy Apa Phoibammon of Jeme the freeing[11] of my son Victor whom I have donated thereto, even if it should seem good to us, to me or any other man at all who may in any way, shape or form at all seek to transgress all the things I have said in this donation document.

For myself or whoever may dare to do this, first of all that man is to have no profit of it, but rather is to be liable to the reproach[12] and the peril of the holy oath. Subsequently he is to become and be a stranger to God Almighty, and be subject to the great curse that the Lord uttered in Deuteronomy,[13] to Moses because he dared to act in this way. But the one who observes this donation to the holy *topos*, the God of the holy Apa Phoibammon will watch over[14] him and all his house.

---

[4] *prosdokein* (προσδοκεῖν): Förster, *WB*, 687.
[5] From the Byzantine *syntelein* (συντελεῖν), as in the earlier documents above.
[6] *despoteia* (δεσποτεία): Förster, *WB*, 165.
[7] *dikaion* (δίκαιον), a technical term: cf. Förster, *WB*, 194–95: really the monastery as a legal person that is entitled to receive donations and own property.
[8] *anatrepein* (ἀνατρέπειν): Förster, *WB*, 53.
[9] Literally "voice."
[10] *aposobein* (ἀποσοβεῖν): Förster, *WB*, 87.
[11] *katharopoiêsis* (καθαροποίησις), literally "cleansing": Förster, *WB*, 359.
[12] *enklêma* (ἔνκλημα): Förster, *WB*, 225.
[13] Deuteronomy 28:15–68, 29:20–27.
[14] The same verb as that just translated "observe", *hareh* (ϨⲀⲢⲈϨ).

It is secured to the governing board of the monastery of Apa Phoibammon in the mountain of Jeme and the oikonomos of the time, who will undertake the holy *oikonomia* of the monastery.

I have drawn up this donation document; I assent to it; and I bear witness [to it.]

+ I John son of Victor, man of Kastron Jeme, I assent to this donation document as it is written.

+ I Pamp(repius) son of Chaêl, I bear witness.

+ Thomas son of N., I bear witness.

+ Menas son of the late John, I bear witness.

+ Pesau son of Pesyntheus, man of Tsê,[15] I bear witness.

---

[15] Timm, *Ägypten*, 6: 2851–52.

P.KRU 104

Document of Self-Oblation by an Adult

DATE: 771/72
PLACE: St Phoibammon monastery
PARTIES: Petronius son of George
OBJECT: himself
WITNESSES: [not preserved]
SCRIBE: [unnamed]
PUBLICATION: Till, *KRUTheb*, 186–89

This document is included here, though a bit late in date (cf. Godlewski, *Phoibammon*, 75) for the present selection, for its value as a unique example of an adult male, in gratitude for miraculous healing from sickness, willingly binding himself as a servant (ϨΜϨΑΛ) to the monastery of St Phoibammon. Though older legal studies linked such a practice all the way back to the Pharaonic Egyptian practice of *hierodulia*, attested in Demotic documents,[1] this phenomenon[2] is better viewed in the context of a late offshoot of Byzantine piety,[3] as well as an economic safety move.[4]

[Invocation lost] [I Petronius son of George, . . . , with no necessity incum]bent upon me, with no [trickery] or intimidation or seizure or cirumscription, but with sober mind and unchanged reasoning and unrepented decision[5] and an un-self-deceived conviction towards God, proceeding in obedience to the laws that our lords

---

[1] Cf. M. Depauw, *A Companion to Demotic Studies* (Brussels, 1997), 136–37; however, sensibly contra, see Richter, "Donation Documents," 248–49.
[2] For "auto-dedition" in medieval western Europe see D. Barthélemy, *La mutation de l'an Mil: a-t-elle eu lieu? Servage et chevalerie dans le France des Xe et XIe siècles* (Paris, 1997), 57–91.
[3] See Papaconstantinou, "Donation d'enfants," 93.
[4] Cf. Richter, "Donation Documents," 241–44.
[5] *gnômê* (γνώμη).

the kings have ordered,[6] (am writing) as follows: It is possible[7] for each person to do what he wishes with what is his own.[8] I too have made a determination according to the ordering[9] of the laws that our lords ordered from the first.[10]

I have proceeded in writing to the governing board of the holy monastery of the prize-bearing, victory-bearing [ho]ly Abba Phoibammon the martyr, that lies in the mountain of Jeme in the nome of the city of Hermonthis, as follows:

WHEREAS: In this year, the 10th indiction D.V. by God's will, God, the good, who judges and works miracles,[11] brought upon me a great sickness. I was overwhelmed; I wasted away as though deathly blight were upon me. Some faithful men said to me, "Beseech the God of the holy Apa Phoibammon: He will have mercy on you." I got myself a sober mind (and) a faithful wish of my heart. I sent to the holy *topos* of the holy Abba Phoibammon. I took water from the holy basin[12] that is before the sanctuary, from the holy hands of that oikonomos. They came, they poured it over me, and straightaway the Lord heard my weeping and my crying out,[13] and He graced me with healing. I rested from the great sickness, and a great joy came upon me. I said to myself, "It is meet and right[14] that I donate my body to him (St Phoibammon), because well-being/salvation[15] came to me through his intercession."

And now, God willing, from today on no man is to be owner/lord[16] over my body, save only the holy monastery of the holy Abba Phoibammon the great martyr that lies in the holy mountain of Jeme, and I, the aforenamed above, shall become and be a servant/slave[17] thereto, performing its commands like a servant/slave bought with money.

Anyone who dares to go to law with the holy *topos* undertaking to undo this offering of this my body that I have donated, first of all he is to have no profit of it, but rather he will be liable to the judgement of God Almighty the true Creator,[18]

---

[6] By the Abbasid period it is not completely clear what may have been intended by the notary who set down this time-honored Byzantine-style phrase. Does it reflect a consciousness that Christian subjects of the Abbasid-ruled state had to justify their practices with one eye on Muslim regulations and the other on their Roman heritage?

[7] *exesti* (ἔξεστι).

[8] Cf. above, *P.KRU* 69; noticed by Richter, "Donation Documents," 242.

[9] *akolouthia* (ἀκολουθία).

[10] Cf. above n. 6.

[11] Cf. Psalm 135:4.

[12] *loutêr* (λουτήρ) (Förster, *WB*, 484); cf. Schmelz, *Kirchliche Amtsträger*, 108.

[13] Cf. Psalm 6:8–9.

[14] *ôshe* (ⲱϣⲉ [= *axion* (ἄξιον)]) *kai dikaion* (καὶ δίκαιον): exactly the words used in the eucharistic liturgy before the Sanctus.

[15] *oujai* (ⲟⲩϫⲁⲓ).

[16] *joeis* (ϫⲟⲉⲓⲥ).

[17] *hmhal* (ϩⲙϩⲁⲗ), here and in the next phrase.

[18] Literally "Demiurge."

and the holy Abba Phoibammon will wreak revenge on him before the fearsome judgement-seat of God. Subsequently he is to become and be a stranger to the Father and the Son and the Holy Ghost. And again I request every authority into whose hands this document may come to see to it that it is established, because the Lord has blessed it since it is an *agapê* for God. And again you are all, my brothers, to know that it is not right for someone to give a gift and then say "I am taking it back." My brothers, do not be like those who break promises to the Lord, and do not inherit their dwelling-place, because this matter did not come about through us, but rather though Samuel the prophet, who donated himself to the temple of the Lord.[19]

This matter stands since we have drawn up this donation document, Abba Sourous the deacon[20] being superior over the holy *topos* of the holy Abba Phoibammon that lies in the mountain of Jeme, and the great pronoêtês and curator, *kyrios* Psmô[21] the great magistrate, being *dioikêtês* over Kastron Jeme.

I Petronius son of George, I have established it with the governing board of the holy monastery. I asked the notary[22] and other trustworthy, credible witnesses to witness it according to the force of the laws. They read it aloud to us, we recognized its validity, we consented together, we approved it and established it. I set it down, God willing.

---

[19] Actually according to 1 Samuel 1:5–28, 2:18, his mother Hannah donated the infant Samuel to the temple in gratitude for her childbearing. This text was always used as a pattern for the practice of child oblation: see M. de Jong, *In Samuel's Image: Child Oblation in the Early Medieval West* (Leiden, 1996); and Richter, "Donation Documents," 246–48, 254–56. Here Petronius changes the story to justify what he himself has done.

[20] As well as Till, *D&P*, 204–5, 236, see Papaconstantinou, *Saints*, 208–9.

[21] So Till, *KRUTheb*, 188; but cf. *D&P* 35.

[22] *siliômatougraphos* (ⲥⲓⲗⲓⲱⲙⲁⲧⲟⲩⲅⲣⲁⲫⲟⲥ) for *synallagmatographos* (συναλλαγματογρά-φος): Förster, *WB*, 728.

P.KRU 106

Donation of Property to a Monastery

DATE: 31 May 734

PLACE: Jeme

PARTIES: Anna, daughter of the late John and Taham, donatrix; monastery of St Paul (represented by Zacharias, its superior, and two other monastic officers, Philotheus and Mena), recipient

OBJECT: One house, portion of another house, part of a bakery, and land

SUM [fine]: 1 lb. gold

WITNESSES: 5

SCRIBE: Chmntsnêu son of Shenoute, priest and hegoumenos[1]

PUBLICATION: Till, *Erb*, 205–12

Here, in strongly scriptural phrases, Anna, a single woman motivated by experience of illness, donates her inherited house property, some land, and part of a bakery to the St Paul monastery of Jeme for the salvation of her soul and for charity to the poor (cf. Schmelz, *Kirchliche Amtsträger*, 170). The properties may be sold and the money used for the charitable purposes she specifies. This text is discussed and a section translated in Wilfong, *Women*, 85–86, 99.

[Traces remain of an Arabic-language protocol datable to A.D. 732.]
 + In the name of the holy, life-giving, consubstantial Trinity, Father, Son and Holy Ghost.[2] + Written in the month of Payni, 6, indiction 3; under Mamet [=Muhammad][3] the *amir*, most renowned *amir* of the pagarchy of Hermonthis, and Chaêl son of Psmô,[4] most magnificent *dioikêtês* of Kastron Memnonion, year of Diocletian the king 451, and year of the Saracens 114.[5] +++ [Greek]

---

[1] Also the scribe of *P.KRU* 13 and 12 above.

[2] Invocation Type **2E**: *CSBE 2*, 100, 104–5, 294 (= *SB* I 5609).

[3] Now the pagarch is a Muslim. See Frantz-Murphy, *Agricultural Leases*, 24, 26; and eadem, "Land-Tenure," 244–45; Sijpesteijn, "Landholding Patterns in Early Islamic Egypt," 121–23, 128–30.

[4] The *lashane* in P.KRU 17, 13, and 12 above.

[5] For both of these designations, newly appeared in our phraseology, see *CSBE 2*, 63–68, 74 with n. 42 (pointing out the discrepancy), 300–2.

+ I Anna daughter of the late John and the late Taham, people of Kastron Jeme in the nome of the city of Hermonthis, subsequently putting in place the subscription[6] by the hand of the one who is to subscribe for me, am writing to the God-honored, honorable brother Abba Zacharias, the great superior,[7] and Abba Philotheus and Abba Mena his fellow officeholders[8] and great monks of the holy place which is the congregation in the holy,[9] holy[10] monastery[11] of St Paul of Koulol in the mountain of Jeme,[12] as follows:

I rejoice and I agree, I, now, this poor Anna the aforewritten, through this written donation document, composed in Egyptian,[13] un-undoable and unshakable for ever, having established it by the laws in place,[14] with no necessity incumbent upon me, with no trickery or intimidation or compulsion or deception or seizure or circumscription at all, but rather in desire unregretted and reasoning unaltered, without duality of heart, in an understanding[15] with no trickery in it, and with an upright heart and established faith that is perfected in every just lordship/ownership,[16] without compulsion,[17] without deception, without seizure, without (undue) influence,[18] free from all danger, but of my very own free will, with unchanged intent[19] and alert mind, being alive, walking to and fro under my body's own power,[20] with my purpose[21] fixed:

I am now asking the scribe to establish for me, by my desire and will, the donation document, by his hand, and again those who will witness it, this donation instrument[22] that is untransgressable and not to be set aside by law, writing from now on for all time: writing now that I am making a donation to the holy monastery of this very one at present who sheds light and shines with his rays of light, by

---

[6] The feminine abstract noun *hypographê* (ὑπογραφή).

[7] Till, *D&P*, 236.

[8] *synkathedros* (συνκάθεδρος): Förster, *WB*, 763.

[9] *hagia* (ϨΑΓΙΑ).

[10] *etouaab* (ⲈⲦⲞⲨⲀⲀⲂ).

[11] Here the Coptic *heneete* (ϨⲈⲚⲈⲈⲦⲈ), not the Greek *monastêrion* (ⲘⲞⲚⲀⲤⲦⲎⲢⲒⲞⲚ).

[12] As above, in *P.CLT* 1, 2, 4, and 5.

[13] Here *Aigyptiakê* (ⲀⲒⲄⲨⲠⲦⲒⲀⲔⲎ), not *rmnkême* (ⲢⲘⲚⲔⲎⲘⲈ).

[14] Cf. Steinwenter, "ⲚⲞⲘⲞⲤ."

[15] Reading *synainesis* (συναίνεσις) (as per Förster, *WB*, 773) for Crum/Steindorff's *synêtesis* (ⲤⲨⲚⲎⲦⲈⲤⲒⲤ) (Till, *Erb*, 206 proposed *syneidêsis* [συνείδησις] as recorded in Förster's lemma, *WB*, 776).

[16] *mntjoeis* (ⲘⲚⲦϪⲞⲈⲒⲤ).

[17] Here *bia* (βία): all four of these "without" phrases are in Greek, including the preposition *chôris* (χωρίς).

[18] *epirhoia* (ἐπίρροια): Förster, *WB*, 282.

[19] *skopos* (σκοπός).

[20] Cf. *P.Lond.* I 77.12; and above, *P.KRU* 68.

[21] *dianoia* (διάνοια): Förster, *WB*, 186.

[22] Literally "sale", *prâsis* (πρᾶσις).

means of his prayers and his holy way of life,[23] reaching up to heaven, the anchorite and citizen (of heaven) and blessed ascetic, the holy Apa Paul,[24] at the hands of your God-honored brother Abba Zacharias the great superior and his other brothers and fellow officeholders with him, Philotheus and Mena, and of those who will come after them at the time, following the succession of administration:

WHEREAS: In these present times into which we have come, God, the good and merciful,[25] opened my heart to cast in this my tiny little mite, according to the word of my Lord that He spoke in the holy gospels about the two mites of the widow that she cast into the treasury [Mark 12:41–44, Luke 21:1–4].[26] She reached for a lot, but did not find that she had a lot to cast in, save for two mites: but the Lord rejoiced over them. Now I too, this poor one, looking at how her time (has come), I have come to know, through the great sickness into which I gave fallen, that I am approaching my end, as the holy prophet said: "Lord, let me know mine end [Psalm 38:4]." Accordingly, in accordance with the will of the good God I was caused to fall into this sickness now, so that I am to go the way of all my ancestors, and I am afraid, lying on my bed and looking around me, back and forth, again and again, yet not finding any way to get a little rest in the place I need. So God put it into my heart that I should make a donation of this little memorial to the holy monastery, this present one aforenamed,[27] whose holy public designation[28] is above in this donation document, the holy Apa Paul's of Kolol, the great anchorite: first of all so that his supplications and his holy intercessions may obtain favor for me before the true Judge, and so that my little memorial may remain concerning the great *agapê* now practiced towards the poor who come to the holy monastery,[29] and concerning what the brothers have said about the poor and needy, as the tongue of sweet-smelling incense, the holy Paul the apostle,[30] said: "Love (*agapê*) never faileth [1 Corinthians 13:8]"

---

[23] *politeia* (πολιτεία) (the usage in hagiography); cf. Förster, *WB*, 661.

[24] See Papaconstantinou, *Saints*, 170–71.

[25] Phraseology possibly influenced, by now, by the Koran that Christian Egyptians would have heard recited around them: cf. T.S. Richter, "Arabische Lehnworte und Formeln in koptischen Rechtsurkunden," *Journal of Juristic Papyrology* 31 (2001): 75–89; and idem, "Emergence of Arabic Words in Coptic Legal Documents;" also idem, "Greek, Coptic, and the 'Language of the Hijra'."

[26] Using the same words, *lepton/lepta* (λεπτόν/λεπτά) and *gazophylakion* (γαζοφυλάκιον).

[27] *-onomaze* (-ⲟⲛⲟⲙⲁⲍⲉ).

[28] *stêliteusis* (στηλίτευσις): not in Förster, *WB*; not translated by Till, *Erb*, 207; an interesting and rare loanword manifesting semantic shift. Earlier on it had developed a negative connotation, meaning public display for purposes of condemnation (and so used in the 5th to 8th centuries according to Lampe and the TLG): but here it is used quite neutrally.

[29] Cf. Papaconstantinou, *Saints*, 317ff., and Schmelz, *Kirchliche Amtsträger*, 170.

[30] On this Pauline designation and image (2 Corinthians 2:14–16) and what underlies them see S. A. Harvey, *Scenting Salvation: Ancient Christianity and the Olfactory*

and "Mercy rejoiceth against judgement [James 2:13]." Accordingly, reflecting on this, I again remembered what our fathers the holy apostles said in the holy Catholic Epistles, "The prayer of a righteous man availeth much and is powerful [James 5:16]." And again so that my little memorial may be an offering for my poverty, because I have no one and I know that my sins are many—for I have examined my thoughts concerning my sins, for there is no person living who has not sinned against You (God) [Romans 3:23]; even if he lived on earth for only a single hour[31] he would not evade sin, according to the saying that our Lord uttered to our father Adam: "Adam, dust thou art and unto dust shalt thou return [Genesis 3:19]";[32] and when I heard these sayings thus on my bed I was afraid[33] owing to the sickness that lay upon me, and I remembered the fear of God and the judgement at which there is no respecting of persons, concerning my poor soul. And this is man's apportionment[34] all the days of his life, as the wise Ecclesiastes said: "There is nothing better for a man than that he should give requital for his soul [Ecclesiastes 3:22]"; and again as our Lord said in the holy gospels, "Watch, for ye know not the day nor the hour; ye know not at what hour the master of the house will come [Matthew 25:13, 24:42]."

When I remembered these things I perceived my sins. I sought with a fixed mind, sitting upon my bed, to reveal my affairs so as not to leave them disordered concerning the clothing of my weak body.[35] And as to my offering, I am now donating and giving away[36] to the holy monastery of the holy Apa Paul the anchorite and holy archimandrite who took pains in apostolic sweat, at your hands, Abba Zacharias and Abba Philotheus and Abba Mena, (to) the superiors and the oikonomoi at (whatever) time from today on and for ever to all time, the little house that belongs to me, which is my little house that came to me from my late father John. This house accordingly I am thus donating to the holy monastery,[37] together with all its utensils reckoned thereto, with its doors and windows, with its upper parts and back parts, simply put, from a small form of article to (even)

Imagination (Berkeley, 2006), 18–19, 114–15, 247 n. 39; and Cyril's commentary on the Pauline passage in PG 74.925B-928A, Cyril being the father whose exegesis carried most weight in the Coptic church.

[31] Compare the sixth-century anaphora attributed to Timothy III of Alexandria: ". . . for there is no man who lives and does not sin, even if his life(-span) on the earth were to be (just) one hour . . .": "Anaphora Syriaca Timothei Alexandrini," ed. A. Rücker, in *Anaphorae Syriacae*, 1.1 (Rome, 1939), 3–47, here 38–39. (Till [*Erb*, 207] translates 2ooy as "day" but it should be "hour.")

[32] Again here literally "you are earth and you will sleep in earth".

[33] Cf. Habakkuk 3:2.

[34] Cf. Ecclesiastes 3:22.

[35] Dunand, "Funerary Practices."

[36] *apotassein* (ἀποτάσσειν): Förster, *WB*, 90–91; here a lay person giving something away, not a monastic person "renouncing" (the other connotation).

[37] Here *heneete* (ϨΕΝΕΕΤΕ).

the least thing, so that it may belong to the holy monastery[38] as an offering on behalf of my poverty of soul, through the Lord God Who transcends all things.

This house, accordingly, I thus give and give away, from now on for ever: this very one that lies in this same Kastron Memnonion in this street that is called Methuselah Street. And these are its neighboring boundaries surrounding it on its four sides in a quadrilateral according to its ancient boundaries: they are: east, Cross Street;[39] south, the street again (Methuselah St.); north, Victor son of Staphôra;[40] west, Main Gate Street, with its door opening thereonto. These are the boundaries of the house, thusly, in quadrilateral, it being the house of my late father John. And likewise again I am donating to the holy place my other portion of the house of my late mother Taham, namely half of that house; this, then, lies in St. Ananias[41] Street; and also again my other portion of the lands that I possess (jointly) with Abraham son of Athanasius;[42] and also again the quarter portion of the bakery that lies in . . . [gap in manuscript].

These are all of them that I have clearly indicated[43] in this written donation document. And now I am donating them for ever, for all time, so they will come to belong to the holy monastery (*m.*) of St Paul. They are to become and be in appurtenance to the holy monastery (*h.*), and are to be under the obedience of the holy place from generation to generation.

And as for you, the superiors of the holy monastery, it is thereby for you to be owners of these structures,[44] in the way I have made plain above, from their foundations up to the air spaces, and of all their utensils reckoned thereto, from a great form of item to a very humble, and from the most valuable to the cheapest, whether door or window or beam or wooden article or ceramic vessel, an item of iron or one of stone, in a word, movable, immovable or self-moving. And yours is to be the possession of and authority over these structures, thusly, you, the God-honored brother Abba Zacharias the superior and Abba Philotheus and Abba Mena, and the other fathers, the superiors who will come after you at whatever time. And you are to be their (the structures') owners in all just

---

[38] Here *monastêrion* (ⲘⲞⲚⲀⲤⲦⲎⲢⲒⲞⲚ).

[39] For these street names in Jeme see Timm, *Ägypten*, 3: 1018–19.

[40] Probably the son of one of the witnesses below. The name Staphora/e is still attested at Jeme in 759, in *P.KRU* 20 = *KSB* II 947.131, a document written by the scribe Mark son of the late Anastasius, who also confuses invocation and oath formulary as we have seen John son of Lazarus do.

[41] Papaconstantinou, *Saints*, 48–49; cf. Schmelz, *Kirchliche Amtsträger*, 94; and H. Behlmer, "Christian Use of Pharaonic Sacred Space in Western Thebes," in *Sacred Space and Sacred Function in Ancient Thebes*, ed. P.F. Dorman and B.M. Bryan (Chicago, 2007), 163–75, here 167–68 for this sainted bishop of Hermonthis.

[42] Nothing is said further about this person or the nature of the co-ownership.

[43] *saphênizein* (σαφηνίζειν).

[44] *oikodomê* (οἰκοδομή): Förster, *WB*, 562.

ownership, to leave them, sell them and take their price to be spent for the sake of the holy monastery and the *agapê* of the poor; to donate them, give them away, exchange them, transform them into workshops, tear them down, build on to them upwards, pledge them as collateral: in short, whatever you intend for them, that to do, in any fashion you wish, without let and without hindrance to you, in any way at all whatsoever. Wherefore this is the way I have set up my memorial: may this also be for a remembrance of me before God and for the repose of my poor soul on the Day of Judgement.

Which—may it not happen![45]—but if this should happen, that someone should say at some time, (someone) of my heirs or of my kin or my kin's kin, or either one from my family or a stranger from outside my family, or any man at all representing me, wishing to put forth any word[46] at all that is in contradiction to this donation document, any person at any time wishing to summon[47] you or bring an action against[48] you over this donation document, or saying that I executed an action that was not mine to execute, or wishing to break or destroy anything of what I said, with which I was satisfied—because this is my offering and I took care over the holy offering for you and for God, speaking with you, the superiors whose names I have revealed—so then, knowing the *agapê* and the spirit[49] within your hearts with regard to the poor, being still in my body and moreover seeing with my eyes that you are perfect monks of God, I undertook to set up this my humble statement for you.

And I adjure you by God and I swear to you that you are not to forget and destroy anything of what I have said concerning my offering. Anyone wishing to destroy anything from this donation document and all matters written therein, whether through an authority of an emperor[50] of this world,[51] or (authority) priestly or lay or monastic, anyone at all who shall call into question this donation document, first of all my holy father St Paul will wreak vengeance on him, and he will be judged at the judgement-seat of God concerning my offering, because it is for the salvation of my soul: but my desire will be fulfilled when you (pl.) are owners of the utensils and of those structures in this way, you, the superiors, these that I have donated, so that you can manage them, cede them, sell them, rent them out, dealing with them, in short, in any fashion that pleases you.

And no one is to be able—neither brother nor sister nor relative in the first or in the second degree, nor stranger nor kin [nor kin of ki]n, nor anyone in any

---

[45] Greek: *hoper mê genoito* (ὅπερ μὴ γένοιτο) (spelled *geneto* [ⲅⲉⲛⲉⲧⲟ]).
[46] Or "discourse", *shaje* (ϣⲁϫⲉ).
[47] *enkalein* (ἐνκαλεῖν).
[48] *anapoiêsthai* (ἀναποιῆσθαι): Förster, *WB*, 64.
[49] Till, *Erb*, 210 prefers *na* (ⲛⲁ) "mercy"; but I opt to read *pn(eum)a* (ⲡⲛ(ⲉⲩⲙ)ⲁ) "spirit."
[50] *autokratôr* (αὐτόκρατωρ): Förster, *WB*, 124; cf. *CSBE* 2, 252–72 for Byzantine emperors.
[51] Now the caliph in Damascus: in 734 it was Hisham.

way, shape or form — to act against this donation document, in court or out of court, or in any praetorium, or by any glorious, venerated religious law,[52] through a great, holy constitution[53] or valid, prevailing rank,[54] in any way at all, in short. But if anyone dares to, now or at any time, first of all that person is to have no profit of it, but rather the curse of the scriptures will come upon him[55] and he will perish together with all that is his, and he will be in fear at this voice saying (as) in the holy gospels it says, "These, for their part, will go away into everlasting punishment [Matthew 25:46]." And secondly, he will be a stranger to the Father and the Son and the Holy Ghost, and will receive the apportionment of Judas Iscariot, the one who betrayed the Lord,[56] and the apportionment of Ananias and Sapphira his wife.[57] And again subsequently he is pay out to account of fine, by law and to the authority in power at that time, a pound of gold as fine, = AV L. 1, one only. And after the paying-in[58] of this fine, this donation document is to be in force and possess an establishedness for ever and from generation to generation. And I adjure you (pl.) by God Almighty, you, every authority into whose hands this donation document shall come, that you not allow anything of it to be destroyed.

Securing it for you (pl.), you, the superiors of the holy monastery (m.) of the holy Apa Paul, the monastery (h.) of the Kolol in the mountain of Jeme, and its oikonomoi at whatever time succeeding, I have drawn up for you this written donation document, being secure and having validity in every place where it may be produced in evidence, (whether challenged) within or without the law.

I requested the notary,[59] he wrote, and some other trustworthy persons witnessed it at my request. Under my supervision it was written in the Egyptian[60] language; they read it aloud to me, I assented to it, I set it down. +++

+ I Anna daughter of the late John and the late Taham, woman of Kastron Jeme, the aforewritten, I assent to this donation document as it is written, and in every matter that I have set down therein.—+ I Chmntsnêu, most humble priest and hegoumenos of the same Kastron Jeme,[61] she, namely Anna,[62] I subscribed for her as she did not know how, at her request. +

---

[52] MacCoull, "ⲧⲩⲡⲟⲥ."
[53] *theia diataxis* (θεῖα διάταξις), imperial law (we have encountered this above, e.g., in *P.CLT* 1, q.v.).
[54] *taxis* (τάξις).
[55] Probably the Deuteronomic curses, as above, *P.CLT* 2, *P.KRU* 78.
[56] Matthew 27:3–5; Acts 1:16–18.
[57] Acts 5:1–10 again.
[58] Here *katabalesis* (ⲕⲁⲧⲁⲃⲁⲗⲉⲥⲓⲥ [sic]), not *katabolê* (ⲕⲁⲧⲁⲃⲟⲗⲏ).
[59] *syngrapheus* (συνγραφεύς): Förster, *WB*, 762.
[60] Here *rmnkême* (ⲣⲙⲛⲕⲏⲙⲉ).
[61] Known from *P.KRU* 13 and 12 above.
[62] He miswrites her name as "Iôanna."

\+ I Noah son of Jeremias, the priest and hegoumenos of the holy church of Jeme,[63] I bear witness.

\+ I Phoibammon son of the late George,[64] I bear witness.

\+ I Staphôre son of the late Victor,[65] I bear witness.—+ Phoibammon son of the late George, he asked me, I wrote for him as he did not know how.

\+ I Samuel son of the late Enoch,[66] I bear witness according as I heard it from those sitting with Anna at the time when she put forth her discourse according to the force of this donation document.

\+ I Isaac son of the late Zacharias,[67] man of the same Kastron Jeme, I bear witness according as I heard from those sitting with Anna at the time when she went to her rest.[68] +

[Docket (in Greek)]: Written donation document, that came about through Anna . . . from Kastron Memnonion, concerning the house of John her father and the portion of a bakery and the half-portion of the house of Taam her mother. Month of Payni, 6, indiction 3. +

\+ I Chmntsnêu, most humble priest and hegoumenos (son of Shenoute) of the holy church of Jeme, I wrote this written donation document with my hand as Anna daughter of John was supervising me, and I executed it. +

Written in the month of Payni, 6, ind. 3 ΑΡΧΗ[69] +++

---

[63] Known from *P.KRU* 45/46, 21, 42, 13, and 12 above.

[64] Same as in *P.KRU* 42 and 44?

[65] Cf. Victor son of Staphôra, whose house forms one of the boundaries specified above.

[66] Same as in *P.KRU* 13 and 12?

[67] Quite possibly the same individual as in *P.CLT* 6, ten years earlier.

[68] This is the first indication we have that the document was framed right at the end of Anna's life. It is formulated explicitly as a donation, yet it functions as a will.

[69] *CSBE* 2, 112 with n. 18.

P.KRU 18

Sale

DATE: 1st 1/3 of 8th c.

PLACE: Jeme

PARTIES: John, priest and oikonomos of St Phoibammon's, seller; Apa Victor son of Athanasius, buyer

OBJECT: House property with appurtenances

SUM [price]: 4 solidi

[fine]: 3 oz. gold

WITNESSES: 5

SCRIBE: Jeremias son of the late Athanasius

PUBLICATION: Till, *KRUTheb*, 116–18

This document records an interesting monastic property transfer in which a priest/oikonomos[1] sells to another priest house property that had earlier been donated to the St Phoibammon monastery (cf. Schmelz, *Kirchliche Amtsträger*, 35, 170). Seller and buyer appear to be related. Compare *P.KRU* 75 above, in which concern that monastic property not fall into the hands of lay relatives is paramount. The phraseology is strongly colored by piety towards St Phoibammon, martyred saint of the holy place (cf. Papaconstantinou, "Donation d'enfants," 85–89).

. . . the crown[-bearing] Apa Phoibammon . . .; [I John,] swearing by the power of the consubstantial Trinity, Father, Son and Holy Ghost, and the pains that the martyr suffered before the (worldly) judgement-seat,[2] and the well-being of our lords, and subsequently asking and beseeching trustworthy witnesses to witness for me, before the well-being of these our lords who rule over the world, seeking for this sale, secure, believable and un-undoable, that cannot be set aside or unmade: I am selling to you, you, Apa Victor son of the late Athanasius, in Jeme in the nome of the city [of Hermonthis,] the portion that George son of Johanna daughter of Elias son of Apa Victor (whose mother was Eudoxia) gave to the holy

---

[1] See Schmelz, *Kirchliche Amtsträger*, 163. Here the name is just too common to identify this individual with any other Jeme priest named John.

[2] Seidl, "Eid," 144.

Apa Phoibammon for the salvation of their mother and his own.[3] May God, by the intercession of the martyr, have mercy on them at His judgement-seat, as that is the place where every Christian needs it (mercy), at that place.

Look, I John the aforewritten am going to write and reveal the places that he (George) donated as a donation to the *topos*. These are: his portion of the house that lies in the street (where the house of) Panias son of Phabô (is). These are its boundaries round about on all four sides—together with all its utensils[4]—from the ground up to the air space: east, the heir (f.); west, Psan son of Pchôl; north, Jacob son of Andrew;[5] south, Jeremias. These are the boundaries round about their portion up to the field and their portion up to the church and their portion up to the tent (?)[6] and their portion up to the village (edge), along with land, courtyard, movable and immovable (property), this which came to me, John, from Johanna[7] and that which came to me by way of the donation George made to the holy Apa Phoibammon.

The price, which you have given to me, me, the seller, is four solidi by the standard {standard}[8] of the *kastron*. You, Apa Victor son of Athanasius, the buyer, may give orders over all portions and places that George son of Johanna gave to the *topos* (they having come to him from his parents), so as to give orders for them, build on them, sell them, give them away, pledge them as collateral, rent them out, give them to your children and your children's children. I am not to proceed against you over them for ever, nor to produce a counter-donation against you over them, (neither myself) nor those who come after me in the holy *topos*.

Anyone who dares to, either myself, John the most humble priest, or oikonomos coming after me in the *topos*, brother or nephew or person on either my father's side or my mother's, or any man at all representing me, or who produces a counter-donation against you over any portion of all the places that George gave to the *topos*, (i.e., against) you, Apa Victor son of Athanasius, over the portion, or who proceeds against you or your[9] son or grandson or uncle on your father's or mother's side, going to law with you, chiefly he is to have no good out of it, nor is the matter to bring him any advantage, but rather he is to be liable to the holy, venerated oath of Christians, (by) the Father and the Son and the Holy Ghost, and is to receive the apportionment of Ananias and Sapphira;[10] and is to pay into

---

[3] I.e., Johanna and Eudoxia. It is unusual for someone (like George here) to be identified by a matronymic, but perhaps this is because the original donation was made on behalf of mothers. This text is not discussed by Wilfong, *Women*.

[4] Seemingly an out-of-place insertion by the scribe.

[5] The one mentioned in *P.KRU* 3 above?

[6] Or "awning"? Cf. Förster, *WB*, 737–38.

[7] Thus John and Victor seem to be related.

[8] Inadvertently repeated by the scribe.

[9] So Till, *KRUTheb*, 117.

[10] Acts 5:1–10 again.

the hand of the magistrate in office at that time three ounces of gold as fine, and is to appear and acknowledge this sale, which is secure as it is written.

I John, oikonomos of the holy Apa Phoibammon {of the holy Apa Phoibammon},[11] I order that no man of your relatives, you, Apa Victor son of Athanasius, is to be able to proceed against you over portions of the places that George son of Johanna gave to the holy *topos* of Apa Phoibammon. The one who proceeds against you the God of the *topos* will wreak vengeance upon; and he will pay the fine of three ounces of gold.

I John, most humble priest of Apa Phoibammon, I assent to this secure sale.

+ I Psêre son of the late Peter, by the mercy of God priest and hegoumenos,[12] I bear witness at the request of John.

+ I Constantine son of the late Solomon,[13] I bear witness.

I Pishate son of Pilish, I bear witness. +++

+ I Pahash son of Elisha, I bear witness. +++—+ I Jeremias son of the late Athanasius,[14] at the request of John, as they asked me to, I wrote for them.

+ I Jeremias son of the late Athanasius, I wrote this sale with my hand at the order of John, most humble priest, and I bear witness.

---

[11] Repeated inadvertently by the scribe.
[12] Known from *P.KRU* 21, 3, and 12 above.
[13] Quite possibly the ex-*lashane* of *P.CLT* 1, *P.KRU* 35 and 10 above.
[14] Also the notary; Victor's brother?

P.KRU 38

Settlement of Inheritance

DATE: 26 February 738

PLACE: Jeme

PARTIES: George son of the late Loula and the late Elizabeth; Isaac and Kyra, his younger half-siblings, and their father Abraham

OBJECT: Inherited property

SUM [fine]: 36 solidi

WITNESSES: 8

SCRIBE: John son of Lazarus[1]

PUBLICATION: Till, *Erb*, 121–23

With this text we return to the family feud of George son of the late Loula, elder son of Elizabeth (who also is now deceased), versus his younger half-siblings Isaac and Kyra, children of Elizabeth's second marriage to Abraham, and the second husband as well. Now George is no longer just worried about getting what is coming to him from his now long-deceased father. Who is going to inherit Elizabeth's money, goods, and property? The widower, and/or the younger children? Or George? Now they have tried to work out a settlement before the "Great Men" of Jeme.

[Traces remain of a Greek-language version of the Bismillah protocol—"in the name [of God] the compassionate, [the merciful]; there is no God [but God alone;] Muhammad [is the messenger of God]"—used by the state factory between 705 and 715; thus there was a long delay for use of the papyrus. A governor's name, 'Abd. . ., was read by Crum/Steindorff; in 705 this would have been 'Abd Allah ibn 'Abd al-'Aziz.]

+ In the name of the Father and of the Son and of the Holy Ghost, consubstantial Trinity,[2] and the rule[3] and establishedness and continuance of our lords

---

[1] Known as the scribe of *P.CLT* 1, *P.KRU* 35, 51, 21, and 42 above.

[2] Invocation Type **2L**: *CSBE 2*, 101, 104–5, 295.

[3] This scribe, John son of Lazarus, has a way of conflating the phraseology of an invocation ("In the name of. . ."), which begins a document, with that of an oath by qualities of ruler(s), that usually comes later. Cf. above.

the kings, these who have power over the whole earth through the counsel of God Almighty:[4] Today being the second day of the month of Phamenoth of the indiction year [6], in the presence of the most honored, the honorable John son of the late Victor[5] and Isaac son of the late Constantine,[6] *lashane*s of Kastron Jeme in the nome of the city of Hermonthis.

+ I George son of the late Loule and the late Elizabeth, persons of Kastron Jeme in the nome of the city of Hermonthis, am writing to my beloved siblings Isaac and Kyra, and their father Abraham, man of the city of Syene. We are setting down this settlement, and I am putting in place someone who will subscribe for me and some credible, trustworthy witnesses who will witness this settlement at my very own request.

WHEREAS: At this time I have gone to law with you (pl.), you, Isaac and Kyra, and Abraham your father, over the inheritance of my late mother Elizabeth. Some God-fearing "Great Men" have with God's help come into the midst of us together over this whole inheritance in all matters: gold, silver, bronze, iron, smith's work, buildings and land, property movable and immovable, from small to large, severally and globally, in the inheritance of my late mother Elizabeth. I came to an agreement with you according as the "Great Men" agreed, as we trusted one another in every way [Greek]. I received and fulfilled with you over the whole inheritance of my late mother Elizabeth, such that I was not to go to law with you, you, Isaac and Kyra and Abraham, over anything, for ever and ever. If I were to reveal (such a lawsuit) in court or out of court, in city or in nome or before any God-fearing man at all, either myself or a brother or sister or child or grandchild or kin or kin of kin or anyone at all appertaining to me, he (sic) is to pay thirty-six gold solidi as fine to the magistrate, = AV sol. 36, pure, by standard of Kastron Memnonion. I received and fulfilled with you my entire portion of the inheritance of my late mother Elizabeth, in all things. Subsequently I have entered in and made acknowledgement of the force of the settlement and all matters written therein. And on top of all these things I swear by the holy, consubstantial Trinity and the rule and establishedness and continuance of our lords the kings, those who have power over us from God,[7] that no transgression of it (the settlement) will occur.

Accordingly for security I have drawn up this settlement, which is secure and has validity in every place where it may be produced in evidence.

+ I George son of the late Loulou [sic] and the late Elizabeth, the aforewritten above, I assent to the settlement with my oath and the fine and all matters written therein, as it stands above.

---

[4] Cf. Seidl, "Eid," 142–43; and compare the oath clause below.
[5] Cf. *P.KRU* 35?
[6] Cf. *P.KRU* 25, 47, 50, 42?
[7] Seidl, "Eid," 140–43.

+ I Pamphilus son of the late Peter, and Joseph son of the late Pinis, and Theodore son of the late Constantine, we bear witness.—John son of Lazarus, I wrote for them.

+ I Pshêre, by the mercy[8] of God most humble priest and hegoumenos[9] of the holy church of Jeme, I bear witness at the request of George.

I Joseph son of the late Peter bear witness at the request of George.

+ I Papnouthios, most humble deacon of the Apostle's,[10] I bear witness at the request [of George.]

+ I Efranke son of the late David,[11] I bear witness to the settlement at the request of the framer. — I Anastasius, most humble deacon of the Mother of God Mary,[12] I wrote for these witnesses, and I bear witness.

+ I John son of Lazarus, with God's help, I executed it with my hand as it stands above. +

IC XC

---

[8] Our scribe, clearly used to writing *nomina sacra*, has written a supralinear stroke above ⲡⲛⲁ making it "*pneuma*"; but formulaically of course this is *p-na* (ⲡ-ⲛⲁ), "the mercy."

[9] Known from *P.CLT* 1, *P.KRU* 35; is he the same person as the priest/hegoumenos Psêre son of the late Peter in *P.KRU* 21, 3, 12, 18? The letters ⲥ and ϣ do not usually interchange in the spelling of names.

[10] Papaconstantinou, *Saints*, 56–58, esp. here 57; here singular.

[11] Is this Frange the monk, known from numerous documents (e.g., *KSB III*, 1336–1348)? See Wilfong, *Women*, 71 n. 4.

[12] Papaconstantinou, "Sanctuaries de la Vierge," 89 (no. 17bis).

P.KRU 19

Transfer of House Property

DATE: 5 November 747

PLACE: Jeme

PARTIES: Hllô son of the late David, donor; his son Mena and daughter Tsône (his children by his late wife Sarra), recipients

OBJECT: House property

SUM: [original sale price] 5 solidi

WITNESSES: 3

SCRIBE: David son of Psate[1]

PUBLICATION: Till, *Erb*, 103–5

In this document a widower transfers to his son and daughter ownership of a house his late wife, their mother, had left. Sarra has died leaving the house to her husband Hllô; he in turn sold that house on to a man named Cosmas for 5 solidi. But this apparently was not the only house property Sarra had owned: she had left a second house to the St Phoibammon monastery. Apparently the two houses have been swapped between Cosmas and the monastery. In a further transfer, St Phoibammon's has apparently allowed Hllô to make the house they now have over to Hllô's motherless children. This is yet another example of interdependence between town-dwellers and religious houses.

[Traces remain of an Arabic-language protocol mentioning a governor 'Abd. . . and a year]

In the name of the holy and life-giving, consubstantial Trinity, Father, Son and Holy Ghost.[2] Written in the month of Hathyr, 8, first indiction. [Greek]
+ I Hllô son of the late David,[3] man of Kastron Jeme in the nome of the city of Hermonthis, am writing to my beloved children Mena and Tsône, my legitimate children, as follows:

---

[1] See Richter, "Zwei Urkunden des Notars David."
[2] Invocation Type **2E**: *CSBE 2*, 100, 104–5, 294 (= *SB* I 5566).
[3] Could he be the grandson of the David son of Hllo (?) in *P.KRU* 65?

WHEREAS: in this year that we are in, the tenth indiction, God (brought) greatly straitened circumstances upon me and your mother and you, I sold the house of your late mother[4] Sarra to Cosmas son of Joseph. I received its price from him, namely five solidi: we took them for ourselves. That house (was) in the Roude Street, as I made its old location clear in the sale.

But now I agree, I Hllô the aforewritten, with you, you my beloved children Mena and Tsône, that the whole house that came from your mother[5] (has gone) to St Phoibammon's in exchange for the one I sold to Cosmas son of Joseph, this one now the old location of which I shall make clear to you now, in quadrilateral: south, Pisrael son of Paul,[6] the brother of my late father; north, Martha the widow,[7] and the place where the main gate opens out on to, and the public street; east, Methuselah son of the late Elias; west, the public street going in. These are the complete boundaries of that house on all sides.

From now on you, my beloved children, are to enter in and take possession and be owners of that whole house. And no one is to be able, neither myself nor a son or brother or sister nor kin nor kin of kin, nor stranger nor man of (our) house, to go to law with you (pl.) over that whole house, for ever. But if anyone goes to law with you, in court or out of court, whether in city or in nome or outside our nome and its boundaries, to make any legal motion against you at all over the whole house that I made plain before above, you are the ones who have acquired it in acquisition, to administer it, manage it, make improvements to it, dwell in it, give it away, confer it, give it to your children, bequeath it to your heirs, in short, deal with it in any way, shape or form you like: for no man at all is to go to law with you over it for ever.

Accordingly, for your security I have drawn up this written document of sale for you, it being secure and valid and warranted in every place where it may be produced in evidence. They asked me, I agreed. They read it aloud to me, I heard it, I established it with subscribers and witnesses. I set it down according to the order[8] of our laws. +

+ I Peter son of the late Pisate, I bear witness.—Peter, most humble priest, I wrote for him as he did not know how to write, and I bear witness.

+ I David son of Karakos, I bear witness.—+ Peter, I wrote for him.

+ Written by me, David son of Psate. + [Greek]

---

[4] I.e., she died in the "straitened circumstances": possibly shortages resulting from tax revolts (cf. Kennedy, "Province," 75–76; Sijpesteijn, "Landholding Patterns in Early Islamic Egypt," 130).

[5] I.e., another house, one that changed ownership through bequest by the deceased mother.

[6] Cf. *P.KRU* 42?

[7] Till, *Erb*, 104 takes *chêra* (ⲭⲏⲣⲁ) as a proper name (a matronymic); but clearly it is "the widow".

[8] *akolouthia* (ἀκολουθία).

[Docket] [Hllô son of the] late⁹ David, writing to Mena and Tsône my children . . . (concerning) the house of your mother that I sold to Cosmas son of Joseph, as far as concerns myself, the house that came from your mother, to the holy Apa Phoibammon, that I shall give to you for the house that I sold to Cosm[as son of Joseph . . .

---

⁹ Crum/Steindorff's reading of *auô* (ⲁⲩⲱ) "and" is clearly nonsense; it should be the framer's patronymic.

P.KRU 54

Acknowledgement of Receipt of Donation

DATE: 24/25 September 748

PLACE: Jeme

PARTIES: The late Tsyros daughter of Takoum, testatrix/donatrix; Senouthios son of the late Philotheus, oikonomos of the St Psate monastery, recipient on the monastery's behalf; Komos son of the late Damian, intermediary

OBJECT: 1 trimesion

WITNESSES: 3

SCRIBE: Senouthios [a.k.a. Shenoute] son of the late Chmntsnêu, priest[1]

PUBLICATION: Till, *Erb*, 150

This text is written on the other side of *P.KRU* 26 (an inheritance settlement, possibly datable to 745?). (Its scribe will write *P.KRU* 4 [a sale of land to Aaron, Jeme's property entrepreneur whom we have met in *P.KRU* 5, 13, and 12] in the following year.) In this document a monastic steward acknowledges receipt of a money bequest from a woman, transmitted by a lay intermediary.

+ In the name of the holy and life-giving, consubstantial Trinity, Father, Son and Holy Ghost.[2] Month of Thoth, 27, indiction 2. + [Greek]
   + I Senouthios son of the late Philotheus, oikonomos of the holy Apa Psate[3] in the mountain of Jeme, am writing to Komos son of the late Damian, man of the same Kastron Jeme in the nome of this same city of Hermonthis, as follows:
   Over the matter of the trimesion that Tsyros daughter of Takoum gave to the holy Apa Psate, this one that she donated in her testament that it should be given to the holy Apa Psate: look, it has come to my hand from your hand, you, Komos son of Damian. And from now on no man of that holy *topos*, neither myself nor brother nor child nor grandchild nor any heir who is of the *topos*, is to be able to proceed against you, nor any man appertaining to me, for ever. For your security I have drawn up this written document. I assent to it, it being secure

---

[1] The former deacon of *P.KRU* 5, seemingly now moved up in clerical rank.
[2] Invocation Type **2E**: *CSBE 2*, 100, 104–5, 294 (also possibly 763[?]; = *SB* I 5585).
[3] Papaconstantinou, *Saints*, 217–19, esp. here 217–18; cf. *P.KRU* 50 above.

and valid in every place where it may be produced in evidence. They asked me, I agreed.

+ I Cosmas son of Mena, I bear witness.—I Isaac son of Constantine,[4] I wrote for him as he did not know how.

I Constantine son of Isaac,[5] I bear witness.—I Isaac wrote for them as they did not know how, and I bear witness.

+I Senouthios son of the late Chmntsnêu,[6] most humble priest, have written this. + [Greek]

---

[4] Cf. *P.KRU* 25, 47, 50, 42; the *lashane* of *P.KRU* 38?

[5] From the same papponymic family?

[6] By inference the scribe of *P.KRU* 13, 12, and 106 above, now deceased; the profession descended in families from father to son, indeed families of priests as here. Cf. Schmelz, *Kirchliche Amtsträger*, 251–54.

Glossary

account	*logos*	λόγος	ΛΟΓΟC
administer	*dioikein*	διοικεῖν	ΔΙΟΙΚΕΙ
administration	*dioikêsis*	διοίκησις	ΔΙΟΙΚΗCΙC
agree	*homologein*	ὁμολογεῖν	ϨΟΜΟΛΟΓΕΙ
agreement	*homologia*	ὁμολογία	ϨΟΜΟΛΟΓΙΑ
allegation	*prophasis*	πρόφασις	ΠΡΟΦΑCΙC
anchorite	*anachôrêtês*	ἀναχωρήτης	ΑΝΑΧⲰΡΗΤΗC
archdeacon	*archidiakonos*	ἀρχιδιάκονος	ΑΡΧΙΔΙΑΚΟΝΟC
archpriest	*archipresbyteros*	ἀρχιπρεσβύτερος	ΑΡΧΙΠΡΕCΒΥΤΕΡΟC
assent (v.)	*stoichein*	στοιχεῖν	CΤΟΙΧΕΙ
ask	*aitein*	αἰτεῖν	ΑΙΤΕΙ
authority	*exousia*	ἐξουσία	ΕΞΟΥCΙΑ
befit	*prepein*	πρέπειν	ΠΡΕΠΕΙ
bishop	*episkopos*	ἐπίσκοπος	ΕΠΙCΚΟΠΟC
body	*sôma*	σῶμα	CⲰΜΑ
cede	*parachôrein*	παραχωρεῖν	ΠΑΡΑΧⲰΡΕΙ
cession	*parachôrêsis*	παραχώρησις	ΠΑΡΑΧⲰΡΗCΙC
chiefly	*prôtotypôs*	πρωτοτύπως	ΠΡⲰΤΟΤΥΠⲰC
circumscription	*perigraphê*	περιγραφή	ΠΕΡΙΓΡΑΦΗ
city	*polis*	πόλις	ΠΟΛΙC
compulsion	*ji nchons*		ϪΙ ΝϬΟΝC [1]
confer	*apocharizein*	ἀποχαρίζειν	ΑΠΟΧΑΡΙΖΕΙ
consent (v.)	*syneudokein*	συνευδοκεῖν	CΥΝΕΥΔΟΚΕΙ
continuance (ruler)	*dianomê*	διανομή	ΔΙΑΝΟΜΗ
court	*dikastêrion*	δικαστήριον	ΔΙΚΑCΤΗΡΙΟΝ
custom	*synêtheia*	συνήθεια	CΥΝΗΘΕΙΑ
dare	*tolman*	τολμᾶν	ΤΟΛΜΑ
deception	*apatê*	ἀπάτη	ΑΠΑΤΗ
define	*horizein*	ὁρίζειν	ϨΟΡΙΖΕΙ
direction	*epitropê*	ἐπιτροπή	ΕΠΙΤΡΟΠΗ
discipline (monastic)	*katastasis*	κατάστασις	ΚΑΤΑCΤΑCΙC
document	*chartês*	χάρτης	ΧΑΡΤΗC

---

[1] See Richter, *Sprache*, 371; renders *bia* (βία).

donate	*dôrizein*	δωρίζειν	ⲆⲰⲢⲒⲌⲈ
donation document	*dôreastikon*	δωρεαστικόν	ⲆⲰⲢⲈⲀⲤⲦⲒⲔⲞⲚ
exchange (v.)	*katallagein*	καταλλαγεῖν	ⲔⲀⲦⲀⲖⲖⲀⲄⲈⲒ
execute	*sômatizein*	σωματίζειν	ⲤⲰⲘⲀⲦⲒⲌⲈⲒ
expectation	*prosdokia*	προσδοκία	ⲠⲢⲞⲤⲆⲞⲔⲒⲀ
fine	*prostimon*	πρόστιμον	ⲠⲢⲞⲤⲦⲒⲘⲞⲚ
free choice	*prohairesis*	προαίρεσις	ⲠⲢⲞⲀⲒⲢⲈⲤⲒⲤ
fulfil	*plêrophorein*	πληροφορεῖν	ⲠⲖⲎⲢⲞⲪⲞⲢⲈⲒ
furnish	*paraskeuazein*	παρασκευάζειν	ⲠⲀⲢⲀⲤⲔⲈⲨⲀⲌⲈⲒ
give away	*charizein*	χαρίζειν	ⲬⲀⲢⲒⲌⲈⲒ
glorious, most	*endoxotatos*	ἐνδοξότατος	ⲈⲚⲆⲞⲜⲞⲦⲀⲦⲞⲤ
go to law	*enagein*	ἐνάγειν	ⲈⲚⲀⲄⲈ, ⲈⲚⲈⲄⲈ
God-bearing	*theophoros*	θεόφορος	ⲐⲈⲞⲪⲞⲢⲞⲤ
God-loving, most	*theophilestatos*	θεοφιλέστατος	ⲐⲈⲞⲪⲒⲖⲈⲤⲦⲀⲦⲞⲤ
guarantee (n.)	*asphaleia*	ἀσφάλεια	ⲀⲤⲪⲀⲖⲈⲒⲀ
habit (monastic)	*schêma*	σχῆμα	ⲤⲬⲎⲘⲀ
half-portion	*hêmisys + meros*	ἥμισυς + μέρος	ⲎⲘⲒⲤⲨⲘⲈⲢⲞⲤ
harm	*harpagê*	ἁρπαγή	2ⲀⲢⲠⲀⲄⲎ
heir	*klêronomos*	κληρόνομος	ⲔⲖⲎⲢⲞⲚⲞⲘⲞⲤ
hindrance	<*kôluein*	κωλύειν	ⲔⲰⲖⲨⲈⲒ
honorable, most	*timiôtatos*	τιμιώτατος	ⲦⲒⲘⲒⲰⲦⲀⲦⲞⲤ
humble, most	*elachistos*	ἐλάχιστος	ⲈⲖⲀⲬⲒⲤⲦⲞⲤ
illustrious, most	*lamprotatos*	λαμπρότατος	ⲖⲀⲘⲠⲢⲞⲦⲀⲦⲞⲤ
improvements, make	*philokalein*	φιλοκαλεῖν	ⲪⲒⲖⲞⲔⲀⲖⲈⲒ
inheritance	*klêronomia*	κληρονομία	ⲔⲖⲎⲢⲞⲚⲞⲘⲒⲀ
intention	*prothymia*	προθυμία	ⲠⲢⲞⲐⲨⲘⲒⲀ
intimidation	*hote*		2ⲞⲦⲈ[2]
judgement-seat	*bêma*	βῆμα	ⲂⲎⲘⲀ
late, the (deceased)	*makarios*	μακάριος	ⲘⲀⲔⲀⲢⲒⲞⲤ
lawsuit	*dikaiologia*	δικαιολογία	ⲆⲒⲔⲀⲒⲞⲖⲞⲄⲒⲀ
lector	*anagnôstês*	ἀναγνωστής	ⲀⲚⲀⲄⲚⲰⲤⲦⲎⲤ
liable, be	*hypokeisthai*	ὑποκεῖσθαι	2ⲨⲠⲞⲔⲈⲒⲤⲐⲈ
life	*bios*	βίος	ⲂⲒⲞⲤ
magistrate	*archôn*	ἄρχων	ⲀⲢⲬⲞⲚ
make plain	*dêloun*	δηλοῦν	ⲆⲎⲖⲞⲨ
manage	*oikonomein*	οἰκονομεῖν	ⲞⲒⲔⲞⲚⲞⲘⲈⲒ
master	*despotês*	δεσπότης	ⲆⲈⲤⲠⲞⲦⲎⲤ
mind	*nous*	νοῦς	ⲚⲞⲨⲤ
monk	*monachos*	μοναχός	ⲘⲞⲚⲞⲬⲞⲤ
necessity	*anankê*	ἀνάνκη	ⲀⲚⲀⲄⲔⲎ

---

[2] See Richter, *Sprache*, 341: renders *phobos* (φόβος).

obedience (monastic)	akolouthia	ἀκολουθία	ⲁⲕⲟⲗⲟⲩⲑⲓⲁ
obedience	hypotagê	ὑποταγή	ϨⲨⲠⲞⲦⲀⲄⲎ
offering	prosphora	προσφορά	ⲠⲢⲞⲤⲪⲞⲢⲀ
order (v.), give orders	keleuein	κελεύειν	ⲔⲈⲖⲈⲨⲈ
ordinance	diastalma	διάσταλμα	ⲆⲒⲀⲤⲦⲀⲖⲘⲞⲤ
penalty	epitimia	ἐπιτιμία	ⲈⲠⲒⲦⲒⲘⲒⲀ
pious, most	eulabestatos	εὐλαβέστατος	ⲈⲨⲖⲀⲂⲈⲤⲦⲀⲦⲞⲤ
portion	meros	μέρος	ⲘⲈⲢⲞⲤ
possessions	chrêmata	χρήματα	ⲬⲢⲎⲘⲀⲦⲀ
priest	presbyteros	πρεσβύτερος	ⲠⲢⲈⲤⲂⲨⲦⲈⲢⲞⲤ
prize-bearing	athlophoros	ἀθλοφόρος	ⲀⲐⲖⲞⲪⲞⲢⲞⲤ
proceed against	ei ebol		ⲈⲒ ⲈⲂⲞⲖ[3]
produce in evidence	emphanizein	ἐμφανίζειν	ⲈⲘⲪⲀⲚⲒⲌⲈ
profit (n.)	ôpheleia	ὠφέλεια	ⲰⲪⲈⲖⲈⲒⲀ
profit, obtain (v.)	ôphelein	ὠφελεῖν	ⲰⲪⲈⲖⲈⲒ
prosecution	proseleusis	προσέλευσις	ⲠⲢⲞⲤⲈⲖⲈⲨⲤⲒⲤ
quadrilateral	tetragônon	τετράγωνον	ⲦⲈⲦⲢⲀⲄⲰⲚⲞⲚ
reasoning	logismos	λογισμός	ⲖⲞⲄⲒⲤⲘⲞⲤ
release	amerimneia	ἀμεριμνεία	ⲀⲘⲈⲢⲒⲘⲚⲈⲒⲀ
renowned, most	eukleestatos	εὐκλεέστατος	ⲈⲨⲔⲖⲈⲈⲤⲦⲀⲦⲞⲤ
represent	rprosôpon	<πρόσωπον	Ⲣ ⲠⲢⲞⲤⲰⲠⲞⲚ
request (v.)	parakalein	παρακαλεῖν	ⲠⲀⲢⲀⲔⲀⲖⲈⲒ
request (n.)	aitêsis	αἴτησις	ⲀⲒⲦⲎⲤⲒⲤ
rule (n.)	archê	ἀρχή	ⲀⲢⲬⲎ
rule over	archein	ἀρχεῖν	ⲀⲢⲬⲈⲒ
sale	prasis	πρᾶσις	ⲠⲢⲀⲤⲒⲤ
seizure	syn(h)arpagê	συναρπαγή	ⲤⲨⲚϨⲀⲢⲠⲀⲄⲎ
settlement	dialysis	διάλυσις	ⲆⲒⲀⲖⲨⲤⲒⲤ
soul	psychê	ψυχή	ⲮⲨⲬⲎ
subscribe	hypographein	ὑπογραφεῖν	ϨⲨⲠⲞⲄⲢⲀⲪⲈ
subscriber	hypographeus	ὑπογραφεύς	ϨⲨⲠⲞⲄⲢⲀⲪⲈⲨⲤ
superior (monastic)	proestôs	προεστώς	ⲠⲢⲞⲈⲤⲦⲰⲤ
take care	spoudazein	σπουδάζειν	ⲤⲠⲞⲨⲆⲀⲌⲈ
testament	diathêkê	διαθήκη	ⲆⲒⲀⲐⲎⲔⲎ
transgress	parabainein	παραβαίνειν	ⲠⲀⲢⲀⲂⲀ
transgression	parabasis	παράβασις	ⲠⲀⲢⲀⲂⲀⲤⲒⲤ
trickery	krof		ⲔⲢⲞϤ[4]
trustworthy	axiopistos	ἀξιόπιστος	ⲀⲜⲒⲞⲠⲒⲤⲦⲞⲤ
warrant (v.)	bebaioun	βεβαιοῦν	ⲂⲈⲂⲀⲒⲞⲨ

---

[3] See Richter, *Sprache*, 195-99 esp. 196-98.
[4] See Richter, *Sprache*, 210-11: renders *dolos* (δόλος).

warrant (n.)	*bebaiôsis*	βεβαίωσις	ⲃⲉⲃⲁⲓⲱⲥⲓⲥ
whereas[5]	*epeidê*	ἐπειδή	ⲉⲡⲉⲓⲇⲏ
will (n.)	*boulêma*	βούλημα	ⲃⲟⲩⲗⲏⲙⲁ
witness (n.)	*martyros/mntre*	μάρτυρος	ⲙⲁⲣⲧⲩⲣⲟⲥ / ⲙⲛⲧⲣⲉ
witness, bear	*martyrizein/rmntre*	μαρτυρίζειν	ⲙⲁⲣⲧⲩⲣⲓⲍⲉ / ⲣ ⲙⲛⲧⲣⲉ
world	*kosmos*	κόσμος	ⲕⲟⲥⲙⲟⲥ
worldly	*kosmikos/-on*	κοσμικός /-όν	ⲕⲟⲥⲙⲓⲕⲟⲛ
written document	*engraphon*	ἔνγραφον	ⲉⲅⲅⲣⲁⲫⲟⲛ

---

[5] Cf. Richter, "Donation Documents," 242.

Bibliography

(other than items in Abbreviations)

Adams, C. E. P. *Land Transport in Roman Egypt.* Oxford, 2007.
Alcock, A., and †P. J. Sijpesteijn. "Early 7th Cent. Coptic Contract from Aphrodito (P.Mich.inv. 6898)." *Enchoria* 26 (2000): 1–19.
Athanassiadi, P. "Antiquité tardive: construction et déconstruction d'un modèle historiographique." *Antiquité tardive* 14 (2006): 311–24.
Axer, J., and K. Tomaszuk. "Central-Eastern Europe." In *A Companion to the Classical Tradition*, ed. C. W. Kallendorf, 132–55. Oxford, 2007.
Bagnall, R. S. *Egypt in Late Antiquity.* Princeton, 1993.
———. *Reading Papyri, Writing Ancient History.* London, 1995.
———. "Periodizing When You Don't Have To: The Concept of Late Antiquity in Egypt." In *Gab es eine Spätantike?*, 39–49. Frankfurt, 2003.
———. "Egypt and the Concept of the Mediterranean." In *Rethinking the Mediterranean*, ed. W. V. Harris, 339–47. Oxford, 2005.
———, ed. *Egypt in the Byzantine World, A. D. 400–700.* Cambridge, 2007.
———, and R. Cribiore. *Women's Letters from Ancient Egypt, 300 BC–AD 800.* Ann Arbor, 2006.
———, and D. W. Rathbone. *Egypt from Alexander to the Copts: An Archaeological and Historical Guide.* London, 2004.
———, and K. A. Worp. "Dating the Coptic Legal Documents from Aphrodite." *Zeitschrift für Papyrologie und Epigraphik* 148 (2004): 247–52.
Ballet, P., et al. *Kellia: l'ermitage copte QR 195: céramique, inscriptions, décors.* Cairo, 2003.
Banaji, J. "Aristocracies, Peasantries and the Framing of the Early Middle Ages." *Journal of Agrarian Change* 9 (2009): 59–91.
Barthélemy, D. *La mutation de l'an Mil: a-t-elle eu lieu? Servage et chevalerie dans la France des Xe et XIe siècles.* Paris, 1997.
Bates, D. "Charters and Historians of Britain and Ireland: Problems and Possibilities." In *Charters and Charter Scholarship in Britain and Ireland*, ed. M. T. Flanagan and J. A. Green, 1–14. New York, 2005.
Bates, M. L. "Coins and Money in the Arabic Papyri." In *Documents de l'islam médiéval: Nouvelles perspectives de recherche*, ed. Y. Ragib, 43–64. Cairo, 1991.
Beaucamp, J. *Le statut de la femme à Byzance, 4e-7e siècles.* 2 vols. Paris, 1990.

———. "Tester en grec à Byzance." In *EYΨYXIA: Mélanges offerts à Hélène Ahrweiler*, ed. M. Balard et al., 1:97–107. 2 vols. Paris, 1998.

———. "Byzantine Egypt and Imperial Law." In *Egypt*, ed. Bagnall, 271–87.

Becker, A. H. *Fear of God and the Beginning of Wisdom: The School of Nisibis and Christian Scholastic Culture in Late Antique Mesopotamia*. Philadelphia, 2006.

Behlmer, H. "Christian Use of Pharaonic Sacred Space in Western Thebes." In *Sacred Space and Sacred Function in Ancient Thebes*, ed. P. F. Dorman and B. M. Bryan, 163–75. Chicago, 2007.

Bell. H. I. "The Byzantine Servile State in Egypt." *Journal of Egyptian Archaeology* 4 (1917): 86–106.

Biedenkopf-Ziehner, A. *Koptische Schenkungsurkunden aus der Thebais*. Wiesbaden, 2001.

Bingen, J. "Normality and Distinctiveness in the Epigraphy of Greek and Roman Egypt." In idem, *Hellenistic Egypt*, ed., trans., and intro. R. S. Bagnall, 256–78. Berkeley, 2007.

Blair, J. *The Church in Anglo-Saxon Society*. Oxford, 2005.

Bogaert, R. "La banque en Égypte byzantine." *Zeitschrift für Papyrologie und Epigraphik* 116 (1997): 85–140.

Boud'hors, A., et al., eds. *Études coptes IX*. Paris, 2006.

———. *Monastic Estates in Late Antique and Early Islamic Egypt: Ostraca, Papyri, and Studies in Honour of Sarah Clackson*. Cincinnati, 2008.

Bowes, K. "Personal Devotions and Private Chapels." In *Late Ancient Christianity*, ed. V. Burrus, 188–210. Minneapolis, 2005.

Bowman, A. K., and E. Rogan, eds. *Agriculture in Egypt from Pharaonic to Modern Times*. Proceedings of the British Academy 96. Oxford, 1999.

Brooks-Hedstrom, D. "Divine Architects: Designing the Monastic Dwelling Place." In *Egypt*, ed. Bagnall, 368–89.

Burrus, V., and R. Lyman. "Shifting the Focus of History." In *Late Ancient Christianity*, ed. Burrus, 1–23.

Calament, F. "Correspondance inédite entre moines dans la montagne thébaine." In *Études coptes IX*, ed. Boud'hors et al., 81–102.

Choat, M. "Language and Culture in Late Antique Egypt." In *A Companion to Late Antiquity*, ed. P. Rousseau, 342–56. Oxford, 2009.

Clackson, S. J. *Coptic and Greek Texts Relating to the Hermopolite Monastery of Apollo*. Oxford, 2000.

———. "Papyrology and the Utilization of Coptic Sources." In *Papyrology and the History of Early Islamic Egypt*, ed. P. M. Sijpesteijn and L. Sundelin, 21–44. Leiden, 2004.

———. "Archimandrites and *Andrismos*: A Preliminary Survey of Taxation at Bawit." In *Akten des 23. Internationalen Papyrologen-Kongresses*, ed. B. Palme, 103–7. Vienna, 2007.

Coquin, R.-G., et al. "Dayr Anbā Shinūdah." In *Coptic Encyclopaedia*, 3:761–69. 8 vols. New York, 1991.

Cribiore, R. *Gymnastics of the Mind: Greek Education in Hellenistic and Roman Egypt*. Princeton, 2001.
Cromwell, J. "Aristophanes Son of Johannes: An 8th-Century Bilingual Scribe?" Paper at the Twenty-fifth International Congress of Papyrologists, Ann Arbor, 2007.
———. "Individual Scribal Practice at Jeme: The Papyri Documents of Aristophanes Son of Johannes." Ph.D. diss., University of Liverpool, 2008.
———. "Another Family Archive from Jeme." Forthcoming.
Daris, S. *Il lessico latino nel greco d'Egitto*. 2nd ed. Barcelona, 1991.
de Jong, M. *In Samuel's Image: Child Oblation in the Early Medieval West*. Leiden, 1996.
Delattre, A. "Les 'lettres de protection' coptes." In *Akten des 23. Internationalen Papyrologen-Kongresses*, ed. Palme, 173–78.
Depauw, M. *A Companion to Demotic Studies*. Brussels, 1997.
Diethart, J. M., and K. A. Worp. *Notarsunterschriften im byzantinischen Ägypten (ByzNot)*. 2 vols. Vienna, 1986.
Dunand, F. "Between Tradition and Innovation: Egyptian Funerary Practices in Late Antiquity." In *Egypt*, ed. Bagnall, 163–84.
Emmel, S. "From the Other Side of the Nile: Shenute and Panopolis." In *Perspectives on Panopolis*, ed. A. Egberts et al., 95–113. Leiden, 2002.
———. *Shenoute's Literary Corpus*. 2 vols. Leuven, 2004.
Feissel, D., and J. Gascou. *La pétition à Byzance*. Paris, 2004.
Firth Green, R. "Literature and Law." In *A Companion to Medieval English Literature and Culture c.1350–c.1500*, ed. P. Brown, 292–306. Oxford, 2007.
Förster, H.. "Ein koptischer Kaufvertrag über Anteile an einem Wagen: Edition von P. Vat. Copt. Doresse 1." *Aegyptus* 84 (2004): 217–42.
———. "The Coptic Papyri of the Doresse Collection in the Vatican Library." Paper at the Twenty-fifth International Congress of Papyrologists, Ann Arbor, 2007.
Foss, C. *Arab-Byzantine Coins*. Washington, DC, 2008.
Fournet, J.-L. "Un nouvel épithalame de Dioscore d'Aphrodité addressé à un gouverneur civile de Thébaïde." *Antiquité tardive* 6 (1998): 65–82.
———. *Hellénisme dans l'Égypte du VIe siècle: La bibliothèque et l'oeuvre de Dioscore d'Aphrodité*. 2 vols. Cairo, 1999.
———. "Disposition et réalisation graphique des lettres et des pétitions protobyzantines: Pour une paléographie 'signifiante' des papyrus documentaires." In *Proceedings of the 24th International Congress of Papyrology*, ed. J. Frösen et al., 1: 353–67. Helsinki, 2007.
———, ed. *Les archives de Dioscore d'Aphrodité cent ans après leur découverte*. Paris, 2008.
———. "The Multilingual Environment of Late Antique Egypt." In *Oxford Handbook of Paprology*, ed. R. S. Bagnall, 418–51. Oxford, 2009.
———. "Sur les premiers documents juridiques coptes." In *Actes des 13e Journées coptes de Marseille (juin 2007)*. Forthcoming.

———, and J. Gascou. "Liste des pétitions sur papyrus des Ve-VIIe siècles." In *La pétition à Byzance*, ed. Feissel and Gascou, 141–96.

Frantz-Murphy, G. "A Comparison of the Arabic and Earlier Egyptian Contract Formularies." *Journal of Near Eastern Studies* 40 (1981): 203–25, 44 (1985): 99–114, 47 (1988): 105–12, 269–80, 48 (1989): 97–107.

———. "Land-Tenure in Egypt in the First Five Centuries of Islamic Rule (Seventh-Twelfth Centuries A.D.)." In *Agriculture in Egypt*, ed. Bowman and Rogan, 237–66.

———. *Arabic Agricultural Leases and Tax Receipts from Egypt*. CPR 21. Vienna, 2001.

———. "The Economics of State Formation in Early Islamic Egypt." In *From al-Andalus to Khurasan: Documents from the Medieval Muslim World*, ed. P. M. Sijpesteijn et al., 101–14. Leiden, 2007.

Fulk, R. D. "Male Homoeroticism in the Old English *Canons of Theodore*." In *Sex and Sexuality in Anglo-Saxon England*, ed. C. B. Pasternack and L. M. C. Weston, 1–34. MRTS 277. Tempe, 2004.

Gabra, G. "Die Münzschätze aus dem Schenute-Kloster bei Sohag." In *Ägypten-Münster: kulturwissenschaftliche Studien*, ed. A. I. Blöbaum and J. Kahl, 125–28 and Plates 5–6. Wiesbaden, 2003.

Gagos, T., and P. van Minnen. *Settling a Dispute: Towards a Legal Anthropology of Late Antique Egypt*. Ann Arbor, 1994.

Gardner, I. "Report on the Editing of both the Coptic and the Manichaean Texts from Ismant el-Kharab." In *The Oasis Papers 3*, ed. G. E. Bowen and C. A. Hope, 201–5. Oxford, 2003.

Gascou, J. "*Ducs, praesides*, poètes et rhéteurs au Bas-Empire." *Antiquité tardive* 6 (1998): 61–64.

———. "L'Égypte byzantine (284–641)." In *Le monde byzantin*, ed. C. Morrisson et al., 403–36. Paris, 2004.

Ghica, V. "Kellis: notes toponymiques." In *Coptica – Gnostica – Manichaica: Mélanges offerts à Wolf-Peter Funk*, ed. L. Painchaud and P.-H. Poirier, 325–37. Québec-Louvain, 2006.

Greenfield, R. "Children in Byzantine Monasteries." In *Becoming Byzantine: Children and Childhood in Byzantium*, ed. A. Papaconstantinou and A.-M. Talbot, 253–82. Washington, DC, 2009.

Grossmann, P. *Christliche Architektur in Ägypten*. Leiden, 2002.

Harvey, A. "Economy." In *Palgrave Advances in Byzantine History*, ed. J. Harris, 83–99. London, 2005.

Harvey, S. A. *Scenting Salvation: Ancient Christianity and the Olfactory Imagination*. Berkeley, 2006.

Hasitzka, M. "Namen in koptischen dokumentarischen Texten." <www.onb.ac.at/sammlungen/papyrus/publ/kopt_namen.pdf>

———. "Einige Korrekturen zu P.Mich.Inv. 6898." *Enchoria* 27 (2001): 200–1.

Henein, N. H., and M. Wuttmann. *Kellia II: l'ermitage copte QR 195: archéologie et architecture*. Cairo, 2000.

Herbert, M. "Before Charters? Property Records in Pre-Anglo-Norman Ireland." In *Charters and Charter Scholarship in Britain and Ireland*, ed. Flanagan and Green, 107–19.

Heurtel, C. *Les inscriptions coptes et grecques du temple d'Hathor à Deir el-Médina*. Cairo, 2004.

Hickey, T. "Aristocratic Landholding and the Economy of Byzantine Egypt." In *Egypt*, ed. Bagnall, 288–308.

———. *Economic Decision Making and Fiscal Participation in Late Antique Egypt*. Forthcoming.

Horden, P. "Mediterranean Plague in the Age of Justinian." In *The Cambridge Companion to the Age of Justinian*, ed. M. Maas, 134–60. Cambridge, 2005.

Humfress, C. "Law and Legal Practice in the Age of Justinian." In *Cambridge Companion to the Age of Justinian*, ed. Maas, 161–84.

———. "Cracking the Codex: Late Roman Law in Practice." *Bulletin of the Institute of Classical Studies* 49 (2006): 251–64.

———. "Judging by the Book: Christian Codices and Late Antique Legal Culture." In *The Early Christian Book*, ed. W. E. Klingshirn and L. Safran, 141–58. Washington, DC, 2007.

———. "Law and Justice in *The Later Roman Empire*." In *A. H. M. Jones and the Later Roman Empire*, ed. D. M. Gwynn, 121–42. Leiden, 2007.

———. *Orthodoxy and the Courts in Late Antiquity*. Oxford, 2007.

———. "Law in Practice." In *A Companion to Late Antiquity*, ed. Rousseau, 377–91.

———. "Roman Law as Social Practice." In *The Cambridge Companion to Roman Law*. Cambridge, forthcoming.

James, E. "The Rise and Function of the Concept 'Late Antiquity'." *Journal of Late Antiquity* 1 (2008): 20–30.

Karalis, V. "Greek Christianity After 1453." In *The Blackwell Companion to Eastern Christianity*, ed. K. Parry, 156–85. Oxford, 2007.

Kennedy, H. "Egypt as a Province in the Islamic Caliphate, 641–868." In *The Cambridge History of Egypt*, 1: *Islamic Egypt, 640–1517*, ed. C. F. Petry, 62–85. Cambridge, 1998.

Keynes, S. "The Fonthill Letter." In *Words, Texts and Manuscripts*, ed. M. Korthammer, 53–97. Munich, 1992.

Kotsifou, C. "Books and Book Production in the Monastic Communities of Byzantine Egypt." In *The Early Christian Book*, ed. Klingshirn and Safran, 48–67.

Krause, M. "Die Testamente der Äbte des Phoibammon-Klosters in Theben." *Mitteilungen des deutschen archäologischen Instituts Kairo* 25 (1969): 57–67.

———. "Zwei Phoibammon-Klöster in Theben-West." *Mitteilungen des deutschen archäologischen Instituts Kairo* 37 (1981): 261–66.

———. "Die Beziehungen zwischen den beiden Phoibammon-Klöstern auf dem thebanischen Westufer." *Bulletin de la Société d'Archéologie Copte* 27 (1985): 31–44.
Krawiec, R. *Shenoute and the Women of the White Monastery*. Oxford, 2002.
Krueger, D. "Monastic Companionship: An Early Byzantine Institution?" *Byzantine Studies Conference Abstracts* 29 (2003): 78–79.
———. "The Practice of Christianity in Byzantium." In *Byzantine Christianity*, ed. idem, 1–15. Minneapolis, 2006.
Laiou, A., ed. *Economic History of Byzantium*. 3 vols. Washington, DC, 2002.
Laniado, A. "Συντελεστής: notes sur un terme fiscale surinterprété." *Journal of Juristic Papyrology* 26 (1996): 23–51.
Layton, B. "Rules, Patterns, and the Exercise of Power in Shenoute's Monastery: The Problem of World Replacement and Identity Maintenance." *Journal of Early Christian Studies* 15 (2007): 45–73.
Lefort, J. "The Rural Economy, Seventh-Twelfth Centuries." In *Economic History of Byzantium*, ed. Laiou, 1:225–304.
Lobdell, J. "Welsh Language." In *J. R. R. Tolkien Encyclopedia: Scholarship and Critical Assessment*, ed. M. D. C. Drout, 705–6. New York, 2007.
Lucas, A. "The Role of the Monasteries in the Development of Medieval Milling." In *Wind and Water in the Middle Ages*, ed. S. A. Walton, 89–127. MRTS 322. Tempe, 2006.
Luisier, P. "ϭⲏⲛ ⲑⲉⲱ: Signification et destin d'une formule d'invocation en Egypte." In *Κορυφαίωι Ἀνδρί: Mélanges offerts à André Hurst*, ed. A. Kolde et al., 339–46. Geneva, 2005.
MacCoull, L. S. B. "Child Donations and Child Saints in Coptic Egypt." *East European Quarterly* 13 (1979): 409–15.
———. "The Coptic Archive of Dioscorus of Aphrodito." *Chronique d'Egypte* 56 (1981): 185–93; repr. in eadem, *Coptic Perspectives*, no. II.
———. "A Coptic Cession of Land by Dioscorus of Aphrodito." In *Acts of the Second International Congress of Coptic Studies (Rome, 1980)*, ed. T. Orlandi, 159–66. Rome, 1985; repr. in eadem, *Coptic Perspectives*, no. VII.
———. "Redating the Inscription of El-Moallaqa." *Zeitschrift für Papyrologie und Epigraphik* 64 (1986): 230–34; repr. in eadem, *Coptic Perspectives*, no. XIV.
———. *Dioscorus of Aphrodito: His Work and his World*. Berkeley, 1988.
———. "ⲧⲩⲡⲟⲥ in Coptic Legal Papyri." *Zeitschrift der Savigny-Stiftung für Rechtsgeschichte, kanonistische Abteilung* 75 (1989): 408–11.
———. "'The Holy Trinity' at Aphrodito." *Tyche* 6 (1991): 109–11.
———. "Law." In *The Coptic Encyclopaedia*, 5: 1428–32.
———. *Coptic Perspectives on Late Antiquity*. Aldershot, 1993.
———. "The Apa Apollos Monastery of Pharoou (Aphrodito) and its Papyrus Archive." *Le Muséon* 106 (1993): 21–63.
———. "Further Notes on Interrelated Greek and Coptic Documents of the Sixth and Seventh Centuries." *Chronique d'Egypte* 70 (1995): 341–53.

———. "Dated and Datable Coptic Documentary Hands Before A.D. 700." *Le Muséon* 110 (1997): 349–66.
———. "*P.Lond.* IV 1494 Revisited." *Aegyptus* 77 (1997): 125–35.
———. "Prophethood, Texts, and Artifacts: The Monastery of Epiphanius." *Greek, Roman, and Byzantine Studies* 39 (1998): 307–24.
———. "Apa Abraham." In *Byzantine Monastic Foundation Documents*, ed. J. P. Thomas and A. C. Hero, 1: 51–58. 5 vols. Washington, DC, 2000.
———. "P.Mich. Inv. 6898 Revisited: A Sixth-Century Coptic Contract from Aphrodito." *Zeitschrift für Papyrologie und Epigraphik* 141 (2002): 199–203.
———. "The Bilingual Written Environment of Late Antique Egypt: Did Gender Have Anything to Do With It?," *DIOTIMA*, http://www.stoa.org/diotima/essays/fc04/MacCoull.html.
———. "Why Do We Have Coptic Documentary Papyri Before A.D. 641?" In *Actes du huitième Congrès international d'études coptes*, ed. N. Bosson and A. Boud'hors, 2: 751–58. 2 vols. Leuven, 2007.
———. "The Aphrodito Estate of Count Ammonios." *Analecta Papyrologica* 16 (2007): 83–90.
———. "More on Documentary Coptic at Aphrodito." *Chronique d'Egypte* 82 (2007): 365–74.
———. "A Date for *P.KRU* 105?" Paper at the Twenty-fifth International Congress of Papyrologists, Ann Arbor, 2007.
———. "Προνόμιον, *Privilegium*, and Precedent in the Law of Christian Egypt." Forthcoming.
Maravela-Solbakk, A. "Monastic Book Production in Christian Egypt." In *Spätantike Bibliotheken, Leben und Lesen in den frühen Klöstern Ägyptens*. Vienna, 2008.
Marcone, A. "A Long Late Antiquity?" *Journal of Late Antiquity* 1 (2008): 4–19.
Maresch, K. *Nomisma und Nomismatia*. Opladen, 1994.
Mayerson, P. "The Port of Clysma (Suez) in Transition from Roman to Arab Rule." *Journal of Near Eastern Studies* 55 (1996): 119–26.
Mirković, M. "*Ktetores, syntelestai* et l'impôt." In *Les archives de Dioscore d'Aphrodité cent ans après*, ed. Fournet, 191–202.
Neville, L. *Authority in Byzantine Provincial Society, 950–1100*. Cambridge, 2004.
Noeske, H.-C. "Finds of Coins and Related Objects from the Monastery of Apa Shenute at Suhag." Forthcoming in *Dumbarton Oaks Papers* 63 (2009).
O'Connell, E. R. "Transforming Monumental Landscapes in Late Antique Egypt: Monastic Dwellings in Legal Documents from Western Thebes." *Journal of Early Christian Studies* 15 (2007): 239–75.
O'Donnell, J. J. *Augustine: A New Biography*. New York, 2005.
Oikonomides, N. "Formularies." *ODB*, 2: 797–89.
Palme, B. "Asyl und Schutzbrief im spätantiken Ägypten." In *Das antike Asyl*, ed. M. Dreher, 203–36. Cologne, 2003.

Papaconstantinou, A. "Sanctuaires de la Vierge dans l'Égypte byzantine et omeyyade." *Journal of Juristic Papyrology* 30 (2000): 81–94.

———. "Notes sur les actes de donation d'enfant au monastère thébain de Saint-Phoibammon." *Journal of Juristic Papyrology* 32 (2002): 83–105.

———. "ΘΕΙΑ ΟΙΚΟΝΟΜΙΑ: Les actes thébains de donation d'enfants ou la gestion monastique de la pénurie." *Travaux et mémoires* 14 (2002): 511–26.

———. "Historiography, Hagiography, and the Making of the Coptic 'Church of the Martyrs' in Early Islamic Egypt." *Dumbarton Oaks Papers* 60 (2006): 65–86.

———. "'They Shall Speak the Arabic Language and Take Pride in It': Reconsidering the Fate of Coptic After the Arab Conquest." *Le Muséon* 120 (2007): 273–99.

———. "Dioscore et la question du bilinguisme dans l'Egypte du VIe siècle." In *Les archives de Dioscore d'Aphrodité*, ed. Fournet, 77–88.

Papagianni, E. "Legal Institutions and Practice in Matters of Ecclesiastical Property." In *Economic History of Byzantium*, ed. Laiou, 3:1037–47.

Papini, L. "Notes on the Formulary of some Coptic Documentary Papyri from Middle Egypt." *Bulletin de la Société d'Archéologie Copte* 25 (1983): 83–89.

Porten, B., ed. *The Elephantine Papyri in English*. Leiden, 1996.

Richter, T. S. "Zwei Urkunden des koptischen Notars David, des Sohnes des Psate." *Archiv für Papyrusforschung* 44 (1998): 69–85.

———. "Arabische Lehnworte und Formeln in koptischen Rechtsurkunden." *Journal of Juristic Papyrology* 31 (2001): 75–89.

———. "O.Crum Ad.15 and the Emergence of Arabic Words in Coptic Legal Documents." In *Papyrology and the History of Early Islamic Egypt*, ed. Sijpesteijn and Sundelin, 97–114.

———. "What's in a Story? Cultural Narratology and Coptic Child Donation Documents." *Journal of Juristic Papyrology* 35 (2005): 237–64.

———. "Coptic Letters." *Asiatische Studien / Etudes Asiatiques* 62 (2008): 739–70.

———. "Greek, Coptic, and the 'Language of the Hijra': Rise and Decline of the Coptic Language in Late Antique and Medieval Egypt." In *From Hellenism to Islam: Cultural and Linguistic Change in the Roman Near East*, ed. H. Cotton. Cambridge, forthcoming.

———. "Greek and Coptic in Late Antiquity." In *Law and Society in Ptolemaic, Roman, and Byzantine Egypt*, ed. J. G. Keenan et al. Cambridge, forthcoming.

Robinson, C. *Abd al-Malik*. Oxford, 2005.

Rücker, A., ed. "Anaphora Syriaca Timothei Alexandrini." In *Anaphorae Syriacae*, 1.1: 3–47. Rome, 1939.

Ruffini, G. *Social Networks in Byzantine Egypt*. Cambridge, 2008.

Sarris, P. "The Justinianic Plague: Origins and Effects." *Continuity and Change* 17 (2002): 169–82.

———. "On Jairus Banaji's *Agrarian Change in Late Antiquity*." *Historical Materialism* 13 (2005): 207–19.

———. *Economy and Society in the Age of Justinian*. Cambridge, 2006.

———. "Bubonic Plague in Byzantium: The Evidence of Non-Literary Sources." In *Plague and the End of Antiquity: The Pandemic of 541–750*, ed. L. K. Little, 119–32. Cambridge, 2007.

Satzinger, H. "ⲕⲁⲑⲁⲣⲱⲥ ⲕⲁⲓ ⲁⲡⲟⲕⲣⲟⲧⲱⲥ in koptischen Urkunden." *Chronique d'Egypte* 45 (1970): 417–20.

Schaten, S. "Ein weiteres Familienarchiv aus Djeme: KRU 66 und KRU 76, die Testamente der Susanna." In *Akten des 21. Internationalen Papyrologenkongresses*, ed. B. Kramer et al., 902–13. Stuttgart, 1997.

Schiller, A. A. "The Coptic ⲗⲟⲅⲟⲥ ⲙⲡⲛⲟⲩⲧⲉ Documents." In *Studi in memoria di A. Albertoni*, 1:303–45. 2 vols. Padua, 1935.

———. "A Family Archive from Jeme." In *Studi in onore di Vincenzo Arangio-Ruiz*, 325–75. Naples, 1952.

———. "The Budge Papyrus of Columbia University." *Journal of the American Research Center in Egypt* 7 (1968): 79–117.

Schmelz, G. *Kirchliche Amtsträger im spätantiken Ägypten*. Leipzig, 2002.

Schroeder, C. T. "Prophecy and *Porneia* in Shenoute's Letters: The Rhetoric of Sexuality in a Late Antique Egyptian Monastery." *Journal of Near Eastern Studies* 65 (2006): 81–97.

———. *Monastic Bodies: Discipline and Salvation in Shenoute of Atripe*. Philadelphia, 2007.

Sharpe, R. "The Use of Writs in the Eleventh Century." *Anglo-Saxon England* 32 (2003): 247–91.

Shepard, J. "The Byzantine Commonwealth 1000–1500." In *The Cambridge History of Christianity*, vol. 5: *Eastern Christianity*, ed. M. Angold, 3–52. Cambridge, 2005.

Sijpesteijn, P. M. "The Arab Conquest of Egypt and the Beginning of Muslim Rule." In *Egypt*, ed. Bagnall, 437–59.

———. "New Rule over Old Structures: Egypt After the Muslim Conquest." In *Regime Change in the Ancient Near East and Egypt*, ed. H. Crawford, 183–200. Proceedings of the British Academy 136. Oxford, 2007.

———. "Landholding Patterns in Early Islamic Egypt." *Journal of Agrarian Change* 9 (2009): 120–33.

Simon, D. "Intestate Succession." *ODB*, 2: 1004.

Sirat, C. *Writing as Handwork*. Turnhout, 2006.

Smyrlis, K. "The Management of Monastic Estates: The Evidence of the Typika." *Dumbarton Oaks Papers* 56 (2002): 245–61.

Stacey, R. C. *Dark Speech: The Performance of Law in Early Ireland*. Philadelphia, 2007.

Stancliffe, C. "Religion and Society in Ireland." In *The New Cambridge Medieval History*, vol. 1: *c.500–c.700*, ed. P. Fouracre, 397–425. Cambridge, 2005.

Steinwenter, A. "Die Rechtsstellung der Kirchen und Klöster nach den Papyri." *Zeitschrift der Savigny-Stiftung für Rechtsgeschichte, kanonistische Abteilung* 50 (1930): 1–50.

———. "Byzantinische Mönchstestamente." *Aegyptus* 12 (1932): 55–64.

———. "Zur Edition der koptischen Rechtsurkunden aus Djême." *Orientalia* 4 (1935): 377–85.

———. "ⲛⲟⲙⲟⲥ in den koptischen Rechtsurkunden." In *Studi in onore di A. Calderini e R. Paribeni*, 2: 461–69. 2 vols. Milan, 1957.

Thirard, C. "Le monastère d'Epiphane à Thébes: nouvelle interprétation chronologique." In *Études coptes IX*, ed. Boud'hors et al., 367–74.

Thomas, J. P. *Private Religious Foundations in the Byzantine Empire*. Washington, DC, 1987.

———, and A. C. Hero, eds. *Byzantine Monastic Foundation Documents*. 5 vols. Washington, DC, 2000.

Till, W. C. "Koptische Schutzbriefe." *Mitteilungen des deutschen archäologischen Instituts Kairo* 8 (1938): 71–146.

———. "ⲉⲗⲉⲩⲑⲉⲣⲟⲥ = 'unbescholten'." *Le Muséon* 64 (1951): 251–59.

Timbie, J. "Shenoute." *ODB*, 3: 1888.

———. "Coptic Christianity." In *Blackwell Companion to Eastern Christianity*, ed. Parry, 94–116.

Torallas Tovar, S. "The Police in Byzantine Egypt." In *Current Research in Egyptology 2000*, ed. A. McDonald and C. Riggs, 115–23. Oxford, 2000.

Treadgold, W. *The Early Byzantine Historians*. New York, 2007.

Urbanik, J. "Dioskoros and the Law (on Succession)." In *Les archives de Dioscore d'Aphrodité cent ans après*, ed. Fournet, 117–42.

van der Vliet, J. "Perennial Hellenism: László Török and the al-Mu'allaga Lintel (Coptic Museum inv. no. 753)." *Eastern Christian Art* 4 (2007): 77–80.

van Minnen, P. "Dioscorus and the Law." In *Learned Antiquity*, ed. A. A. MacDonald et al., 115–33. Leuven, 2003.

Watts, E. J. *City and School in Late Antique Athens and Alexandria*. Berkeley, 2006.

Vycichl, W. *Dictionnaire étymologique de la langue copte*. Leuven, 1983.

Wickham, C. *Framing the Early Middle Ages*. Oxford, 2005.

Wilfong, T. G. "The Non-Muslim Communities: Christian Communities." In *The Cambridge History of Egypt*, 1: *Islamic Egypt, 640–1517*, ed. Petry, 175–97.

———. "Agriculture among the Christian Population of Early Islamic Egypt: Practice and Theory." In *Agriculture in Egypt*, ed. Bowman and Rogan, 217–35.

———. "'Friendship and Physical Desire': The Discourse of Female Homoeroticism in Fifth-century CE Egypt." In *Among Women*, ed. N. S. Rabinowitz and L. Auanger, 304–29. Austin, 2002.

———. "Women's Things and Men's Things: Notes on Gender and Property at Jeme." *Bulletin of the American Society of Papyrologists* 40 (2003): 213–21.

———. "Gender and Society in Byzantine Egypt." In *Egypt*, ed. Bagnall, 309–27.

Wipszycka, E. "Les ordres mineurs dans l'Église d'Égypte du IVe au VIIIe siècle." *Journal of Juristic Papyrology* 23 (1993): 181–215; repr. in eadem, *Études sur le christianisme dans l'Égypte de l'antiquité tardive*, 225–55. Rome, 1996.
Wood, S. *The Proprietary Church in the Medieval West*. Oxford, 2006.
Wormald, P. *Legal Culture in the Early Medieval West: Law as Text, Image and Experience*. London, 1999.
Worp, K.A. "Witness Subscriptions in Documents from the Dioscorus Archive." In *Les archives de Dioscore d'Aphrodité*, ed. Fournet, 143–53.
Zuckerman, C. *Du village à l'empire: autour du registre fiscal d'Aphroditô (525/526)*. Paris, 2004.
———. "Learning from the Enemy and More: Studies in 'Dark Centuries' Byzantium." *Millennium* 2 (2005): 79–135.

Index

Personal Names

A

Aaron, son of Andrew, *P.KRU* 42
Aaron, son of the late Cyriac, brother of Peter, *P.CLT* 5
Aaron, son of the late Shenoute, brother of Victor and Pelotare, *P.KRU* 5, 13, 12
Aaron, son of Shoumara, *P.KRU* 13
Abessa, daughter of the late Zacharias and Abigaia, sister of Takoum, widow of George, mother of Tsherkah (Thekla) and Arsenios, *P.KRU* 25, 47, 50, 45/46
Abigaia, daughter of Samuel (deacon and monk, son of Chareb) and Tshenoute, wife of Daniel son of Komes, sister of Stephen and Chareb, *P.KRU* 35, 36
Abigaia, wife of Zacharias, mother of Abessa and Takoum, *P.KRU* 47, 45/46
Abraham, son of Athanasius, *P.KRU* 106
Abraham, son of the late Constantine, *P.KRU* 37
Abraham, son of the late Cyriac, *P.KRU* 74
Abraham, son of the late David, brother of Theodore, scribe, *P.KRU* 68, 37
Abraham, son of Enoch, *P.KRU* 105
Abraham, son of Lelou, priest, *P.KRU* 105
Abraham, son of Theodore, husband of Elizabeth, *P.KRU* 68, 36, 37, 38
Abraham, son of the late Theodore, *P.CLT* 5, *P.KRU* 44 (?)
Abraham, son of Tobias, *P.KRU* 67
Abraham (Apa), bishop, monastic founder, *P.KRU* 75, 65
Abraham, P.Vat.Copti Doresse 3
Agnatius, son of the late Matthias, brother of Ezekiel, *P.CLT* 6
Amanias, widow of John (deacon), *P.Lond.* V 1709
Ammonius (Apa), *P.KRU* 75
Ananias, son of the late Abraham, *lashane*, *P.KRU* 35
Ananias, son of the late Psês and Tmanna, *P.KRU* 27
Anastasia, daughter of Jacob and Thaumastê, P.Mich. inv. 6898
Anastasius, son of Victor, P.Mich. inv. 6898
Anastasius, deacon, *P.KRU* 38
Anatolius, son of the late Samuel and Rebecca, *P.KRU* 50, 3
Anchên, son of George, brother of Zebedee, *P.KRU* 9
Andrew, son of the late Lazarus, brother of John (?), *P.KRU* 35
Andrew, son of Phêr, *P.CLT* 2
Andrew, son of the late Pser, *P.CLT* 1
Andrew, son of Secundinus, *P.KRU* 45/46
Andrew, son of the late Phoibammon, *P.KRU* 69
Anna, daughter of the late John and the late Taham, *P.KRU* 106
Anoup, son of Apollo and Mesianê, half-brother of Julius, monk, *P.Cair.Masp.* II 67176r + P.Alex. inv. 698
Antony, son of Paul, *P.KRU* 35, 25, 36

Apatêr, son of Sarapion, P.Mich. inv. 6898
Aphous, husband of Victorinê, *P.Lond.* V 1709
Aristophanes, son of John, scribe, *P.KRU* 10, 25, 47, *P.CLT* 6, *P.KRU* 17, 45/46, 27
Aroou, son of the late Daniel, brother of George, *P.KRU* 21
Arsenios, son of the late George and Abessa, *P.KRU* 50
Athanasius, son of the late Antony, *P.CLT* 1
Athanasius, son of Daniel, *P.CLT* 2
Athanasius, son of David, *meizoteros* (*lashane*), *P.KRU* 10
Athanasius, son of George, *lashane*, *P.CLT* 5, *P.KRU* 68, 36, 37
Athanasius, son of the late Jeremias, *P.KRU* 35
Athanasius, son of the late Papnouthios, *P.CLT* 1
Athanasius, son of Peter, *P.KRU* 34
Athanasius, son of Pillustris and Thêre, brother of Enoch, *P.KRU* 9
Athanasius, son of Sanchêm, *P.CLT* 6
Athanasius, monk, *P.CLT* 1, 4, 2
Athanasius, patrician, *P.Lond.* V 1709
Athanasius, *P.KRU* 51

B
Bartholomew, son of the late John, *P.CLT* 1
Barach, *P.KRU* 44

C
Chaêl, son of Psmô, *lashane*, *P.KRU* 17, 13, 12, 106
Chaêl, son of Severus, *P.KRU* 5
Chareb, son of Samuel and Tshenoute, brother of Abigaia and Stephen, *P.KRU* 36
Chmntsnêu, son of Shenoute, priest, hegoumenos, scribe, *P.KRU* 13, 12, 106

Christopher, contributor (*syntelestês*), father of Colluthus and Mark, P.Mich. inv. 6898, P.Vat.Copti Doresse 5, 1
Christopher, of Aphrodito, deceased, P.Vat.Copti Doresse 1
Colluthus, son of Christopher *syntelestês*, brother of Mark, P.Mich. inv. 6898, P.Vat.Copti Doresse 5, 1
Colluthus, son of the late John, *P.KRU* 12
Constantine, son of Cyrus, honey-seller, *P.Lond.* V 1709
Constantine, son of Philotheus, *P.CLT* 6
Constantine, son of the late Solomon, brother of John, ex-*lashane*, *P.CLT* 1, *P.KRU* 35, 10, 18
Constantine, (deceased) husband of Thaumastê, P.Mich. inv. 6898, P.Vat.Copti Doresse 2
Constantine, P.Vat.Copti Doresse 3
Cosmas, son of Joseph, *P.KRU* 19
Cosmas, son of Mena, *P.KRU* 54
Cosmas, son of Victor, *P.KRU* 51
Cyriac, son of the late Abraham, *P.KRU* 44
Cyriac, son of the late Andrew, *P.KRU* 36
Cyriac, son of Demetrius, superior, *P.KRU* 13
Cyriac, son of Joseph, *P.CLT* 1
Cyriac, son of the late Peter, *P.CLT* 6, *P.KRU* 50
Cyril, son of Elias, *P.CLT* 5
Cyril, son of the late Phoibammon, brother of Isaac, hegoumenos, *P.KRU* 67
Cyrus, son of Chaêl, *lashane*, *P.KRU* 88
Cyrus (Fl.), son of Colluthus, *archon*, *P.KRU* 27

D
Damian, *grammatikos*, scribe, *P.KRU* 105
Daniel, son of Andrew, priest, *P.KRU* 105
Daniel, son of David and Tellole, *P.KRU* 74
Daniel, son of the late Isidore, *P.KRU* 47
Daniel, son of Komes, husband of Abigaia, *P.KRU* 36

Daniel, son of Phoibammon, *P.CLT* 6
Daniel, son of Saul, *P.KRU* 3
Daniel, son of the late Zacharias, *P.KRU* 55
Daniel, monk, *P.CLT* 1, 4, 2
Daniel, priest, *P.KRU* 105
Daniel, *P.KRU* 51
David, son of (the late) Christopher and Tsyra, P.Vat.Copti Doresse 1
David, son of Ezekiel, deacon, *P.KRU* 105
David, son of Hllo (or: elder), *P.KRU* 65
David, son of Karakos, *P.KRU* 19
David, son of Paul and Sarra, *P.KRU* 74
David, son of Peter, *P.KRU* 3
David, son of Psate, scribe, *P.KRU* 5, 19
David, son of Severus, *P.CLT* 1, 6
David, son of Shoi, *P.KRU* 44
David, son of the late Victor, *P.KRU* 21
David, *P.CLT* 1
Demetrius, son of the late Leontius, *P.KRU* 21, 12
Dioscorus, son of David, brother of Job, *P.CLT* 1, 2
Dioscorus of Aphrodito, lawyer and scribe, *P.Cair.Masp.* II 67176r + P.Alex. inv. 689, *P.Lond.* V 1709

E
Efranke, son of the late David, *P.KRU* 38
Eiôt, son of Shenoute, priest, *P.CLT* 1
Elias, son of Moses, priest, scribe, *P.KRU* 74
Elias, son of Samuel, monk, *P.KRU* 75
Elias, son of Zacharias, *P.CLT* 6, *P.KRU* 37, 49
Elisha, son of Elias, *lashane*, *P.KRU* 74
Elisha, son of Hatre, deacon, *P.KRU* 105
Elisha, (deceased) archdeacon, *P.KRU* 66/76
Elizabeth, daughter of the late Epiphanius and Mary, widow of Loule (Loula), mother of George, wife of Abraham son of Theodore, mother of Isaac and Kyra, *P.KRU* 35, 68, 36, 37

Enoch, son of Pillustris and Tthêre, brother of Athanasius, *P.KRU* 9
Ephraim, son of the late Psate, *P.KRU* 10
Epiphanius, son of the late Zacharias, *P.KRU* 35
Epiphanius (Apa), *P.KRU* 75
Epiphanius (deceased), *P.KRU* 47
Ezekiel, son of the late Matthias, brother of Agnatius, *P.CLT* 6, *P.KRU* 50, 45/46
Ezekiel, son of Pahom, *P.KRU* 105

F
Faustus, son of the late Andrew, *P.KRU* 42, 27

G
Gamoul, son of the late Elisha, *P.CLT* 1
George, son of Chmntsnêu, *lashane*, *P.KRU* 42
George, son of the late Cosmas, *P.KRU* 3
George, son of Daniel, *P.KRU* 17, (21?), 27
George, son of (the late) Isaac (?), P.Mich. inv. 6898
George, son of Johanna daughter of Apa Elias (son of Apa Victor and Eudoxia), *P.KRU* 18
George, son of the late Loule (Loula) and Elizabeth, *P.KRU* 68, 37, 38
George, son of the late Matthew, *P.KRU* 55
George, son of Patermoute, monk, priest, *P.KRU* 75
George, son of Phêu, *P.KRU* 10
George, son of the late Samuel, *P.KRU* 69
George, archdeacon, *P.KRU* 44
George (?), scribe, P.Vat.Copti Doresse 2
George, (deceased) husband of Abessa, *P.KRU* 50
George, P.Vat.Copti Doresse 3
Gera, *P.KRU* 67
Germanos, bishop, *P.KRU* 3

Germanos, deceased father of Shenoute, Hemai, Stephen, Tsône, and Victorine, *P.KRU* 66/76, 10, 21
Geton, son of John, *P.KRU* 105

H
Hamôs, son of the late Peter, *P.KRU* 36
Hemai, son of the late Germanos, brother of Shenoute, Stephen, Tsône, and Victorine, *P.KRU* 66/76, 10, 21
Hêu, son of Antony, *P.KRU* 45/46
Hllô, son of the late David, widower of Sarra, *P.KRU* 19

I
Isaac, son of Abraham and Elizabeth, *P.KRU* 37, 38
Isaac, son of Constantine, *P.KRU* 25, 47, 50, 42, 54; *lashane*, *P.KRU* 38
Isaac, son of the late Papnouthios (Papnoute), *P.CLT* 4
Isaac, son of the late Phoibammon, brother of Cyril, *P.KRU* 67
Isaac, son of the late Zacharias, *P.CLT* 6, *P.KRU* 106
Isaac, monk, priest, *P.KRU* 75
Isaac (Apa), *P.CLT* 1
Isidore, son of Tribunus (?), *P.KRU* 3

J
Jacob, son of Andrew, *P.KRU* 3, 18
Jacob, son of David, monk, *P.KRU* 75
Jacob, son of George, scribe, P.Vat.Copti Doresse 1
Jacob, son of Isaac, *pragmateutês* (businessman), *P.CLT* 5
Jacob, son of Paham (monk/priest) and the late Susanna, *P.KRU* 67
Jacob, son of Pashêm, *P.KRU* 74
Jacob, son of Simon, *P.KRU* 74
Jacob, monk, *P.CLT* 1, 4, 5
Jacob, superior, *P.KRU* 65
Jacob, husband of Thaumastê, P.Mich. inv. 6898, P.Vat.Copti Doresse 2
Jacob, P.Vat.Copti Doresse 3

Jeremiah, archpriest, *P.KRU* 105
Jeremias, son of the late Athanasius, brother of Victor (?), scribe, *P.KRU* 18
Jeremias, son of the late Basil, *P.CLT* 1
Jeremias, son of the late Elias, *P.CLT* 5
Jeremias, son of Moses, *P.KRU* 34
Joannake, son of John, *P.KRU* 13
Job, son of Alexander, scribe, *P.KRU* 88
Job, son of David, brother of Dioscorus, *P.CLT* 1, 2
John, son of David, *lashane*, *P.KRU* 77
John, son of John, scribe, *P.KRU* 46
John, son of Joseph, *P.KRU* 105
John, son of Kalearios (?), *P.KRU* 68
John, son of (the late) Lazarus, brother of Andrew (?), scribe, *P.CLT* 1, *P.KRU* 35, 51, 21, 42, 38
John, son of Mathias, *lashane*, *P.KRU* 51, 21
John, son of Papnoute, archpriest, *P.KRU* 75
John, son of the late Papnouthios, *P.KRU* 5
John, son of the late Solomon, brother of Constantine, ex-*lashane*, *P.CLT* 1, *P.KRU* 10
John, son of Victor, *P.KRU* 78
John, son of the late Victor, *P.KRU* 35; *lashane*, *P.KRU* 18
John, (deceased) deacon, *P.Lond.* V 1709
John, priest, *P.KRU* 25, 47
John, priest and hegoumenos, P.Vat.Copti Doresse 1
John, priest and oikonomos, *P.KRU* 18
Joseph, son of Abraham, priest, *P.KRU* 105
Joseph, son of Mythia, priest, *P.KRU* 105
Joseph, son of Palêtheos, *P.KRU* 74
Joseph, son of the late Peter, *P.KRU* 38
Joseph, son of the late Pinis, *P.KRU* 38
Julius, son of Sarapammon and Mesianê, monk, *P.Cair.Masp.* II 67176r + P.Alex. inv. 689

K
Kalapêsios, son of Sinouthios, priest, scribe, *P.CLT* 4
Kalê, son of Kalêl, *P.KRU* 66/76
Kale, son of Matoi, ex-*lashane*, *P.KRU* 65
Kame, son of Pabos, *P.KRU* 105
Kanênê, *P.KRU* 66/76
Koloje, daughter of Paham (?), *P.KRU* 3
Komes, son of Hatre, *P.CLT* 5
Komes, priest, scribe, *P.KRU* 35, 66/76
Komos, son of the late Damian, *P.KRU* 54
Komos (Komes), son of the late Hatre, *P.KRU* 9, 35, 68
Komes, son of the late Samuel (*lashane*), *P.CLT* 5
Kos, son of David, butcher, *P.KRU* 3
Kyra, daughter of Abraham and Elizabeth, *P.KRU* 37, 38
Kyri (Apa), son of Enoch, brother of Samuel, *P.KRU* 42
Kyrikos, son of Joseph, priest, *P.KRU* 105

L
Lala, son of the late Matthew, *P.CLT* 6
Lasan, son of Paman (?), *P.KRU* 13, 12
Leontius, son of the late Cyriac, *P.CLT* 1
Leontius, *lashane*, *P.KRU* 69
Lole, deacon, *P.KRU* 37
Loule (Loula), deceased husband of Elizabeth, *P.KRU* 68, 37, 38

M
Mark, son of Christopher *syntelestês*, brother of Colluthus, P.Mich. inv. 6898, P.Vat.Copti Doresse 5
Mark, son of Papnoute, deacon, *P.KRU* 17, 27 (?)
Mark, son of [N.], P.Vat.Copti Doresse 5
Martyria, daughter of Victor, *P.KRU* 34
Mary, daughter of the late Psate, *P.KRU* 10
Mary, daughter of the late Theodore, sister of Sophia, wife of Peter son of Pheu, *P.KRU* 44
Mary, wife of Theodore son of Aaron, mother of Sonchêm, *P.KRU* 88
Mathias, son of the late Ezekiel, brother of Victor, *P.CLT* 1
Megethos (?), son of Paul, P.Vat.Copti Doresse 3
Mena, son of Abraham, *P.KRU* 55
Mena, son of Hllô and the late Sarra, *P.KRU* 19
Mena, son of Fl. [N.], *P.Lond.* V 1709
Mena, son of Sie, *P.Lond.* V 1709
Mena, *lashane*, *P.KRU* 69
Mena, monk, *P.KRU* 106
Menas, son of the late Abraham, *P.KRU* 51
Menas, son of the late John, *P.KRU* 78
Menas, son of the late Paam, *meizoteros* (*lashane*), *P.KRU* 10
Menas, son of Philotheus, *P.KRU* 3
Mercurius, son of the late Zacharias, *P.CLT* 4
Mesianê, mother of Anoup and Julius (monks), *P.Cair.Masp.* II 67176r + P.Alex. inv. 689
Methuselah, son of the late Elias, *P.KRU* 19
Moses, son of the late Joseph, brother of Pesate, *P.KRU* 42
Moses, son of Matthew, priest, oikonomos, *P.KRU* 75
Moses, son of the late Plouj and Tasia, monk, father of monk Theodore, *P.CLT* 1, 2
Moses, son of archpriest Shenoute, deacon, *P.KRU* 3

N
Nabernoukios, priest, *P.KRU* 67
Niharau, son of Peha..., *P.CLT* 6
Noah, son of Jeremias, priest, hegoumenos, *P.KRU* 45/46, 21, 42, 13, 12, 106
Nonne, daughter of [N.], *P.KRU* 17

P
Paham, son of Epiphanius and Thatre, widower of Susanna, father of

Papnoute (deceased), Jacob, and Thatre, monk, priest, P.KRU 67
Paham, son of Constantine, P.CLT 5
Pahash, son of Elisha, P.KRU 18
Pahôm, son of Apollo, priest, hegoumenos, P.Mich. inv. 6898
Pamphilus, son of the late Peter, P.KRU 38
Pamprepius, son of Chaêl, P.KRU 78
Panachôre, son of Joseph, P.KRU 51
Panias, son of Phabô, P.KRU 18
Papas, son of Stephen, P.KRU 88
Papas (Apa), P.CLT 1
Papas, deacon, P.KRU 66/76
Papnoute (Apa), official of monastery of Apostles, Pharoou (Aphrodito), P.Cair. Masp. II 67176r + P.Alex. inv. 689
Papnoute, son of Isaac, deacon, P.KRU 105
Papnoute (Papnouthi), lashane, P.KRU 105
Papnoute, priest, P.KRU 66/76
Papnouthios, son of Cyriac, P.KRU 10
Papnouthios, son of the late Peter, brother of Psêre (?), archdeacon, P.KRU 3
Papnouthios, deacon, P.KRU 38
Patermoute, son of John, lector, P.KRU 75
Patermoute, son of the late Pestinos, brother of the late Peshate (?), P.KRU 13
Patermoute, archpriest, P.KRU 68
Patermoute, priest, P.KRU 44
Patermouthios, son of the late Constantine, P.KRU 12
Paul, son of Ananias and Sarra, husband of Sarra, father of Susana and David, P.KRU 74
Paul, son of Azarias, deacon, P.Lond. V 1709
Paul, (deceased) son of the late Constantine and Thaumastê, P.Mich. inv. 6898
Paul, son of Kabiou, P.KRU 34
Paul, son of Kanah, P.KRU 88
Paul, son of the late Moses and Tsia, brother of Susanna, P.KRU 66/76
Paul, (deceased) father of Thaumastê, P.Mich. inv. 6898
Pchêr, son of the late Cyriac, brother of Aaron, P.CLT 5

Pcher, son of the late Epiphanius, P.KRU 21
Peêu, son of the late Thomas, P.KRU 5
Pekosh, son of Psmo (lashane), P.KRU 65
Pelotare, son of the late Shenoute, brother of Victor and Aaron, P.KRU 5
Pesate, son of the late Constantine, P.KRU 10
Pesate, son of the late Joseph, brother of Moses, P.KRU 42
Pesau, son of Pesyntheus, P.KRU 78
Peshate, son of the late Elias, P.KRU 35
Peshate, son of Joseph, P.KRU 45/46
Peshate, (deceased) son of Pestine (Pestinos), brother of Patermoute, P.KRU 13
Pesyntheus, son of Paul, P.KRU 10, 21
Pesyntheus, son of Psyrus (builder), P.KRU 42
Pesyntheus, son of Stephen, P.KRU 35, 3
Peter, son of [N.], lashane, P.KRU 74
Peter, son of Andrew, P.KRU 35
Peter, son of Constantine, P.Mich. inv. 6898
Peter, son of Isaac, P.CLT 6
Peter, son of Jeremiah, P.KRU 105
Peter, son of the late Komos (Komes), lashane, P.CLT 1, P.KRU 9, 35, 55, 51, 50, 21
Peter, son of Moses, deacon, P.KRU 105
Peter, son of the late Patermouthios, P.KRU 37
Peter, son of the late Permô, priest, P.Mich. inv. 6898
Peter, son of Pheu, husband of Mary, P.KRU 44
Peter, son of the late Pisate, P.KRU 19
Peter, son of the late Severus, P.KRU 50, 42
Peter, son of Theophilus, P.KRU 74
Peter, son of Zacharias, grandson of Petale, P.KRU 27
Peter (Apa), (deceased) priest, P.KRU 65
Peter, superior, P.KRU 88
Peter, priest, P.KRU 19
Petronius, son of George, P.KRU 104

Petronius (Apa), *P.CLT* 5
Philadelphia, daughter of John and Amanias, *P.Lond.* V 1709
Philemon, son of Joseph, *P.KRU* 51, 49
Philochristos, son of [N.], deacon, *P.KRU* 45/46
Philotheos, son of Pesynthios, *P.CLT* 4
Philotheus, son of Komos, *P.KRU* 51
Philotheus, son of Meus, *P.KRU* 67
Philotheus, son of the late Solomon, *P.KRU* 21
Philotheus, monk, *P.KRU* 106
Phil..., deacon, *P.KRU* 47
Phoibammon, son of the late George, husband of Mary, *P.KRU* 42, 44, 106 (?)
Phoibammon, son of the late John (deacon), *P.Lond.* V 1709
Phoibammon, son of the late Pisês, *P.CLT* 6
Phoibammon, son of Stephen, priest, *P.KRU* 3
Phoibammon, son of Victor, *P.KRU* 65
Phoibammon, priest, *P.KRU* 25, 47
Pishate, son of Pilish, *P.KRU* 18
Pisrael, son of Paul, *P.KRU* 42, 19
Pisrael, son of Psate, *P.KRU* 65
Plêin, son of Patermoute, *P.KRU* 44
Pmai, son of the late Hllô, *P.KRU* 10
Premnhot, son of Athanasius, *P.KRU* 49
Prese, son of Joseph, *P.KRU* 51
Prêshe, son of the late Jeremias, *P.CLT* 6
Psaiô, son of the late Athanasius, *P.KRU* 66/76
Psan, son of Pchôl, *P.KRU* 18
Psan (Apa), monk, *P.KRU* 75
Psate, son of Pisrael, scribe, *P.CLT* 1, 5, *P.KRU* 35, 36, 37, 44
Psêre, son of the late Peter, priest, hegoumenos, *P.KRU* 21, 3, 12, 18
Pshêre, priest, hegoumenos, *P.CLT* 1, *P.KRU* 35, 38, 66/76
Pshêre, deacon, *P.KRU* 36
Psmô, son of Patermoute, *P.KRU* 47
Psmô, *lashane*, *P.KRU* 65, 88

Psousire, P.Vat.Copti Doresse 5

R
Rasios (Apa), scribe, P.Mich. inv. 6898

S
Samuel, son of Enoch, brother of Apa Kyri, chief of police, *P.KRU* 42
Samuel, son of the late Enoch, *P.KRU* 13, 12, 106
Samuel, son of Joses, *P.KRU* 65
Samuel, son of Mena, *lashane*, *P.KRU* 42
Samuel, son of Menas, *P.KRU* 74
Samuel, son of Philotheus, *P.CLT* 6
Samuel, priest, *P.CLT* 4
Sanagapê, son of the late Menas, *P.KRU* 21
Sarra, wife of Paul son of Ananias, mother of Susana and David, *P.KRU* 74
Sarra, (deceased) wife of Hllô son of David, *P.KRU* 19
Senouthios, son of the late Apa Dios, *P.KRU* 13
Senouthios, son of Elias, *P.KRU* 55
Senouthios, son of the late Philotheus, oikonomos, *P.KRU* 54
Sergius, *P.KRU* 55
Severus, son of the late Moses, *lashane*, *P.CLT* 1, 5
Severus, son of the late Samuel, scribe, *P.KRU* 69
Severus, son of the late Souai, *lashane*, *P.CLT* 1
Severus, monk, *P.CLT* 2
Shenetôm, son of the late Jacob, *lashane*, *P.CLT* 1
Shenetom, son of the late Menas, *P.KRU* 66/76
Shenoute, son of the late Chmntsnêu, deacon, then priest, scribe, *P.KRU* 5, 13, 12, 106, 54
Shenoute, son of the late Germanos, brother of Hemai, Stephen, Tsône, and Victorine, priest, *P.KRU* 66/76, 10, 21

Shenoute, son of the late Phoibammon, P.KRU 17, 3
Shenoute, archpriest, P.KRU 3
Shenoute, monk, P.CLT 5
Shenoute, priest, P.CLT 1, P.KRU 68, 36, 37, 49
Shmntsnêu, P.CLT 5
Sina, son of Thesê, P.CLT 74
Solomon, son of the late Moses, P.KRU 3
Sonchêm, son of Theodore and Mary, oblate, P.KRU 88
Sophia, daughter of the late Psate, P.KRU 10
Sophia, daughter of the late Theodore, wife of Phoibammon son of the late George, P.KRU 44
Souai, son of George, P.KRU 88
Souai, son of Zacharias, P.KRU 51
Souros, *lashane*, P.KRU 44
Sourous, deacon, superior, P.KRU 104
Sourous, camelherd, P.KRU 66/76
Stephen, son of the late Germanos, brother of Shenoute, Hemai, Tsône, and Victorine, P.KRU 66/76, 10
Stephen, son of the late Moses, P.KRU 36, 37
Stephen, son of Pchol, P.KRU 5
Stephen, son of Samuel, brother of Abigaia and Chareb, P.KRU 36
Stephen, archpriest, P.KRU 9
Stephen, monk, P.KRU 75
Susana, daughter of Paul (son of Ananias) and Sarra, P.KRU 74
Susanna, daughter of the late Moses and Tsia, sister of Paul, mother of (the late) Germanos, P.KRU 66/76, 10, 21
Symeon, son of Tbenê, P.KRU 74

T
Tachel, daughter of Martha, P.KRU 3
Taham (Taam), daughter of Prômauô, P.Vat.Copti Doresse 5
Takoum, daughter of the late Psate, P.KRU 10

Takoum, daughter of the late Zacharias and Abigaia, sister of Abessa, P.KRU 47, 45/46
Thatre, daughter of monk Paham and the late Susanna, sister of Papnoute (deceased) and Jacob, P.KRU 67
Thaumastê, daughter of (the late) Paul, widow of Constantine, mother of (the late) Paul, widow of Jacob, mother of Anastasia, P.Mich. inv. 6898, P.Vat. Copti Doresse 2
Theodore, son of Aaron, husband of Mary, father of Sonchêm, builder, P.KRU 88
Theodore, son of Anatole, *lashane*, P.KRU 42
Theodore, son of the late Constantine, P.KRU 38
Theodore, son of the late David, brother of Abraham, P.KRU 68, 44
Theodore, son of Moses, monk, P.CLT 1, 2
Theodore, son of Solomon, P.CLT 5
Theodore, archpriest, P.KRU 65
Theodore, *grammatikos*, scribe, P.KRU 65
Theodore (?), scribe, P.Vat.Copti Doresse 5, 3 (?)
Theodore, P.KRU 51
Theodosius, son of the late Macarius, P.Vat.Copti Doresse 1
Theodosius, son of Menas, P.Vat.Copti Doresse 5
Theophanes, son of the late Joannake, P.KRU 67
Theophilus, son of [N.], P.CLT 6
Theopistos, lector, P.KRU 69
Thomas, son of the late John, P.CLT 5
Thomas, son of the late Mark, P.KRU 42
Thomas, son of Souai, P.CLT 4
Thomas, son of the late Victor, P.CLT 6, P.KRU 45/46, 42 (?)
Thomas, *lashane*, P.CLT 5
Tsacho, daughter of Blind Jacob, P.KRU 27

Tsherkah (Thekla), daughter of the late George and Abessa, *P.KRU* 50
Tsible, daughter of Hypatius, *P.KRU* 69
Tsible, *P.KRU* 67
Tsône, daughter of the late Germanos, sister of Shenoute, Hemai, Stephen, and Victorine, *P.KRU* 66/76
Tsône, daughter of Hllô and the late Sarra, *P.KRU* 19
Tsyra, daughter of Sabine and N., widow of Christopher, mother of David, P.Vat.Copti Doresse 1
Tsyros, (deceased) daughter of the late Takoum, *P.KRU* 54

U
Umai, son of Zaêl, *P.KRU* 88

V
Victor, son of Apatêr, priest, P.Vat.Copti Doresse 5, 1
Victor (Apa), son of Athanasius, *P.KRU* 18
Victor, son of Cyriac and Sanêth, priest, superior, *P.KRU* 77, 65
Victor, son of the late Ezekiel, brother of Mathias, *P.CLT* 1
Victor, son of John, oblate, *P.KRU* 78
Victor, son of the late Joseph, *lashane*, *P.KRU* 36, 37, 42 (?)
Victor (Apa), son of the late Papnoute, *P.CLT* 1
Victor (Apa), son of the late Phoibammon, P.Vat.Copti Doresse 5, 1
Victor (Apa), son of Pouôhe, priest, *P.KRU* 105
Victor, son of the late Shenoute, brother of Pelotare and Aaron, *P.KRU* 5
Victor, son of Staphôra, *P.KRU* 106
Victor, son of the late Theodore, monk, *P.KRU* 65
Victor, son of the late Thomas, *lashane*, *P.KRU* 35, 42 (?)
Victor (Apa), archpriest, *meizoteros*, *P.KRU* 37

Victor, priest, hegoumenos, *P.CLT* 5
Victorine, daughter of the late Germanos, sister of Shenoute, Hemai, Stephen, and Tsône, *P.KRU* 66/76
Victorinê, daughter of John (deacon), wife of Aphous, *P.Lond.* V 1709

Z
Zacharias, son of Apa Victor, *P.CLT* 5
Zacharias, son of John, *P.KRU* 74
Zacharias, son of the late Kalakôlf, *P.CLT* 6
Zacharias, son of the late Peter, *P.CLT* 6
Zacharias, son of the late Psate, *P.KRU* 10
Zacharias, son of the late Samuel, *P.CLT* 5
Zacharias, archpriest, *P.KRU* 66/76
Zacharias, priest, *P.CLT* 1, *P.KRU* 10, 68
Zacharias, superior, *P.KRU* 106
Zael, son of the late Theodore, *P.KRU* 51
Zebedee, son of George, brother of Anchên, *P.KRU* 9, 37

Scribes

Abraham, son of the late David, *P.KRU* 68, 37
Aristophanes, son of John, *P.KRU* 10, 25, 47, *P.CLT* 6, *P.KRU* 17, 45/46, 27
Chmntsnêu, son of Shenoute, priest, hegoumenos, *P.KRU* 13, 12, 106
Damian, *grammatikos*, *P.KRU* 105
David, son of Psate, *P.KRU* 5, 19
Dioscorus of Aphrodito, lawyer, *P.Cair. Masp.* II 67176r + P.Alex. inv. 689
Elias, son of Moses, priest, *P.KRU* 74
George (?), P.Vat.Copti Doresse 2
Jacob, son of George, P.Vat.Copti Doresse 1
Jeremias, son of the late Athanasius, brother of Victor (?), *P.KRU* 18
Job, son of Alexander, *P.KRU* 88
John, son of John, *P.KRU* 46

John, son of (the late) Lazarus, *P.CLT* 1, *P.KRU* 35, 51, 21, 42, 38
Kalapêsios, son of Sinouthios, priest, *P.CLT* 4
Komes, priest, *P.KRU* 35, 66/76
Paham, son of Epiphanius and Thatre, monk, priest, widower of Susanna, father of Papnoute (deceased), Jacob, and Thatre, *P.KRU* 67
Psate, son of Pisrael, *P.CLT* 1, 5, *P.KRU* 35, 36, 37, 44
Rasios (Apa), P.Mich. inv. 6898
Severus, son of the late Samuel, *P.KRU* 69
Shenoute, son of the late Chmntsnêu, deacon, then priest, *P.KRU* 5, 13, 12, 106, 54
Theodore, *grammatikos*, *P.KRU* 65
Theodore (?), P.Vat.Copti Doresse 5, 3 (?)

Clerics

bishops: Abraham, of Hermonthis, *P.KRU* 75, 65
Germanos, *P.KRU* 3

archpriests: Jeremiah, *P.KRU* 105
John, son of Papnoute, *P.KRU* 75
Patermoute, *P.KRU* 68
Shenoute, *P.KRU* 3
Stephen, *P.KRU* 9
Theodore, *P.KRU* 65
Victor (Apa), also *meizoteros*, *P.KRU* 37
Zacharias, *P.KRU* 66/76

priests: Abraham, son of Lelou, *P.KRU* 105
Chmntsnêu, son of Shenoute, also hegoumenos and scribe, *P.KRU* 13, 12, 106
Daniel, son of Andrew, *P.KRU* 105
Daniel, *P.KRU* 105
Eiôt, son of Shenoute, *P.CLT* 1
Elias, son of Moses, also scribe, *P.KRU* 74
George, son of Patermoute, also monk, *P.KRU* 75

Isaac, also monk, *P.KRU* 75
John, *P.KRU* 25, 47
John, also hegoumenos, P.Vat.Copti Doresse 1
John, also oikonomos, *P.KRU* 18
Joseph, son of Abraham, *P.KRU* 105
Joseph, son of Mythia, *P.KRU* 105
Kalapêsios, son of Sinouthios, also scribe, *P.CLT* 4
Komes, also scribe, *P.KRU* 35, 66/76
Kyrikos, son of Joseph, *P.KRU* 105
Moses, son of Matthew, also oikonomos, *P.KRU* 75
Nabernoukios, *P.KRU* 67
Noah, son of Jeremias, also hegoumenos, *P.KRU* 45/46, 21, 42, 13, 12, 106
Paham, son of Epiphanius and Thatre, also monk, *P.KRU* 67
Pahôm, son of Apollo, also hegoumenos, P.Mich. inv. 6898
Papnoute, *P.KRU* 66/76
Patermoute, *P.KRU* 44
Peter, son of the late Permô, P.Mich. inv. 6898
Peter (Apa) (deceased), *P.KRU* 65
Peter, *P.KRU* 19
Phoibammon, son of Stephen, *P.KRU* 3
Phoibammon, *P.KRU* 25, 47
Psêre, son of the late Peter, also hegoumenos, *P.KRU* 21, 3, 12, 18
Pshêre, also hegoumenos, *P.CLT* 1, *P.KRU* 35, 38, 66/76
Samuel, *P.CLT* 4
Shenoute, son of the late Chmntsnêu, earlier deacon, also scribe, *P.KRU* 5, 13, 12, 106, 54
Shenoute, *P.CLT* 1, *P.KRU* 68, 36, 37, 49
Victor, son of Apatêr, P.Vat.Copti Doresse 5, 1
Victor, son of Cyriac and Sanêth, also superior, *P.KRU* 77, 65
Victor (Apa), son of Pouôhe, *P.KRU* 105
Victor, also hegoumenos, *P.CLT* 5
Zacharias, *P.CLT* 1, *P.KRU* 10, 68

archdeacons: Elisha (deceased), *P.KRU* 66/76
George, *P.KRU* 44
Papnouthios, son of the late Peter, *P.KRU* 3

deacons: Anastasius, *P.KRU* 38
David, son of Ezekiel, *P.KRU* 105
Elisha, son of Hatre, *P.KRU* 105
John (deceased), *P.Lond.* V 1709
Lole, *P.KRU* 37
Mark, son of Papnoute, *P.KRU* 17, 27 (?)
Moses, son of archpriest Shenoute, *P.KRU* 3
Papnoute, son of Isaac, *P.KRU* 105
Papnouthios, *P.KRU* 38
Paul, son of Azarias, *P.Lond.* V 1709
Peter, son of Moses, *P.KRU* 105
Philochristos, son of [N.], *P.KRU* 45/46
Phil..., *P.KRU* 47
Pshêre, *P.KRU* 36
Shenoute, son of the late Chmntsnêu, later priest, also scribe, *P.KRU* 5, 13, 12, 106, 54
Sourous, also superior, *P.KRU* 104

lectors: Patermoute, son of John, *P.KRU* 75
Theopistos, *P.KRU* 69

hegoumenoi: Chmntsnêu, son of Shenoute, also priest and scribe, *P.KRU* 13, 12, 106
Cyril, son of the late Phoibammon, *P.KRU* 67
John, also priest, P.Vat.Copti Doresse 1
Noah, son of Jeremias, also priest, *P.KRU* 45/46, 21, 42, 13, 12, 106
Pahôm, also priest, P.Mich. inv. 6898
Psêre, son of the late Peter, also priest, *P.KRU* 21, 3, 12, 18
Pshêre, also priest, *P.CLT* 1, *P.KRU* 35, 66/76, 38
Victor, also priest, *P.CLT* 5

monks: Anoup, son of Apollo and Mesianê, *P.Cair.Masp.* II 67176r + P.Alex. inv. 689
Athanasius, *P.CLT* 1, 4, 2
Daniel, *P.CLT* 1, 4, 2
Elias, son of Samuel, *P.KRU* 75
George, son of Patermoute, also priest, *P.KRU* 75
Isaac, also priest, *P.KRU* 75
Jacob, son of David, *P.KRU* 75
Jacob, *P.CLT* 1, 4, 5
Julius, son of Sarapammon and Mesianê, *P.Cair.Masp.* II 67176r + P.Alex. inv. 689
Mena, *P.KRU* 106
Moses, son of the late Plouj and Tasia, father of monk Theodore, *P.CLT* 1, 2
Paham, son of Epiphanius and Thatre, also priest, *P.KRU* 67
Philotheus, *P.KRU* 106
Psan (Apa), *P.KRU* 75
Severus, *P.CLT* 2
Shenoute, *P.CLT* 5
Stephen, *P.KRU* 75
Theodore, son of Moses, *P.CLT* 1, 2
Victor, son of the late Theodore, *P.KRU* 65

oblates: Petronius, son of George, *P.KRU* 104
Sonchêm, son of Theodore and Mary, *P.KRU* 88
Victor, son of John, *P.KRU* 78

oikonomoi: John, also priest, *P.KRU* 18
Moses, son of Matthew, also priest, *P.KRU* 75
Senouthios, son of the late Philotheus, *P.KRU* 54

superiors: Cyriac, son of Demetrius, *P.KRU* 13
Jacob, *P.KRU* 65
Peter, *P.KRU* 88
Sourous, *P.KRU* 104

Victor, son of Cyriac and Sanêth, also priest, *P.KRU* 77, 65
Zacharias, *P.KRU* 106

uncertain: Papnoute (Apa), official of monastery of Apostles, Pharoou (Aphrodito), *P.Cair.Masp.* II 67176r + P.Alex, inv. 689

Churches (see also Monasteries)

Apostles, Thebes (Jeme), *P.KRU* 105, 66/76, 36, 38
Catholic (Holy) Church, Jeme, *P.KRU* 75, *P.CLT* 1, *P.KRU* 35, 66/76, 68, 36, 37, 21, 42, 3, 13, 12, 106, 38
Colluthus, St., *P.KRU* 67
Cosmas and Theodore, Sts., *P.CLT* 1, 4
Cyriac, St., *P.CLT* 1, *P.KRU* 68, 37
Isidore, St., *P.KRU* 9
Mary, Virgin, Mother of God, Thebes (Jeme), *P.KRU* 105, 75, 74, 38
Patermouthis (Patermoute), St., *P.KRU* 35, 66/76, 10, 21
Victor, St., Thebes (Jeme), *P.KRU* 105, 36, 44, 3

Monasteries (see also Churches)

Apostles, Pharoou (Aphrodito), *P.Cair. Masp.* II 67176r + P.Alex. inv. 689
Epiphanius, *P.KRU* 75
Menas, St., *P.KRU* 75
Patermouthios, St., *P.KRU* 66/76
Paul, St., Koulol, *P.CLT* 1, 2, 4, 5, *P.KRU* 106
Phoibammon, St. (Apa), *P.KRU* 105, 77, 75, 65, *P.CLT* 5, *P.KRU* 44, 13, 74, 88, 78, 104, 18, 19
Psate, St., *P.KRU* 50, 54

Shenoute (Apa), Pachme, *P.KRU* 75
Shenoute (Apa), Panopolite ("White Monastery"), P.Mich. inv. 6898

Officials

lashane: Abraham, son of the late Psês, *P.CLT* 6, *P.KRU* 42, 44
Ananias, son of the late Abraham, *P.KRU* 35
Athanasius, son of David, *P.KRU* 10
Athanasius, son of George, *P.CLT* 5, *P.KRU* 68, 36, 37
Chaêl, son of Psmô and Tshenoute, *P.KRU* 17, 13, 12, 106
Constantine, son of the late Solomon, *P.CLT* 1, *P.KRU* 35, 10, 18
Cyrus, son of Chaêl, *P.KRU* 88
Elisha, son of Elias, *P.KRU* 74
George, son of Chmntsnêu, *P.KRU* 42
Isaac, son of Constantine, *P.KRU* 38
John, son of David, *P.KRU* 77
John, son of Mathias, *P.KRU* 50, 21
John, son of the late Solomon, *P.CLT* 1, *P.KRU* 10
John, son of the late Victor, *P.KRU* 18
Kale, son of Matoi, *P.KRU* 65
Leontius, *P.KRU* 69
Mena, *P.KRU* 69
Menas, son of the late Paam, *P.KRU* 10
Papnoute (Papnouthi), *P.KRU* 105
Peter, son of [N.], *P.KRU* 74
Peter, son of the late Komos (Komes), *P.CLT* 1, *P.KRU* 9, 35, 55, 51, 50, 21
Psmô, *P.KRU* 65
Psmô, *P.KRU* 88 [same as previous?]
Samuel (deceased), *P.CLT* 5
Samuel, son of Mena, *P.KRU* 42
Severus, son of the late Moses, *P.CLT* 1, 5
Severus, son of the late Souai, *P.CLT* 1
Shenetôm, son of the late Jacob, *P.CLT* 1
Souros, *P.KRU* 44
Theodore, son of Anatole, *P.KRU* 42
Thomas, *P.CLT* 5

Victor, son of the late Joseph, *P.KRU* 36, 37, 42 (?)
Victor, son of the late Thomas, *P.KRU* 35, 42 (?)
Victor, also archpriest, *P.KRU* 37 (?)

chief of police: Samuel, son of Enoch, brother of Apa Kyri, *P.KRU* 42

Titles

archon: Fl. Cyrus, son of Colluthus, *P.KRU* 27
patrician: Athanasius, *P.Lond.* V 1709
syntelestês (contributor): Christopher, P.Mich. inv. 6898, P.Vat.Copti Doresse 5, 1

Trades

builders: Psyrus, *P.KRU* 42
Theodore, son of Aaron, *P.KRU* 88
businessman (*pragmateutês*): Jacob, son of Isaac, *P.CLT* 5
butcher: Kos, son of David, *P.KRU* 3
camelherd: Sourous, *P.KRU* 66/76
honey-seller: Constantine, son of Cyrus, *P.Lond.* V 1709

Rulers

Justin II, *P.Cair.Masp.* II 67176r + P.Alex. inv. 689, *P.KRU* 105 (?)
Heraclius and Heraclius "New Constantine", *P.KRU* 77

'Abd al-Homar, *P.KRU* 42
'Amr, pagarch, *P.KRU* 25
Argama b. Ered, *P.KRU* 13, 12
Justin, pagarch, *P.KRU* 44
Mamet, pagarch, *P.KRU* 106

Pahal, *P.KRU* 42
Fl. Saul b. 'Abdullah, pagarch, *P.KRU* 50, 45/46
'Ubayd Allah, governor, *P.KRU* 13

Place Names

Antinoopolis (Antinoe), *P.Lond.* V 1709, P.Vat.Copti Doresse 2 (?), *P.KRU* 10
Aphrodito, *P.Cair.Masp.* II 67176r + P.Alex. inv. 189, *P.Lond.* V 1709, P.Mich. inv. 6898, P.Vat.Copti Doresse 2, 5, 3, 1
Aswan (Syene), *P.KRU* 68, 38
Clysma, *P.KRU* 68
Coptos, *P.CLT* 4, *P.KRU* 67
Côs, *P.KRU* 67
Diospolis, *P.KRU* 50, 45/46
Hermonthis (see also Jeme), *P.KRU* 75, 65, *P.CLT* 4, *P.KRU* 34, 9, 35, 55, 10, 25, 47, 68, 51, 36, 50, 17, 45/46, 21, 44, 27, 5, 13, 12, 74, 104, 106, 18, 38, 19, 54
Jeme, *P.KRU* 77, 75, 65, *P.CLT* 1, 4, 2, 5, *P.KRU* 34, 9, 35, 55, 66/76, 10, 25, 47, 68, *P.CLT* 6, *P.KRU* 51, 36, 37, 50, 17, 45/46, 21, 67, 42, 44, 3, 69, 27, 5, 13, 12, 74, 88, 78, 104, 106, 18, 38, 19, 54
Justinianopolis Kato, *P.CLT* 5
Latopolis, *P.KRU* 45/46
Memnonion, *see* Jeme
Nê, *P.KRU* 68
Pakothis, *P.CLT* 1
Pauê, *P.CLT* 1
Pi-Sinai, *P.KRU* 67
Psenantonius, *P.KRU* 67
Pshenhiai, *P.CLT* 1
Romoou, *P.KRU* 88
Shensiôn, *P.CLT* 1, 4
Thebes (*see also* Jeme), *P.KRU* 105, 75, 27
Timeshor, *P.KRU* 88
Tsê, *P.KRU* 78
Tsei, *P.KRU* 3

Biblical Passages

Genesis 3:19, *P.CLT* 5, *P.KRU* 66/76, 68, 69, 106
Genesis 18:27, *P.KRU* 66/76
Deuteronomy 27, 28, 29, *P.CLT* 2, *P.KRU* 78, 106
1 Samuel 1, *P.KRU* 104
Job 12:10, *P.CLT* 5, *P.KRU* 66/76
Job 17:1, *P.KRU* 65
Job 30:19, *P.KRU* 66/76
Psalm 38:4, *P.KRU* 66/76, 106
Psalm 38:6, *P.KRU* 66/76
Psalm 38:12(-13), *P.KRU* 65, 66/76, 74
Psalm 101:11, *P.KRU* 66/76
Psalm 103:29, *P.KRU* 65
Psalm 108:23, *P.KRU* 66/76
Psalm 135:4, *P.KRU* 67
Psalm 143:4, *P.KRU* 66/76
Proverbs 14:8, 16:25, 19:3, *P.KRU* 67
Proverbs 20:24, *P.KRU* 67
Ecclesiastes 1;4, *P.KRU* 74
Ecclesiastes 3:22, *P.KRU* 106
Daniel 5:23, *P.CLT* 5
Habakkuk 3:2, *P.KRU* 106
Matthew 3:17, *P.KRU* 67
Matthew 16:24, *P.KRU* 65
Matthew 16:27, *P.CLT* 1
Matthew 17:5, *P.KRU* 67
Matthew 19:21, *P.KRU* 65
Matthew 24:42, *P.KRU* 74, 106
Matthew 25:13, *P.KRU* 74, 106
Matthew 25:(31-)46, *P.KRU* 65, 68, 106
Matthew 27:3-5, *P.KRU* 106
Mark 1:7, *P.KRU* 37
Mark 1:11, *P.KRU* 67
Mark 8:34, *P.KRU* 65
Mark 9:43-48, *P.KRU* 65
Mark 10:21, *P.KRU* 65
Mark 12:41-44, *P.KRU* 106
Mark 13:33, *P.KRU* 74
Luke 1:51, *P.KRU* 67
Luke 3:16, *P.KRU* 37
Luke 3:22, *P.KRU* 67
Luke 9:23, *P.KRU* 65
Luke 11:5-8, *P.CLT* 1
Luke 12:20, *P.KRU* 74
Luke 14:27, *P.KRU* 65
Luke 18:22, *P.KRU* 65
Luke 21:1-4, *P.KRU* 106
John 1:27, *P.KRU* 37
John 5:29, *P.CLT* 1
John 13:2, *P.CLT* 5
Acts 1:16-18, *P.KRU* 106
Acts 5:1-10, *P.CLT* 1, 2, *P.KRU* 17, 13, 88, 106, 18
Romans 3:23, *P.KRU* 106
1 Corinthians 13:8, *P.KRU* 106
2 Corinthians 2:14-16, *P.KRU* 106
James 2:13, *P.KRU* 106
1 Peter 1:17, *P.KRU* 74
1 John 3:8, *P.CLT* 5